Enville · Hagley · The Leasowes

Three Great Eighteenth-Century Gardens

Visiting the gardens

Enville is open only by appointment, and confined to group visits a few times per year. www.envilleestate.com

Hagley Hall (the house) is open at certain times but special permission is needed to see the grounds. www.hagleyhall.com

The Leasowes is a public park maintained by Dudley Borough Council, and part is a private golf course. www.dudley.gov.uk

The Leasowes as it appeared in 1758, from a Drawing by Mr T. Bond.

First published in 2010 by Redcliffe Press Ltd.,

81g Pembroke Road, Bristol BS8 3EA

www.redcliffepress.co.uk

E: info@redcliffepress.co.uk

© Text and photographs: Michael Symes and Sandy Haynes

ISBN 978-1-906593-53-7

British Library Cataloguing-in-Publication Data

A catalogue record for this book is available from the British Library

Design and typesetting by Stephen Morris www.stephen-morris.co.uk

Printed and bound in the Czech Republic by Akcent Media

front cover: Enville Hall, Estate Survey of 1688
back cover: the Lower Cascades at Enville in a watercolour by Anthony Devis (c.1765)

Enville · Hagley · The Leasowes
Three Great Eighteenth-Century Gardens

Michael Symes

Sandy Haynes

 redcliffe

Acknowledgements

MANY PEOPLE HAVE HELPED IN VARIOUS WAYS IN THE COMPILATION OF THIS BOOK.
Drafts of some of the chapters have been read by Jane Bradney, Jennifer Meir,
Tim Richardson, Katy Myers, Liz Light and Chris Gallagher, and we have prof-
ited greatly from their comments. We should also like to thank David Lambert
and Chris Gallagher for the provision of material. We are most grateful to Peter
and Diana Williams especially for access to the archives at Enville, to Michael
and Judy Scott-Bolton for all their interest, enthusiasm and encouragement,
and to James Rothwell for his help and advice. The staff of the Shropshire and
Worcestershire Record Offices have been most helpful, as have the keepers of
the Manuscripts and Special Collections at the University of Nottingham and
the John Rylands Library, Manchester, who have allowed access to their
archives. References to the Drummonds Bank customer account ledgers have
been permitted by the Royal Bank of Scotland Group Archives. We also thank
Rupert Dugdale, who has been involved with the restoration of The Leasowes,
Michael Cousins, who shared information on Hagley, and John Sutton, who
provided information on Enville and the Civil War.

For permission to reproduce illustrations, we are grateful to the Shropshire
Record Office for the images from David Parkes' portfolio; to Wellesley College,
Massachusetts, for Shenstone's watercolours; to Peter and Diana Williams for
paintings, prints and sketches; to the British Library for the print of Virgil's
Grove at The Leasowes; to the estate of Priscilla Matthews for some early nine-
teenth-century views of Hagley and The Leasowes; to the Bodleian Library,
University of Oxford, for the print of Hagley; to the Conway Library, The Cour-
tauld Institute, London, for the view of the Palladian Bridge at Hagley; to the
Victoria and Albert Museum for the Robins sketch of Enville; and to Michael
Raeburn and The State Hermitage Museum, St. Petersburg, for the 'Green Frog'
dinner service views. We thank English Heritage for allowing us to reproduce
photographs from the National Monuments Record. Sketches by John Parnell
in his ms travel journal are reproduced by permission of the British Library of
Political and Economic Science (London School of Economics and Political
Science), who have also permitted quotations from the text.

The Latin inscriptions at Hagley and The Leasowes have been freshly translated
by the late Gordon Symes (father of Michael).

Sandy Haynes would particularly like to thank the Wingate Trust for awarding
her a generous scholarship which enabled her to make a detailed search of the
archives at Enville Hall.

The encouragement of John Sansom at Redcliffe Press has made it a pleasure
for both authors to work on this publication.

CONTENTS

List of illustrations

towards Wolverhampton c.1760. Watercolour by Anthony Devis

col 14: The Lower Cascades at Enville in a watercolour by Anthony Devis (c. 1765) The water falls in three cascades into the Temple Pool. In the trees above the Cascades there is a dark, arched feature – the end doors of Shenstone's Chapel

col 15: View over the Upper Pool to the Rotunda at Enville in a watercolour by Anthony Devis (c.1765)

col 16: Shenstone's Chapel in Priest Wood, Enville. It was built in the 1750s and dedicated to Shenstone after his death in 1763

col 17: The Shepherd's Bridge, Enville, at the head of Jordan's Pool. Anthony Devis, watercolour, c.1765

col 18: A view of the park at Hagley. Unknown artist

col 19: Thomson's Seat at Hagley, designed by John Pitt (1749-50). Unknown artist

col 20: The pools above the Palladian Bridge at Hagley. Unknown artist

col 21: The Rotunda at Hagley designed by John Pitt (1748-49). Unknown artist

col 22: Hagley: a view of the park

col 23: Hagley: column of Frederick, Prince of Wales in Roman habit c.1739. Moved to its present site in 1751

col 24: The Dairy at Hagley designed by Sanderson Miller (1752-3)

col 25: The Greenhouse at Hagley designed by Sanderson Miller (1752)

col 26: The Temple of Theseus at Hagley designed by James 'Athenian' Stuart (1758-62)

col 27: Shenstone's Urn at Hagley which has been moved from its original place between two streams to a site by the Hall

col 28: The pools above the Palladian Bridge at Hagley looking up towards the Rotunda

col 29: The Rotunda at Hagley

col 30: The Rotunda at Hagley

col 31: The Ruined Castle at Hagley

col 32: View from Milton's Seat to Hagley Hall

col 33: The Leasowes: the farm with hayricks and barn by William Shenstone

col 34: Looking downstream towards the bridge in Virgil's Grove, The Leasowes

col 35: The Hermit at the Priory Gate, The Leasowes, by William Shenstone

col 36: The Leasowes: the Priory and the house. David Parkes, watercolour

col 37: The Leasowes: the Priory by moonlight, 1791. David Parkes, watercolour

col 38: The Priory Pool, The Leasowes

col 39: Gothic Seat at The Leasowes. David Parkes, watercolour

col 40: The Leasowes: Virgil's Grove looking towards Wychbury Hill, William Shenstone

col 41: The Leasowes: a seat, from the far side of the serpentine stream, William Shenstone

col 42: The Leasowes: Shenstone's summer-house or writing hut on a small island in the Beech Water with the spire of Halesowen Church in the distance, William Shenstone

col 43: The Leasowes: Virgil's Grove, William Shenstone

col 44: The Leasowes: Virgil's Grove, William Shenstone

col 45: The Leasowes: Shenstone's summer-house or writing hut

col 46: A view of the Beech Water at The Leasowes

col 47: The restored High Cascade at The Leasowes

Foreword

THIS PROJECT AROSE ORIGINALLY OUT OF AN ARCHIVAL INVESTIGATION INTO ONE of the gardens that are the subject of the book. It soon became clear that, although such an investigation could be justified in its own right on scholarly grounds, so much more would be gained by making it part of a wider study embracing all three. As the title of Joseph Heely's *Letters on the Beauties of Hagley, Envil and The Leasowes* (1777) shows, the gardens form a triptych that was generally recognised at the time. This was an idea which was explored during a weekend visit by the Garden History Society to Enville and Hagley entitled 'Walking with Heely'.

The book has several purposes. First, it considers the three gardens in question as a trio, since they were often visited and discussed as such in the eighteenth century. This enables common features and topography to be explored, together with the remarkable extent of networking between the owners and friends who had an input into the design of the landscape. The evolution of the three gardens was contemporaneous and they cannot be treated in isolation from each other.

Another, more particular purpose is to tell the story of eighteenth-century Enville in a degree of detail which it has not hitherto enjoyed. This chapter provides much previously unpublished archival material.

One aim is to offer a history of the *ferme ornée*, a concept that requires some discussion and explanation. The reputation of The Leasowes is as one of the two great examples of the genre, and an appreciation of the implications is essential to an understanding of the estate. Enville, too, has elements that have caused it to be labelled as a *ferme ornée* from time to time.

The approach is to try to reconstruct the original experience of going round the gardens, both in terms of how they looked physically and how contemporary visitors reacted to them. Although much has changed and been lost, all three sites are intact in the sense of not having been built over, and it is still possible today, with some imagination, to trace the eighteenth-century visitor's footsteps and to share some of the excitement that the gardens provoked.

The book may be seen in some way to complement the Historic Gardens of England series by Timothy Mowl, published by Redcliffe Press, especially the volume on Staffordshire gardens (2009). While the focus has been on the three gardens, it is also important to locate them in a general history of the development of the English landscape garden, from formal to more naturalistic appearance and towards the romantic and the Picturesque. They are unmistakably of their time, but they are important examples of the Georgian landscape garden, and they cling together in a fascinating part of the country, steeped in tradition and history and looking westward to the eternal hills and mountains of Wales.

1

A Trio of Landscape Gardens

❊

HOUSES, GARDENS AND ESTATES DO NOT STAND IN ISOLATION FROM THE COUNTRY-side around them. They are the product of their landscape, evolving through centuries of social and economic change, as well as design trends and land management. From the middle of the eighteenth century Enville, Hagley and The Leasowes were the three great West Midland gardens to admire. Their visitors came from a wide range of society, the good, the famous and the merely curious. William Shenstone in particular loved to show his creation at The Leasowes to friends and all comers, though the more aristocratic the better. The three gardens are contemporaneous with Stourhead in Wiltshire and Painswick in Gloucestershire, but were well advanced by the time Lancelot Brown began his early commission at Croome Court in Worcestershire twenty miles away.

All three have much in common, and were started within a few years of each other. In 1736 Shenstone went to live with his tenants at The Leasowes, and it is difficult to believe that, even if he did not start some of the actual work, he was not planning what to do with the grounds when he took over the estate around 1743. The earliest conjectural date for garden operations at Hagley is 1739, with the buildings in Hermitage Wood,[1] while work at Enville began in the early 1740s with the re-siting of the stable block adjacent to the Hall. All three owners knew each other well and visited each others' gardens. Shenstone almost certainly advised Lord Stamford and stayed at Enville Hall.[2] The properties are within ten miles of each other, with Hagley and The Leasowes only two or three miles apart, and they all have similar topographies, being on steep sloping sites cut by streams. The personal links between the owners and their circles are striking, as the diagram of social network demonstrates (fig. 2).

Enville, Hagley and The Leasowes lie near the junction of the county boundaries of Worcestershire, Shropshire and Staffordshire. The original county boundaries were established in the tenth century and have remained fairly stable ever since, with only minor changes. The most notable alteration has been to the area around Halesowen which includes The Leasowes.

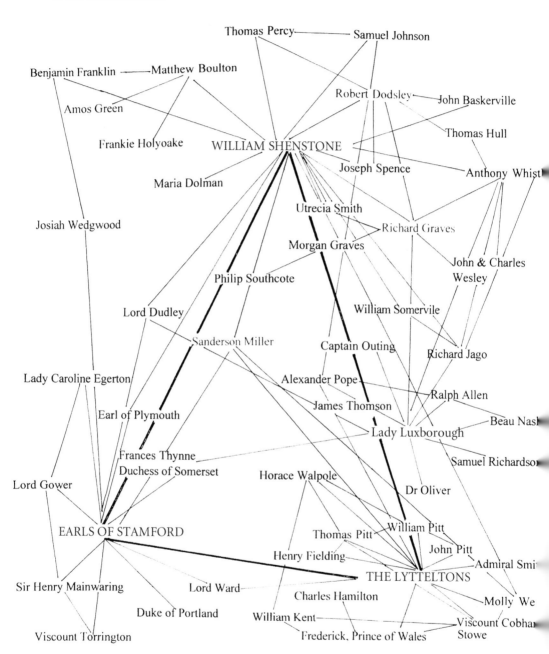

Originally it fell within Worcestershire, but by the thirteenth century it had become part of Shropshire when the manor was annexed by the powerful Earl of Shrewsbury.[3] It remained there until the mid-nineteenth century, when it reverted to Worcestershire.[4] For the purposes of this book The Leasowes will be considered to be in Shropshire as it was in the eighteenth century.

Geology

This area forms part of the eastern section of a region of England which is known as the Mid Severn Sandstone Plateau. It is dissected by the River Stour, which runs from north to south to join with the River Severn a few miles south of Kidderminster. It is an area of complex geology of sedimentary rocks which were laid down between 200 and 300 million years ago. They comprise a mixture of sandstones, limestone, clay and coal measures which have been deeply fractured and twisted by earth movements and then finally overlain with fluvio-glacial gravels deposited by the meltwaters from the retreating ice sheets at the end of the last ice age 10,000 years ago.[5]

On either side of the Stour valley lie the oldest and hardest rocks of the Carboniferous sandstones which are known as the Enville Beds. They form the erosion-resistant uplands of the Sheep Walk at Enville, which rise to over 200 metres, and the Clent Hills, which form the backdrop to Hagley at 298 metres. Between them, and nearly 100 million years younger, are the softer Triassic sandstones of the Bunter Pebble Beds and Upper Mottled Sandstone. At the boundaries of these two rock types are deep faults which run in a north-south direction – the Enville Fault to the west and, confusingly, the West Boundary Fault to the east, which runs from near Stoke-on-Trent down to the west of Evesham (fig. 3). Both these earth movements have been exploited in the design of the gardens, where the change in level across the fault line has been used to help create cascades. Both Hagley and Enville, although they are located on either side of the wide Stour valley, are similarly situated with the house at the lowest part of the grounds on the Triassic sandstone and the park laid out above their respective fault lines on the higher grounds of the Enville Beds.

The Leasowes, although only a short distance to the north-east of Hagley, is situated on the Upper Coal Measures of the Halesowen Beds. Here the coal outcrops are quite thin, being sandwiched between layers of sandstone, clay and limestone. There was, however, enough coal as well as charcoal to provide the energy source for local Halesowen industry just one

3. A simplified geological map of north Worcestershire and south Staffordshire

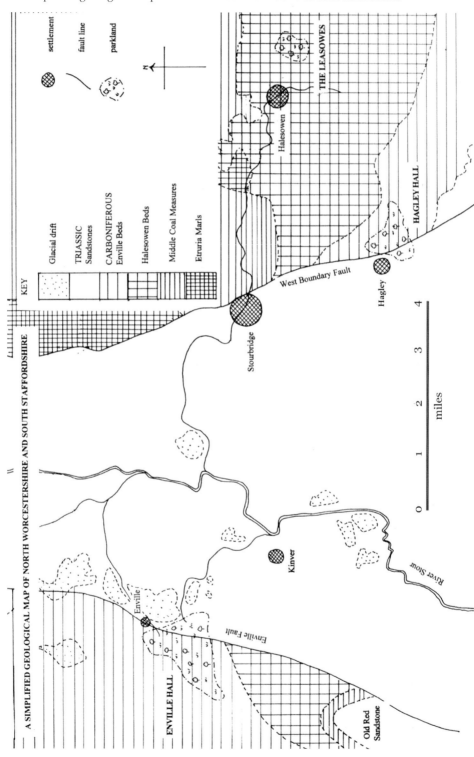

A SIMPLIFIED GEOLOGICAL MAP OF NORTH WORCESTERSHIRE AND SOUTH STAFFORDSHIRE

KEY

settlement

fault line

parkland

Glacial drift

TRIASSIC
Sandstones

CARBONIFEROUS
Enville Beds

Halesowen Beds

Middle Coal Measures

Etruria Marls

THE LEASOWES

Halesowen

HAGLEY HALL

West Boundary Fault

Hagley

Stourbridge

ENVILLE HALL

Enville

Enville Fault

Kinver

River Stour

Old Red Sandstone

0   1   2   3   4
miles

mile away. Although most people were employed in agriculture in medieval times, iron bloomeries were in existence by the end of the thirteenth century. Nail making was first recorded in the early seventeenth century,[6] and during the Civil War they provided lead shot to a garrison stationed at Dudley Castle.[7] Better deposits of coal further north fuelled the industries of the Industrial Revolution which so transformed much of the landscape in the area that was to become known as the Black Country. The iron waste, or slag, from the furnaces found a use in gardens as material from which to decorate cascades and grottoes. William Marshall described the resulting landscape:

> Enville, in situation, is similar to Hagley and the Leasowes. The immediate site is the precipitous face of an extended hill, broken into furrows and watered by rills; of which there are two, as at the Leasowes, that unite near the house, at the foot of the slope. The site of Enville is the steepest, most lofty and largest of the three.[8]

The soils which resulted from the weathering of the underlying rocks would have supported a vegetation of oak woodland on the Carboniferous sandstones and marls, while the Triassic rocks broke down to form a sandy loam creating an open heathland of gorse, bracken, birch and some oak. In order to get from Hagley and The Leasowes to Enville it was necessary to cross these softer and lower lying Triassic sandstones which often made travel difficult, as William Shenstone complained in a letter of 6 March 1750 to Lady Luxborough: 'Lord Stamford lives about Six Miles from hence yᵉ direct Road (betwixt me & Stourbridge) is almost one continu'd Grotto, in other terms a *hollow*-way; practicable for an Horse, but for no wheel-carriage.'[9] The soft sandstone was easily broken down by feet and wheels, and then washed away in the next heavy rain. This resulted in tracks cut deep into the surrounding countryside known as holloways. Things had not improved by 1789, when the author of *A Companion to The Leasowes, Hagley and Enville* wrote:

> Our approach toward Enville is over wild heath, nearly barren. As we get sufficiently near to discover his Lordship's grounds, the contrast is extremely fine; opposed to the bleak desart, the verdant sloping lawns of Enville appear with ten-fold lustre, edged and interspersed with luxuriant woods.[10]

As with other designed eighteenth-century landscapes, Enville created an island of order and peace within the unplanned, disordered 'ancient countryside.'

Geography

Originally much of this area was covered with thick woodland. Evidence of early human occupation is sparse. A few Palaeolithic flint tools have been found alongside river valleys, and there are Iron Age forts near Enville at Solcum Farm, Woverley, and Wychbury Hill above Hagley. This hill takes its name from the local Anglo-Saxon tribe, the Hwicce, but is famed more as a Roman encampment. Roman coins were found in the fields, and the site is celebrated locally for a battle between the Romans, based at Wychbury Hill, and the Britons on Clent Hill.[11] At Greensforge in the Stour valley are the remains of a Roman marching camp with a road which connected with the Roman road between Droitwich (Salinae) in the south and Penkridge (Pennocrucium) in central Staffordshire. During the Anglo-Saxon period the area became part of the kingdom of Mercia, and it was then that people started to make a noticeable impact on their environment.

Settlement was mainly small scale. Clearings or assarts were made in the woodland for arable crops. Fields were made by cutting down the surrounding woodland, leaving narrow strips of woodland to form the boundaries. Many of the field names like Stockings (Old English *stoccing*, meaning a piece of ground cleared of stumps) or Rudding (OE *ryding*, cleared land) reflect this.[12] Today, in spring, the base of the hedgerows is filled with dog's mercury and bluebells, indicating their woodland past. The hill tops of the Clent hills at Hagley and the sheep walk at Enville provided summer pasture. This piecemeal clearance of the land has resulted in a pattern of dispersed settlement with isolated farmsteads and hamlets, and only a few medium-to-large villages. Small irregular hedged fields, containing many species of plants and trees, numerous woodlands and many winding, sunken lanes characterise this type of settlement pattern. It is often referred to as 'ancient countryside' to differentiate it from 'planned countryside', which is characterised by large regular fields, nucleated villages and little woodland. Margaret Gelling writes that 'at Enville the number and distribution of open fields ... reflects a gradual process of bringing forest woodland into cultivation. Each of the three manors had its own set of fields ... and there was a separate set for Lyndon.'[13]

Many place names reflect these events, such as Hagley, Frankley and Lutley, all of which end in 'leah' (Old English), or 'ley', meaning a clearing, as well as specific tree names like The Hollies, Four Ashes, Broad Oak and Nash Elm. Enville, Hagley and Halesowen are all recorded in the Domesday Book. Envil or Enville was earlier written as Evenfeld: here the suffix 'feld' does not mean field but indicates the presence of woodland.[14] Oliver Rackham's analysis of 'Woodland areas by counties in the Domesday Book' shows that Worcestershire and Staffordshire had the second and third highest percentage of woodland as a total of land use in England after the Weald.[15] The manor of Morfe which formed part of the parish of Enville was recorded as having woodland two leagues long by two leagues wide, in other words covering most of the manor – the rest was waste. The manor of Enville covered an area of three hides, or about 360 acres. There was land for four ploughs, with four acres of meadow and woodland that was one league long and half a league wide, which was held by the King in the Forest. The landscape was not one of impenetrable wildwood, but of woodland and wood-pasture interspersed with small settlements. In the mid-seventeenth century Essex Wood and Priest Wood at Enville were already old woodland and may well have been the remnants of that earlier forest. The woodlands also provided the raw material for the production of charcoal, which was used for iron making around Halesowen from the fourteenth century.

By the twelfth century the land use would be described as wood-pasture: tree density is lighter, and there are open grassland areas or launds where animals can be grazed. This required careful management to prevent over-grazing, which would result in all new tree growth being eaten. Areas were often delineated with wood banks and pollarded trees which can still be seen at Enville. As the population increased, so did the amount of land cleared for agriculture. Enville and Hagley, with Halesowen on the eastern edge, had become part of the Royal Forest of Kinver with a hunting lodge just north of Kinver at what is now Stourton Castle. A forest was a piece of land on which the King had the right to kill deer. It was not necessarily thickly wooded, and often had more open areas of rough pasture with scattered trees. The King might not own the land, but had hunting rights over it. Forest laws were complex and strict. Infringement of the laws, including poaching the King's deer, was an offence that was severely punished. Enforcement of Forest Law decreased in the fourteenth century, and wealthy people could apply for a licence to have their own deer parks. As Oliver Rackham writes: 'Parks were status symbols ... They symbolised a higher status than a moat, but lower than one's private gallows.'[16] Costs of maintenance could probably exceed returns unless other uses for the land could be found. To keep a park primarily for the hunting of deer, however, meant that there were relatively few other economic uses of the park that were compatible with its main purpose. Some income could be derived from timber and brushwood, and grazing could be found for other animals, especially pigs. Parks could also include fishponds and rabbit warrens. Deer parks are found within the grounds of both Enville and Hagley, whilst a park was created by the abbot and convent of the Premonstraterian Abbey at Halesowen not far from The Leasowes.[17]

Historical background

The early fourteenth century saw a series of poor harvests and famine. This was followed by the Black Death, which arrived in the Midlands in the spring of 1349 and killed about 40% of the population over the next few years.[18] There was no population increase for nearly two centuries. On many manors shortage of labourers gave the tenants bargaining rights so that they were able to negotiate with the lord of the manor the right to pay rents for their holdings rather than to have to perform feudal duties. At Hagley John Lyttelton (1541-1599) was one who gave his tenants leaseholds and tenancies.[19] There was an increasing move to expand the amount of pastoral farming, and this resulted in the enclosure of what had previously been open or common land. Many enclosures were implemented by agreement, and small pieces of land were often exchanged between neighbours and then enclosed. In September 1638 William Hale, gentleman, who lived at The Hollies in Enville exchanged two selions of land in the Nether Hoo and two fields for a pasture, a close and an orchard belonging to John Leigh, gentleman, of Leigh House, Enville.[20] Disputed cases were settled in the manorial court. Enclosure changed the face of Britain and created a more regulated landscape. From the seventeenth century onwards some landowners began to enclose large areas of the surrounding land without being challenged. The land was usually of poor quality, being heath or woodland, but nevertheless it interfered with local people's rights to collect fuel and graze animals on the open land. Clent Common at Hagley was enclosed in 1675 and converted to arable, and Kinver and Enville commons were enclosed in 1774. The land of Britain was slowly becoming privatised.

Parish registers show that from the middle of the sixteenth century the general trend was for the population to increase rapidly, although local outbreaks of plague and disease occurred from time to time. This increase put pressure on food resources and employment opportunities, resulting in famine in years of bad harvest. The Civil War (1642-1648) affected the area as it did elsewhere in the country. Some families such as the Greys were divided. On 2 August 1650 the County Commissioners were asked to examine reports that Henry Grey had kept a garrison at his own house at Enveild and 'if causes of delinquency appear, to secure [his] estates.'[21] These estates were confiscated, though later returned. His nephew Thomas Grey fought for the Parliamentarians under Oliver Cromwell, and was one of the twelve regicides whose signature is on King Charles I's death warrant.

The peace which followed the Restoration of Charles II in 1660 slowly prepared people for changes in almost all spheres of life. The larger landowners like the Lytteltons at Hagley and the Greys at Enville owned more than one manor. Their holdings did not form a nucleated unit but consisted of property and land spread over a wide area. The Greys not only owned land in Enville and Morfe, but also Amblecote and Whittington in Staffordshire, Kinlet in Shropshire, a large estate based around Bradgate Park in Leicestershire, plus manors and land in Nottinghamshire, Lincolnshire and Derbyshire. Throughout the seventeenth century there was a trend, followed by both the Lytteltons and the Greys, to purchase more land around their main houses, often financed by selling land and property in outlying manors.

The eighteenth century

Life in Britain became more secure following the Glorious Revolution in 1688, although there was still some factional infighting during the reign of Queen Anne and the Jacobite uprising in 1715. It was the accession of George I, combined with Sir Robert Walpole's long period of government, that produced significant stability, though power and advancement depended on having the right contacts and sympathies.[22] Property gave not only social status but political power as well. The powers of the monarchy had been curtailed, and it was maintained that the country should be ruled by the consent of 'the people', though universal suffrage was a long way off. The King was responsible to the House of Lords, whilst the House of

4. Sir George Lyttelton.
Engraving after a painting by
Benjamin West

GEORGE LORD LYTTELTON.

*From a Painting by M.r West in the Possession of the
Bishop of Bristol.*

Commons kept the upper House in check. There followed a long period of
Whig government which lasted till 1762. Most members had aristocratic
backgrounds and supported the Hanoverian settlement. Religious tolerance
and a strong foreign policy were promoted, with commercial and industrial
development at home and overseas. Sir George Lyttelton was the most polit-
ically active of the three garden owners and was appointed 'Cofferer of the
Household', a post he held between 1754 and 1756. This meant he was in
charge of all the accounting for the Royal Household below stairs. Harry,
4th Earl of Stamford, appears not to have been active or interested in life at
Court and only occasionally seems to have sat in the House of Lords.[23]

As people became accustomed to the peace following the Restoration,
so the high brick walls around their houses came down and they
surrounded their homes with land. This meant that the house was no longer
part of the community of the village and fields, but stood in isolated splen-
dour. Estates were run as economic units as well as somewhere to live,
although new houses were rarely designed with that purpose in mind. In
the early eighteenth century the designed grounds which surrounded the
house and its owners created a landscape of pleasure distinct from the landscape of production, and this made for a social exclusivity that has lasted
till the present day. The great country house became a dominant feature in
the landscape and came to represent not just wealth and status but also

power on an ascending scale of size. Estates like Enville and Hagley owned much of the parish and some of the neighbouring ones as well. They rented out the land and provided employment not only directly for servants on the estate but also for those who offered services to the community such as waggoners or shoemakers.

From the early years of the eighteenth century there was a gradual increase in the population of Britain as birth rates increased and death rates fell.[24] There was also a new social divide. The lesser gentry and professional class were becoming wealthier and more independent, and there 'was a growing gap between the polite world of the gentry and the impolite world of servants, farmers and smallholders.'[25] The rules of hospitality, too, were changing. Anyone who called at the Hall was not automatically given food or drink, and tenants were no longer entertained in the same rooms used by the family. The gentry, however, like Shenstone or the chaplain, would stay at the Hall and eat with the family. For the tenants Enville still held twice-yearly dinners when the rents were paid on Lady Day and at Michaelmas, and there were also celebratory meals for christenings and special birthdays. These were held at the Swan Inn, which was located beside the Hall drive.

Farming techniques and production had improved from the sixteenth century, while small cottage industries were starting up on the coalfields, mainly making iron goods and, in nearby Stourbridge, glass. The Hearth Tax returns of 1662 and 1679 show an increase in both the number and the quality of houses. In 1730 Charles, Viscount Townshend (1675-1738) introduced crop rotation as a means of improving soil fertility and increased yields. Three years later Jethro Tull published a scientific treatise entitled *The Horse-Hoeing Husbandry*, and the Agricultural Revolution was on its way, leading to improved techniques in arable and pastoral husbandry, higher yields and bigger profits. It was linked to national identity: George Sheeran claims that there was a 'direct association made between aristocratic improvement in agriculture and patriotism.'[26] The population and economic structure based on agriculture remained fairly constant in Hagley and Enville, but the population of Halesowen expanded fivefold when the Industrial Revolution took hold.[27] Before then, coal mining in the early part of the eighteenth century was largely confined to the same areas that had been worked since medieval times and which supplemented charcoal as the fuel source in the nail-making industry.

The first half of the eighteenth century saw a building boom which prompted Daniel Defoe to write in his *Tour Through England and Wales*:

> Even while the sheets are in the press, new beauties appear in several places, and almost to every part we are oblig'd to add appendixes, and supplemental accounts of fine houses, new undertakings, buildings &c. and thus prosperity will be continually adding; every age will find an increase of glory.[28]

The eighteenth century saw an escalation in the way country house design reflected the status of the owner. At first a house, generally Palladian in style, would be complemented by a formal geometrical layout of the grounds, but as a more naturalistic and pictorial style took over, the setting would sometimes assume more importance than the house. Thus, at Whitton, Middlesex, the 3rd Duke of Argyll planned and worked on his gardens a dozen years before he built the house. Similarly, for Lord Stamford, Sir Thomas Lyttelton and William Shenstone, the grounds took precedence. The new Hagley Hall was built to a design by Sanderson Miller between 1756 and 1760, while Enville was not 'improved' until 1775-1780, long after the grounds had been completed. Shenstone's house, though central in the estate, was always modest and of far less interest and significance than his gardens. The reasons for such priorities would be partly aesthetic and partly financial, income proceeding from tenancies, land rentals, agriculture and timber production.

One of the greatest cultural influences in the eighteenth century was the Grand Tour. Of the three estate owners, only George Lyttelton went on the tour (1728-30), when he travelled through France and to all the major towns of Italy, reaching as far south as Naples. The other two experienced the classical world of Rome and Greece in their heads, as Alexander Pope had done since infirmity had always prevented him from making the tour. Although the 4th Earl of Stamford, as far as we know, never travelled abroad, he was well versed in classical literature, and his son and grandson made extensive tours not only of Italy but France, Holland, Germany and Switzerland as well. The Grand Tour had enormous consequences in terms of architectural and scenic influence.

Apart from Europe, the Far East held a special fascination. Knowledge of Chinese gardens was limited, and often distorted, but British owners

Three Great Eighteenth-Century Gardens

embraced the distinctly westernised form of *chinoiserie* enthusiastically. Shenstone was suspicious, however, and it fell to Lord Stamford to introduce a Chinese temple in the middle of a pool at Enville.

Taste was a key word of the day – whether applied to paintings, sculpture, buildings or gardens, and much was written on the subject, though no firm or abiding conclusions could ever be reached. It is, of course, a subjective matter, though there were those who set themselves up as arbiters of taste and tried to lay down principles. Baroque might well be 'bad taste' for being too showy and foreign, while Palladianism was 'good taste' for its function, symmetry and restraint. Some years later, as tastes changed, there was a seeking for emotional response to one's surroundings which reached its climax in the picturesque and the sublime. Addison, writing in 1712, acknowledged the difficulty of laying down rules for acquiring taste. He felt that although some were born with it, others might acquire it by reading 'the most Polite authors' and by having conversation with 'men of a Polite Genius'. They ought also to be aware of the 'Works of the best *Criticks* both Ancient and Modern.'[29] But the essence was the ability to make informed and critical judgments.

Taste would be brought into play in visiting other people's properties, where you could not only exhibit your own opinions but make a critical appreciation of what you were seeing. So in diaries and published accounts of tours there was an explosion of this kind of approach to visiting. The earliest guide book to gardens was that written for Stowe in 1744 by Benton Seeley, and others soon followed. In the 1770s there were several pamphlets on Enville, Hagley and The Leasowes, of which the most popular was Joseph Heely's *Letters on the Beauties of Hagley, Envil and The Leasowes*. This served to increase public interest. On a visit to Wilton House, Wiltshire, Mrs Lybbe Powys noted that 'in the porter's lodge, where he desired us to set down our names and the number of our company, we saw by the book there had been to see it in the last year 2,324 persons.'[30] The growing numbers were such that some owners such as Horace Walpole drew up a list of rules for admission, and not every visitor was always able to gain admittance. At first the prospective visitor just turned up and expected to be shown around by the housekeeper or gardener, but the later volume of visitors might cause the owners to specify the days of the week on which the properties were open.[31] Taste had a political dimension, too, for the landscape gardens that prevailed in the middle and later parts of the century were almost all Whig gardens that would claim a monopoly of taste in garden design.

Visitor conduct was not always what it should be. William Shenstone

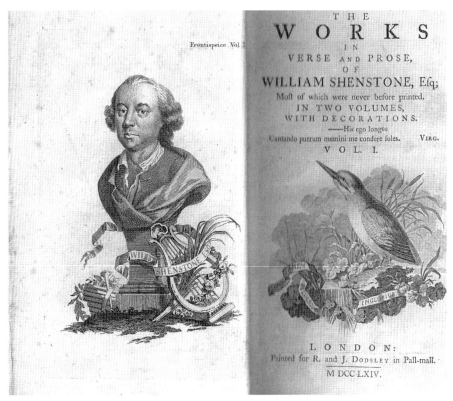

5. William Shenstone: engraving from *The Works in Verse and Prose of William Shenstone Esq. Vol I* (1764)

welcomed visitors, especially the aristocracy or the famous, but was not always so pleased with the behaviour of some of the 'lower classes'. In a letter to Lady Luxborough he wrote 'What do you think, Madam, of my publishing verses once a week upon my skreens or garden-seats, for the Amusement of my good Friends yᵉ Vulgar?', followed by a poem signed by Oberon, King of the Fairies, which extols the virtues of Virgil's Grove but adds a cautionary note for visitors whose behaviour might ruin it:

> Then fear to spoil these sacred Bowers;
> Nor wound yᵉ Shrubs, nor crop yᵉ Flow'rs;
> So may yʳ Path wth Sweets abound!
> So may yʳ Couch wth Rest be crown'd!
> But ill-betide or Nymph or swain
> Who dares these hallow'd Haunts profane![32]

Lyttelton had a similar problem at Hagley. At the entrance to the park there was a notice requesting visitors to keep to the paths and not to scribble on the buildings.[33] Unfortunately this did not prevent the occurrence of graffiti on some of the buildings and inscriptions. The problem was a long-standing one: the owners of Italian Renaissance gardens often set out rules for conduct along with the responsibilities of the owner towards the public in a so-called *Lex Hortorum*.[34]

One development that had a particular effect on gardens was the expansion of the interest in antiquarianism. The study of ancient native literature, buildings and prehistoric earthworks had begun in the sixteenth century with such scholars as John Leland and William Camden. It was continued by William Dugdale, Robert Plot and others in the seventeenth century and then by William Stukeley and William Borlase in the eighteenth. Not only did they record their visits in sketches and engravings, but used information from their libraries to corroborate their fieldwork. The scope of their work was broad, and included looking at historical remains, local customs and natural history whilst asking questions about the origins of the human race, religion and scientific advances. The problems posed by structures such as Stonehenge, which had plainly not been erected by the Romans, gave rise to thinking about pre-Roman Britain and the people who had lived then. The term Druid was often used to embrace all those early pagan communities. In 1717 the Society of Antiquaries was founded, and it later received a Royal Charter from George II. This interest found its way into gardens in the form of hermitages, root houses and grottoes, with the principal exponent, Thomas Wright, revealing a lively interest in the Druids and making fanciful connections with them.

The three gardens

Enville, Hagley and The Leasowes form a trio with much in common yet each with its distinctive character. There are bonds and interconnections that unite them, and topography ensures that their distant panoramas stretching across to the Welsh mountains are similar, even if the basic orientation of the sites is in a different direction. They were all developed in the middle years of the eighteenth century, at a time when the pictorial approach to landscaping – naturalistic park-making with ornamentation by buildings and other features – was at its height. The three acted as a group which visitors to gardens in that area would wish to see and to write about. The most notable instance of the contemporary view that they were a nexus of three

6. People and places: showing who lived where around Birmingham

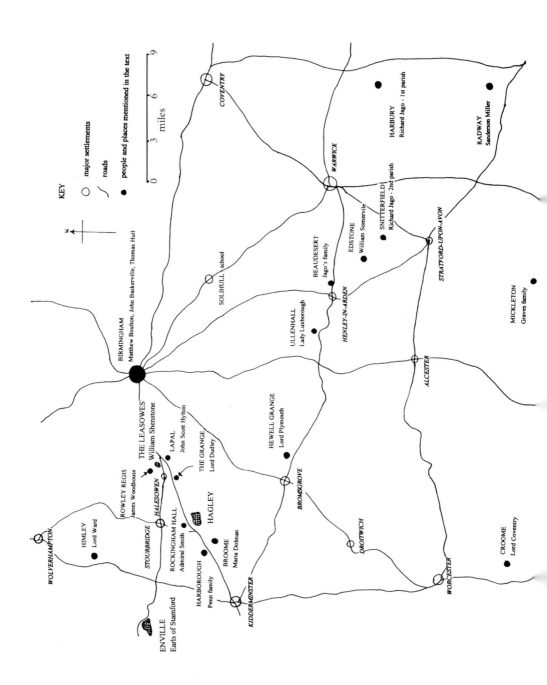

KEY

○ major settlements

〜 roads

● people and places mentioned in the text

miles
0   3   6   9

COVENTRY

WARWICK

HARBURY
Richard Jago - 1st parish

RADWAY
Sanderson Miller

SNITTERFIELD
Richard Jago - 2nd parish

EDSTONE
William Somervile

STRATFORD-UPON-AVON

BEAUDESERT
Jago's family

HENLEY-IN-ARDEN

ULLENHALL
Lady Luxborough

MICKLETON
Graves family

ALCESTER

SOLIHULL school

BIRMINGHAM
Matthew Boulton, John Baskerville, Thomas Hull

THE LEASOWES
William Shenstone

LAPAL
John Scott Hylton

THE GRANGE
Lord Dudley

HEWELL GRANGE
Lord Plymouth

ROWLEY REGIS
James Woodhouse

HALESOWEN

BROMSGROVE

DROITWICH

WOLVERHAMPTON

HIMLEY
Lord Ward

STOURBRIDGE

ROCKINGHAM HALL
Admiral Smith

HAGLEY

BROOME
Maria Dolman

HARBOROUGH
Penn family

KIDDERMINSTER

WORCESTER

CROOME
Lord Coventry

ENVILLE
Earls of Stamford

was that of Joseph Heely, who published his *Letters on the Beauties of Hagley, Envil, and The Leasowes* in 1777, but he was followed by similar accounts.

Heely, a somewhat shadowy figure, lived in Moseley Hall, King's Norton, which is only eight miles from The Leasowes, though later he seems to have moved west, nearer Enville, and the burial register (31 March 1798) records him as 'Joseph Heely of Stourport'. He also owned properties in Birmingham. He was thus well placed to visit and document the three estates over a period of time. His *Letters* supersede an earlier publication of his which had been plagiarised, thus prompting the expanded treatment given in the *Letters*.

One of the features in common is that each estate was developed by its owner and that no professional designer was brought in. Capability Brown was active from c.1750, and he was soon joined by others, working largely in his style, who were also professionals to be hired by owners anxious for the latest in garden fashion. However, no such consultants were employed in the three gardens, which says much for the brio and creativity of their owners.

The estates were within a radius of about ten miles, and one could see the other two from any of them. Indeed, there is a story of Lord Lyttelton becoming annoyed by visitors who arrived at Hagley thinking they had come to The Leasowes, and asking for directions. Lyttelton exacted his revenge on the strays by sending them the wrong way round Shenstone's carefully worked-out circuit, though the poet's friend Richard Graves denied such a story, which had emanated from Dr Johnson.[35]

Hagley and The Leasowes were often compared. Viewing them in 1785, when they were no longer pristine, William Marshall said:

> Indeed the two places are evidently of the same *genus*; their *specific difference* consisting in Hagley's being on a larger scale, more strongly featured, and more fully wooded. Their embellishments, as well as the views from them, are very similar. Their ages, too, are similar: they are both of them growing *seedy*. While they flourished under the eyes of their designers, they were probably in better keeping.[36]

It may well be that, precisely because no outside professional was employed, the gardens flourished while they were actively created and cared for by their designer-owners, whose vision they were. Certainly in the case of The Leasowes the name of William Shenstone is indissolubly

7. Hagley: one of 'James' Views' published by H F James, Master of the Academy, Stourbridge, 1796. [EA]

8. Enville: one of 'James' Views', published by H F James, Master of the Academy, Stourbridge, 1796. [EA]

9. The Leasowes: one of 'James' Views' published by H F James, Master of the Academy, Stourbridge, 1796. [EA]

linked with the creation of that landscape.

The estates are unified geologically, geographically and topographically. The terrain is of long, slow hills – no dramatic crags or precipices – but providing sufficient ascent for breathtaking views, tumbling woodland and series of cascades and pools. A chart of features to be found in the three gardens is on p.31, from which it will be seen that a number of elements relating to land form (views, hills, water) co-exist with many of the artefacts (buildings) beloved of garden-makers of the time. From the latter group it may be deduced that constructions often went up in response to something of a similar kind in one of the other estates. This may or may not have been friendly rivalry – Shenstone, the impecunious one among the three owners, was jealous of Lord Lyttelton's expenditure on garden works at Hagley.[37]

A good many of the features noted in the chart are common to other gardens elsewhere. However, their physical proximity suggests a degree of interaction and response. The chart further reveals sometimes the particular closeness of two rather than all three places, for instance the especially literary nature of Hagley and The Leasowes. There is also some interchange of design: Shenstone advised at Enville as well as creating The Leasowes, and Sanderson Miller worked both at Enville and Hagley.

The 1740s was a time at which the pictorial landscape – naturalistic but composed as a series of pictures or tableaux – reached its apex. Other gardens which were being developed at this period included Painshill, Surrey; Stourhead, Wiltshire; Shugborough, Staffordshire; West Wycombe, Buckinghamshire; Halswell, Somerset; Painswick, Gloucestershire; and Stoke Park (Bristol), while Stowe, Buckinghamshire, was becoming steadily naturalised after a formal baroque start. The essence of such gardens was a combination of appreciation of the physical site from a landscape point of view with the creation of a number of scenes, many of which were focused on buildings. John Harris has coined the word 'templescape' to describe this kind of garden,[38] which had originated much earlier in the century through the work of (in particular) Sir John Vanbrugh and William Kent.

The pictorial landscape would often involve a set circuit, a route which would reveal the pictures not only in a sequential way but with cumulative effect. Some of the circuits could be immensely subtle, as at Painshill, where buildings vanish and reappear at different distances in the view. Sometimes the 'circuit' would be a set walk, such as the terrace walk at Farnborough Hall, Warwickshire which afforded views across a vast valley and also took in buildings en route.

The pictorial approach to creating gardens continued to flourish for two or three decades. However, it was challenged by the more abstract park-making of Capability Brown from around 1750, where form was everything. He tended to reduce landscaping to a simple, though effective and hugely influential, formula – the ingredients were water, lawn and trees, and buildings were reduced drastically in number, often being banished altogether. The essence of a Brown landscape is a foreground of well-kept lawn coming up to the house, a lake in the middle ground, rolling parkland beyond (perhaps pastured by sheep or deer) and a distant belt of trees to indicate the boundary of the estate. Plantings within the estate would be mainly native (beech was favourite) and grown in groups ('clumps'), singly or more densely as woodland. The effect (and presumably the intention) was to create a serene, English scene, looking as if it were the natural countryside though in fact it was carefully manipulated, an idealised nature. Brown had many followers who designed landscapes in a similar way, such as William Emes, Thomas White and Richard Woods.

When we turn to the three gardens, the pictorial concept is uppermost,

10: Features of the three gardens

	Enville	Hagley	The Leasowes
Deer Park	✓	✓	
Grotto	✓	✓	✓
Greek temple		✓	
Bridge	✓	✓	✓
Mock ruins		✓	✓
Old bldg made Gothic	✓		
Hermitage/root house	✓	✓	✓
Chapel	✓		
Far-reaching views	✓	✓	✓
Obelisk		✓	✓
Water and pools	✓	✓	✓
Cascades	✓	✓	✓
Chinoiserie	✓		
Cold bath	✓		
Urns	✓	✓	✓
Boathouse	✓		
Doric portico	✓	✓	
Rustic seat/hut		✓	✓
Literary inscriptions		✓	✓
Eyecatcher	✓		
Turning seat	✓		
Aviary/menagerie	✓		
Gothic seat	✓		✓
Shrubbery	✓	✓	✓
Statuary	✓	✓	✓
Stables	✓	✓	✓
Home farm	✓	✓	
Ice house	✓		
Greenhouse	✓	✓	
Slopes and combes	✓	✓	✓
AREA IN HECTARES	300	180	64

though with Sanderson Miller being a friend of Brown's by 1750, there may have been some colouring from the latter's ideas of a park: it is just as likely, however, that Miller influenced Brown. But in all these gardens there is a substantial presence of buildings or other artefacts, and the views are of distant hills far beyond the perimeter belt of a Brown estate. The circuit is an important concept too – more pronounced in the case of The Leasowes, but discernible in the other two although the route would vary and there was no single preferred way of encompassing all the points of interest (see Lord Gray's Walks, page 214).

The three gardens are all associationist, that is to say an educated eighteenth-century visitor would have responded to many of the buildings or other artefacts by reflecting on what historical associations they evoked. The Druidic 'henge' at Hagley would thus elicit thoughts of the distant native past and perhaps of comparable structures such as Stonehenge. Ruins had their own complex set of associations, both historical (an imagined history in the case of the sham ruins at Hagley and The Leasowes) and emotional, provoking feelings of sadness at decay and the passing of strength and glory. The two ruins were differentiated for calculated effect, one supposedly secular (the castle) and the other supposedly religious (the priory).

Other themes would have been more apparent at the time than they are today. One is nostalgia for a long-vanished and in any case fancifully-imagined past, the classical world of pastoral poetry, the Golden Age. This was specifically evoked by Latin inscriptions at both Hagley and The Leasowes, where quotations particularly from Virgil and Horace abounded. At a time when the classics still held enormous sway, the influence of Virgil is strong, explicitly so in the case of Hagley and The Leasowes, implicitly in regard to Enville. The inspiration was twofold: Virgil's *Eclogues* created an imaginary pastoral world of shepherds and shepherdesses, while the *Georgics* was a practical work on farming.

Another theme is the idea of solitude and contemplation, a retreat from the world of business and from society. This in itself was no new theme and dates back at least as far as the Roman world.[39] Not only would such ideas be evinced by a building such as a hermitage or root-house, which were designed for withdrawal and meditation, but the garden as a whole might be seen as a retreat, a paradise constructed by, and for the main enjoyment of, the owner. Visitors (singly or in small numbers) could partake in this experience of seclusion.

Another major related factor was the role of the fancy, or imagination. It is clear from the comments of visitors that a significant part of the experience of going round the gardens was to imagine, or conjure up ideas or pictures in the mind, which the scenes viewed would evoke. The poet Thomson, for example, spoke of the park at Hagley releasing the faculty of fancy.[40] David Lambert has written about the vivid visual sense of 'imagination' as the term was used at the time, and how Shenstone's 'fairy world' meant the world pictured in the mind. The actual landscape was but a means, a channel to the more exciting, inner world which could be summoned as the visitor proceeded.[41] This idea stems back to Joseph Addison at the beginning of the century, who developed the notion that the imagination could be formed and trained to respond to stimuli, particularly of a natural kind.[42] Although it might appear to us now that artefacts, with their possible symbolism and associations, would be a more obvious means of activating the imagination, the facility of 'picturing' was deemed to be more suitable for scenes of nature. In such vein, it was said of Hagley, though it would apply equally to the other two gardens, 'through a gate you enter the *Fairy Ground*, where you will be disposed to indulge the pleasing fancy, which the mind will be apt to take up, that every thing here is enchantment.'[43]

To illustrate how the imagination might work at this time, William Beckford's description of a visit to the Boboli gardens in Florence, in a letter of 14 September 1780, will suffice. It might well be claimed that Beckford suffered from an overheated imagination, but the process would have been familiar to his contemporaries:

> ... [the amphitheatre] brought the imagery of an antique Roman garden so vividly to mind that, lost in the train of recollections this idea excited, I expected every instant to be called to the table of Lucullus hard by, in one of the porticos, and to stretch myself upon his purple *triclinias*; but waiting in vain for a summons until the approach of night, I returned delighted with a ramble that had led my imagination so far into antiquity.[44]

Visitors' descriptions

The three sites were highly regarded. Where visitors wrote about them, having also seen a number of other major landscaped works, they did not suffer by comparison. The principal authors of the day, such as Thomas

Whately and William Gilpin, deemed them worthy of visiting and commenting on at some length. The earliest account of all three was the manuscript travel diary by Richard Pococke (1751-6).

Thomas Whately's *Observations on Modern Gardening* was first published in 1770 and had run through six editions by 1800. It was translated into French and German, and pillaged for descriptions in various gazetteers such as *The Ambulator*. Visitors to gardens would carry it round with them like a guide book, since it contains detailed descriptions of many of the important sites of the day. But it was not intended as a comprehensive guide, and to ask why Whately describes Hagley and The Leasowes but not Enville is to miss the point of the book. *Observations* is a discussion about different aspects of the landscape garden, and the descriptions given are to illustrate points the author wishes to make. So Hagley is included as an example of a park and The Leasowes as an instance of a 'farm'. Enville is not omitted because it is in any way less important, but presumably it was not needed to illustrate any of Whately's categories.

William Gilpin commented on all three estates in various of his writings. There are 'picturesque' elements in each of the gardens which would have appealed to him and which will be discussed further later. His curate and follower in picturesque taste, Richard Warner, wrote about Hagley though not the others.

RJ Sulivan (Sir Richard Joseph Sullivan), East India merchant and later politician, published *Observations Made during a Tour through Parts of England, Scotland and Wales in 1778* in 1780. The second edition ran to two volumes in 1785 and was reprinted in Mavor's *The British Tourist's or Traveller's Pocket Companion*, six vols. from 1798, attesting to the growing popularity of books about the new industry of domestic tourism and also to the size of pockets if they were intended to accommodate six volumes. Like Heely, Sullivan encompassed all three sites.

Other publications on the three gardens followed. *A Companion to The Leasowes, Hagley and Enville* appeared in 1789, while other descriptions in the next decade showed that the interest in the three as a group was as strong as ever. More general gazetteers proliferated from the 1770s and 1780s, such as *The Modern Universal British Traveller* (1779) and *A New Display of the Beauties of England* (1787), which described Hagley and The Leasowes. Often, however, they were based on (or plagiarised verbatim) earlier accounts such as that by Thomas Martyn in *The English Connoisseur*

(1766). Tours continued to be described for a number of years, such as Henry Skrine's *Two Successive Tours throughout the Whole of Wales with Several of the Adjacent English Counties* (1798), covering the three.

Sometimes an author would come to the subject with a particular approach. Thus, Arthur Young was an agricultural author, although he was also a general describer of gardens visited, and William Marshall's interest is revealed in the title of *On Planting and Rural Ornament* (1796), in which he considered all three gardens.

Many of these descriptions come from the period 1780-1800, which in garden terms would be expected to demonstrate a change of sensibility and taste, away from the mid-century pictorial style which the three gardens exhibited. It is a testament to their enduring qualities of landscape, and also to the prescience of exploiting the romantic and picturesque elements of the sites, that they could be enjoyed in an era which had rather left behind the Arcadian templescapes of earlier years. The descriptions also reflect the growth in tourism and in seekers of the Picturesque.

Other mid-century gardens did not necessarily have 'picturesque' components, and thus lacked the staying power of the trinity. Even the most famous of all, Stowe, was sometimes regarded as too cluttered with buildings. Also, although many areas of England contained fine landscape gardens, nowhere else was there a tightly-knit group which demonstrated such unity.

The 'Green Frog' dinner service ordered by Catherine the Great from Wedgwood included no fewer than twenty-two views of Enville on assorted plates, dishes and covers, making it the single most illustrated site apart from Stowe and Kew.[45] No doubt the proximity to Wedgwood's factory at Etruria, Staffordshire, helped, but the abundance of illustration of that particular garden was clearly intended to appeal to Catherine's anglomania and her love of romantic and naturalistic scenes. Hagley was also illustrated, with three views, but surprisingly not The Leasowes.

Heely suggested the three properties together constituted the acme of modern gardening design:

> If a pre-eminence is to be given to places that include all the variety the science of gardening has to shew in perfection – that pre-eminence belongs to Hagley, Envil, and The Leasowes: Each may be called a school for taste – together, an accomplished one.[46]

What follows is a discussion of the three estates considered as they were in the eighteenth century, taking into account archival material, contemporary descriptions and the milieu and connections of those who created them. Something of the experience of going round them at the time will be re-created, including the responses of visitors. Although this suggests a description of an 'ideal moment' that telescopes the development of the garden, changes and the chronology of individual features will also be discussed. Apart from The Leasowes they may have been overshadowed by more high-profile contemporary gardens, but it is time to reassert their former greatness.

2

The *Ferme Ornée*

✻

THE LEASOWES HAS REGULARLY, SINCE THE BEGINNING, BEEN DESCRIBED AS A *FERME ornée*, and it is appropriate to enquire into the meaning and usage of this term. Nor has it been applied solely to The Leasowes: Enville has been so labelled, and even Hagley creeps in at the end of a chapter on the *ferme ornée* in Miles Hadfield's *The English Landscape Garden*, with the cryptic comment that it is 'not strictly' one.[1] Definitions of the term at the time and since have been fluid and variable, and it is not possible (or even desirable) to arrive at a categorical statement. What follows in this chapter is an exploration of the several strands that go to make up the concept of the *ferme ornée* without attempting a definition. Sometimes the term has been used with hindsight, even leading to the claim that 'most estates' at the time were *ferme ornées* 'if often known by other names'.[2]

The first problem is a simple one of translation. 'Ferme ornée' ought to mean 'ornamented farm', but it is often rendered as 'ornamental farm'. There is a difference, even if a subtle one. An ornamented farm suggests a pre-existing farm that has had something done to it to make it decorative. An ornamental farm, on the other hand, suggests that the farm was created to be decorative. But in either case the farm is the basis and starting-point.

The main difficulty is that the *ferme ornée* was a matter of fashion, and the phrase was used loosely and sometimes playfully at the time (as by Shenstone himself). Contemporary usage, indeed, was often general, descriptive rather than prescriptive. Even though it might be inappropriate to seek a set definition, Thomas Whately will be cited as a leading contemporary commentator who tried. The term was used flexibly, especially on the continent, where several countries adapted it to their own situations.

One of the underlying ideas of the *ferme ornée* is combining the (agriculturally) productive with the pleasurable, the profitable with the agreeable. This in itself was by no means a new idea and can be traced back at least as far as the 'utile dulci' of the ancients. The Roman poet Horace, in retiring to his farm, enjoyed a life of peace and contentment (with some personal

11. Woburn Farm, Surrey. An engraving from *England Displayed* (1769)

labour, though the real toil would have been carried out by slaves). In this case the joys of the countryside were natural, not deliberately enhanced. Nevertheless the seeds of the concept that a farm could be more than utilitarian had been sown. Another sign of the combination of use and pleasure in Roman gardens was the planting of fruit trees not only in orchards but as decorative and shade-giving in the pleasure areas.[3] The pergola, too, with its trained and climbing vines, was an object of visual appeal in the garden. Virgil's *Georgics*, that hugely influential classical work on practical husbandry, spoke of the glory of the countryside and the pleasures of rural retirement, foreshadowing some of the feelings that would lie behind the creation of the eighteenth-century *fermes ornées*. It was not by chance that Shenstone celebrated Virgil as the climax to the circuit at The Leasowes, and that a dozen seats carried inscriptions from Virgil.[4]

In Renaissance Italy some of the ancient Roman ideas concerning the use of pergolas and fruit trees (especially orange trees) in the laid-out garden were applied extensively.[5] The concept of the vigna, literally a vineyard but used as a term to indicate parkland that might not actually be developed for the cultivation of vines, spread widely[6] so that, even where the result was aesthetic or for such purposes as hunting, the term would still carry a flavour of productivity. But for the first glimmerings of the farm as part of the increasingly developed garden landscape we must turn to the Medici villas, particularly the early ones. The illustrations in lunette form, commissioned by Grand Duke Ferdinand I and executed by the Flemish artist Giusto Utens, show fourteen of the villas as they were c.1600, although several of the layouts date from much earlier.[7] The first, for example, was Il Trebbio (see colour fig. 3), surrounded by a large farming estate of twenty-eight smallholdings. A small (surviving) garden with pergola and flowerbeds was created close to the house, but the lunette shows the garden as virtually a *hortus conclusus*, walled off and dwarfed by the farm landscape with its outbuildings round about.[8] Several of the lunettes depict a villa close up with the adjacent garden only, but it must have been a conscious decision in the case of Il Trebbio to forefront the farm elements. No doubt there was some political reason (all the lunettes portray Medici power in one way or another), but we are left with an artist displaying a farm as a visually desirable landscape as well.

Another early Medici estate was Cafaggiolo, dating from the fourteenth century. By the time Utens depicted it, it contained a fortified villa with a small garden (as at Il Trebbio) surrounded by a large game preserve, woods and a rich agricultural area. The farm buildings are again prominent.[9] A third early villa, Careggi, was not painted by Utens but it was surrounded by an area that was substantially farmland.

The source of the *ferme ornée* was seen by some English authors as coming from the northern half of Italy. Joseph Spence suggested: 'Woburn [Surrey] (whence did Mr Southcote take his idea of a Ferme Ornée – Fields going from Rome to Venice)',[10] while a 'Mr T' in 1741 was more specific: 'The country by the road from Ferrara to Padua grows more and more cultivated ... and in some parts of it the cultivation of the fields has a good deal of the air of a garden. They have a level border of eight or ten foot on each side of the cornfields, which is sown with grass and after mowing makes a handsome grass walk round each field.'[11] The Palladian villa farms in the same region might have contributed to the impression.

If some ideas about making fields more like gardens came from post-Renaissance Italy, parallel impulses were stirring in seventeenth-century Britain. David Jacques has noted the spread of the notion of combining profit with pleasure in pastorals and in practical treatises.[12] He cites John Smith, an Officer of the Royal Forests, who in 1670 spoke glowingly of making farmland delightful to look at and to walk through, creating something resembling Paradise.[13] Aesthetics were changing: the taste for geometrical gardens was being challenged by such works as Sir William Temple's *Upon the Gardens of Epicurus* (1685), which uses the word 'sharawadgi' for the first time, indicating Chinese irregularity. Andrew Marvell's poem *The Mower Against Gardens* is anticipatory in preferring fields to formal gardens:

> Tis all enforc'd; the Fountain and the Grot;
> While the sweet Fields do lye forgot[14]

In 1668 John Worlidge's *Systema Agriculturae* went further than John Evelyn's encouragement of planting in *Sylva* by celebrating rural life and the delights and pleasures of fields.

It was in the early part of the eighteenth century that ideas that would lead to the creation of recognisable *fermes ornées* gathered momentum. At the very turn of the century, a book by Timothy Nourse, *Campania Foelix*, was published a year after his death in 1699. Although largely a practical text on the 'benefits and improvements of husbandry', it opens with the statement that the subject is 'both pleasant and profitable', followed by a rapturous exclamation of the extreme delight that country scenes can bring to the senses and provide for the thoughtful viewer: 'so must it needs be a ravishing Pleasure for the Contemplative to consider.'[15] Although Nourse was writing at a time when formality still reigned in gardens, there is just a hint that the countryside beyond the wilderness was a desirable part of the scene, and also that it could be adorned with walks and cross-walks of lime, elm, oak etc., 'For to see the Campain [countryside] without Garniture would look a little too bald, and to have it choakt up with little Enclosures would look too Yeoman-like ... and be stoppage also to the wholsome Air, and to the Prospect of the remoter Countrys.'[16] The frontispiece to the book shows a horse and plough juxtaposed with parterres, an image with a clear message.

Joseph Addison (1672-1719), in a well-known essay in *The Spectator*, no. 414, 25 June 1712, argues that we find the works of nature the more agreeable if they resemble art: 'Hence it is that we take Delight in a Prospect which is well laid out, and diversified with Fields and Meadows; Woods and Rivers.' He goes on to ask 'why may not a whole Estate be thrown into a kind of Garden by frequent Plantations, that may turn as much to the Profit, as the Pleasure of the Owner? ... Fields of Corn make a pleasant Prospect, and if the Walks were a little taken care of that lie between them, if the natural Embroidery of the Meadows were helpt and improved by some small Additions of Art, and the several Rows of Hedges set off by trees and Flowers, that the Soil were capable of receiving, a Man might make a pretty Landskip of his own Possessions.'[17] Here at last we see a full marriage of the profit/pleasure combination with the conversion of fields into quasi-gardens.

Later that year Addison returned to his themes, once more in *The Spectator*. A supposed reader (though almost certainly Addison himself) describes his own garden (whether real or not) as a mixture of flowers, wilderness, kitchen and orchard gardens and parterres, where all run into each other, the productive with the aesthetic, but producing (to him) a pleasurable overall effect: '[I] am pleased that when I am walking in a Labyrinth of my own devising, not to know whether the next Tree I shall meet with is an Apple or an Oak, an Elm or a Pear-tree.'[18] We are on the way to the *ferme ornée*.

The most important figure behind the full-blown concept of the *ferme ornée* was Stephen Switzer (1682-1745), who expanded Addison's ideas and put them into practice as a designer. He was in fact the first to use the term. Although it was published in the second edition of his *Ichnographia Rustica* (1742), internal textual evidence indicates that the passage in question was written in the late 1720s.[19] His ambition was 'to mix the profitable Part of a Country Seat with the pleasurable, that one may pay the Expence of the other.'[20] Switzer promoted his ideas of Rural and Extensive Gardening to achieve this goal, 'where a whole Estate will appear as one great Garden, and the *Utile* harmoniously wove with the *Dulci*; and I believe, I am not singular in my Opinion, if I affirm, that an even decent Walk carry'd thro' a Corn Field or Pasture, thro' little natural Thickets and Hedge Rows, is as pleasing, as the most finish'd Partarre [sic] that some moderns have been so fond of.'[21]

Interestingly, Switzer traces the lineage of his ideas back to the Romans. He contrasts the Roman villa gardens, as described by Pliny (in Robert Castell's version of 1728), with the 'stiff *Dutch* Way, which has been for some time exploded', and declares that 'it is visible, that the *Roman* Genius, which was once the Admiration of the World, is now making great advances in *Britain* also.'[22] He speaks also of Horace exulting in his Sabine villa.[23] So, although Switzer is promoting the beauties of indigenous agriculture and plantings, he, like a good Augustan, still seeks classical authority and precedent.

Switzer believed that fields, orchards and kitchen gardens should lie close to and be connected with the parterres and walks of the pleasure grounds: 'This Taste, so truly useful and delightful as it is, has also for some time been the Practice of some of the best Genius's of *France* under the Title of *La Ferme Ornée*.'[24] The problem is that it hadn't. There is no evidence that the French farm-gardened in this manner when Switzer wrote these words, nor was the term *ferme ornée* used in France till as late as 1774. William Brogden speculates that Switzer gave a French provenance to make his theories more acceptable,[25] but the delay in publication until 1742, when anti-French feeling was running high, makes this problematic. Switzer had already, however, in his *Practical Husbandman and Planter* (1733), used an anglicised form, 'ornamental farm'.

Switzer's typical *ferme ornée* would be a series of fields with decorative hedgerow walks at the side and woods in the form of a labyrinth at the corners of the fields. His thoughts on what would constitute elements of the *ferme ornée* keep darting through volume III of the book: 'And why, is not a level easy Walk of Gravel or Sand shaded over with Trees, and running thro' a Corn Field or Pasture Ground, as pleasing as the largest Walk in the most magnificent Garden one can think of?' or 'Besides as these Hedge Rows, little natural Coppices, large Woods, Corn Fields, &c. mix'd one amongst another, are as delightful as the finest Garden.'[26] The walks were important for establishing communication between all the parts of a property '... little Gravel or Sand Walks [should] be extended quite thro' this Estate, for as the Pleasure of walking and viewing the Fields, &c., is early in the morning, or late in the Evening, the Dews are commonly so great, that 'tis impossible to walk therein; on the contrary, were there little Sand Walks, about 6 or 8 Foot wide; how clean and decently might the Owner, his Friend and Family walk, and view the Produce of Nature, the Blessings of the great God of Heaven and Earth.'[27] The emphasis on walking and viewing is significant: this also accords with the idea of the circuit garden.

The first edition of Switzer's book came out in 1718. A decade later Batty Langley (1696-1751), gardener, architect and Freemason, made similar comments (probably following Switzer) in his *New Principles of Gardening*. After criticising what he called stiff, regular gardens he proposed that walks should lead from water and flower gardens 'through small Inclosures of Corn, open Plains, or small Meadows, Hop-Gardens, Orangeries, Melon-Grounds, Vineyards, Orchards, Nurseries, Physick-Gardens, Warrens, Paddocks of Deer, Sheep, Cows, &c. with the rural Enrichments of Hay-Stacks, Wood-Piles, &c.', musing that 'Little Walks by purling Streams in Meadows, and through Corn-Fields, Thickets, &c. are delightful Entertainments.'[28]

These ideas were put into practice from the 1720s onwards. Riskings, Buckinghamshire (variously Riskins, Richings) was described by Switzer in 1727, but may have dated from earlier. Abbs Court (Apps Court), Surrey, and Dawley in Middlesex, were contemporary developments by Lord Halifax and Lord Bolingbroke respectively. In the 1730s further estates styled in this way included Warlies, Essex; Sugnall, Staffordshire; and Woburn Farm, most celebrated of all. In the 1740s The Leasowes can be added to the list. Some time during the mid-century Whiteknights, Berkshire (now the main campus of the University of Reading), was said to have been laid out in similar fashion.[29] In terms of importance, the two early estates of Riskings and Dawley have traditionally been seen as establishing the model, and the later, better-known estates of Woburn (the work of Philip Southcote) and The Leasowes as stretching and optimising it.

In general the landscape garden was moving in a direction which was at least compatible with the development of the *ferme ornée*, namely the inclusion of farm scenery in the view. Horace Walpole described how Bridgeman (at his height in the 1720s and '30s) in Richmond Gardens 'dared to introduce cultivated fields, and even morsels of a forest appearance, by the sides of those endless and tiresome walks [straight axial walks].'[30] This approach would continue to apply in a widespread way in the more naturalistic landscape gardens to come.

Not a great deal is known about Abbs Court, near Walton-on-Thames, Surrey, the seat of the 1st Earl of Halifax. Switzer described it as an example of the 'Farm-like Way of Gardening', where the farm was walled and fenced. It also contained an orchard,[31] and Alexander Pope described it as 'delightful'.[32] Halifax was one of the first landowners to follow Jethro Tull's principles of crop rotation, improved stock breeding and plant selection. Switzer's *Practical Husbandman and Planter* is dedicated to him. As with Bathurst and Bolingbroke (the Tories to be considered below), so Halifax is praised by Switzer for patriotism and productive use of land as opposed to the 'vanity of expense'.[33]

Two of the other early estates are better documented and enable us to build up a picture of why they were considered to be ornamented farms. One was Riskings, the second seat of Lord Bathurst, whose main residence was Cirencester Park, Gloucestershire, where, with the help of Switzer and others, a huge estate with three woods was linked by a central avenue of between five and six miles. That was certainly Forest and Extensive Gardening as promoted by Switzer at its grandest, a kind of *forêt ornée*. Switzer, however, really preferred a smaller estate. At Riskings a central canal provided the axis, with hedgerow walks leading to it at angles and mostly regular (though asymmetrical) compartments on each side which included a melonry and several kitchen gardens within wildernesses, with a serpentine perimeter drive round the whole. Fields lay beyond the drive, but the flavour of Riskings was more what Switzer called 'rural kitchen gardening' than Whately's idea of a *ferme ornée*. But it was also something of a literary garden, foreshadowing The Leasowes and Hagley. It was a focal point for Bathurst's literary friends – Pope, Swift, Gay, Congreve, Prior, Addison and others – who recorded verses on a bench in the gardens.[34] A labyrinth and grotto contributed to the 'garden' effect.

Henry St. John, first Viscount Bolingbroke, was a Tory who fell from grace at the accession of the Hanoverians and was exiled to France between 1715 and 1725, with visiting rights from 1723. On his return he purchased Dawley Manor, near Uxbridge, Middlesex, only four miles from Riskings, and, immediately and significantly, called it Dawley Farm. It became the political epicentre of the Tory Opposition in the same way that Stowe was to become the focus of the Whig Opposition. The place itself was turned into a productive farm which embodied much of the Tory ideology: 'To the leading Opposition gardeners, Bolingbroke's return to his homeland and his subsequent landscaping illustrated the redemptive power that enlightened landscape gardening could have on the country.'[35] The point was that Dawley Farm represented good and fruitful use of land while some of the Whig grandees such as the Duke of Chandos at Canons might be held up as examples of the prodigal waste of potentially productive land by forming monumentally expansive and expensive gardens. At Dawley, accordingly, 400 acres of parkland were converted into farmland, and paintings in the hall of the house conveyed the iconography; rakes, scythes, harrows, together with scenes of agricultural activity among the corn. Into the farmland at Dawley stretched avenues of lime or other trees, while some decorative features such as a short canal were accessible only by passing through the fields. Whately would have concluded that Dawley was more *ferme* than *ornée*, but equally one could say that it was *sui generis* and should be viewed according to its own parameters.

Both Riskings and Dawley had been Tory visions and enterprises, but there was another imperative at work, and that was agricultural improvement. Nowhere is that better illustrated than in Scotland, especially in the first half of the century. As early as 1720 the Society of Improvers in the Knowledge of Agriculture was founded in Edinburgh and was active for 25 years. Under the energetic secretaryship of Robert Maxwell of Arkland it built up a membership of 300 by 1743, including many of the Scottish aristocracy who were involved in farming and a good number of gentry who held land.[36] The purpose of the Society was to introduce and spread new techniques of farming and land reclamation, following the innovations of Jethro Tull, and Stephen Switzer was a member (possibly the only non-Scot). Several names well known to garden historians were in the membership: Archibald Campbell, 3rd Duke of Argyll, famed for his nursery at Whitton; Sir John Dalrymple, author of the *Essay on Landscape Gardening* (c.1756); Sir John Clerk of Penicuick; and Lord Kames, author of *Elements of Criticism* (1762).[37] The great revolution in agricultural methods was, however, still to come.

Sir John Clerk developed his own riverside estate of Mavisbank, five miles south-east of Edinburgh, with some elements of a 'Rurall Garden'. His poem *The Country Seat* (1731) suggests that fields were desirable objects in the view as one went round a garden, but that they should not be visible all at once; hiding and revealing was the key.[38] A relevant example would be North Merchiston, a small enclosed estate close to Edinburgh, purchased by William Adam in 1730. His son John remodelled the estate in the 1750s with shrubberies and with walks surrounding the fields, forming 'the most splendid Ferme Ornée that can be imagined.'[39] It may be significant that John Adam visited Shenstone at The Leasowes and that Shenstone already knew about North Merchiston. A further feature worth mention was at Newhailes, where there was a 'Ladies' Walk', a straight, raised terrace walk across the middle of a field, by the 1750s.

This last notion, of a walk to give a view of a field, brings us to a type of garden related to the *ferme ornée* though none of the following properties were described as such at the time. The type in question, picking up on some of the ideas mentioned above, might be termed the field circuit, consisting usually of pasture with a decorative walk around it. The archetype was Kew, where, as a plan of 1763 makes clear, a very flat site was utilised to create a long belt walk through plantings and past buildings of various sorts which encompassed a vast lawn divided into three, largely grazed by sheep.[40] The walk itself, accordingly, contained plenty to interest the mind and to please the eye, but all the time the cross views were of the sheep lawn. Another example would be Wotton, Buckinghamshire, where the walks round the large lake and the grounds constantly afford views of pasture and cattle.

On a smaller scale Horace Walpole developed at Strawberry Hill, Twickenham, a serpentine wood and path around a field, on the other side of which were meadows stretching down to the Thames. The sylvan path wound through all kinds of trees and flowering shrubs, with features such as the Chapel in the Woods and a Shell Bench along the way. The shrubs and flowers included lilacs, tulips, jonquils, acacias and syringas, and the meadows were grazed by Turkish sheep and two cows expressly chosen for their colouring to enhance the view. Whether Robert Adam knew of this when he made one of his few known garden plans, for Kedleston, Derbyshire, in 1759 is not known, but he devised a circuit round two pasture fields (reduced to one in practice) where the occupants were to include red deer, Scottish cattle and Indian sheep, again presumably for visual effect. The Long Walk itself was, as at Strawberry Hill, through plantings of flowering and fragrant trees and shrubs, which in the case of Kedleston included laburnums, syringas, lilacs, honeysuckle, jasmine, broom and many others.[41]

At another estate where Adam worked, Osterley, Middlesex, there was also a Long Walk through shrubberies and along a shaded gravel path, where fields with cattle formed a prominent part of the view, as a pair of paintings at the house by Anthony Devis (1784) shows. 'Dickie' Bateman had, much earlier, laid out an ornamental perimeter walk at his estate of Grove House, Old Windsor, around a large expanse of what appears in a painting by Thomas Robins to be meadow rather than pasture.[42] The walk itself incorporated two separate flower gardens.

On a wider scale, a park could have the feeling of a *ferme ornée* even if the term might not be applied to the whole estate. At Shugborough, Staffordshire, the animals grazing in the park were ornamental, such as milk-white cattle and Corsican goats – Walpole would have approved. They were complemented from time to time by perambulating ladies from the Anson family circle dressed as shepherdesses. On Cannock Chase Thomas Anson established sheep pastures and arable fields in addition to planting

12. Kedleston, Derbyshire – a view of the Home Farm looking out from the circuit walk designed by Robert Adam (1759)

hundreds of acres of various trees.[43]

To return to the *ferme ornée*. Mickleton, Gloucestershire, and Warlies are sometimes proposed as having influenced Shenstone when he came to design The Leasowes. The connection was the two brothers Morgan Graves (1707-70), bencher of the Middle Temple, and Richard Graves (1715-1804), poet, novelist and rector. The family seat was at Mickleton, and Shenstone met Richard in 1737 while up at Oxford, subsequently staying at Mickleton for long periods. It is said that Shenstone's first essay in landscape design was the planting of an avenue between Mickleton and Kiftsgate, up the hill from the village.[44] The friendship with Richard was particularly close, and when Richard became rector at Claverton, Somerset, Shenstone visited him frequently. The Graves's maternal family was the Morgans, and the elder brother (who inherited Mickleton) took that as his first name. Morgan Graves was supposedly influenced by Southcote of Woburn Farm, to whom he was related, and is said to have introduced Shenstone to Southcote's new ideas in garden and *ferme ornée* design. Shenstone visited him in 1743 to see the improvements at Mickleton.

The Morgan family's own seat was at Warlies, near Waltham Abbey (not to be confused with Warley Place), and Richard Graves said that it had been laid out in park-like fashion 'from hints which he had borrowed from Mr Southcote's, and other places',[45] so that Shenstone, via the Graves brothers, could himself have taken a great deal from the designer of Woburn Farm.

When we move across the Channel, however, perspectives on the *ferme ornée* were rather different, with continental landscape gardens showing elements of pictorial templescapes, pasture, the Brownian park and their own traditions. The situation in France, despite Switzer's claim, was that ideas about the ornamented farm gathered force only slowly. There were isolated cases such as the farm at Chanteheux which was given some architectural decoration probably in the late 1730s, but it was not until 1774 that the term *ferme ornée* was actually used in France, in Claude-Henri Watelet's *Essai sur les jardins*, and it was confirmed as a 'nouveau genre' by A N Duchêne shortly afterwards.[46] Watelet himself instituted a kind of proto-*ferme ornée* at his estate of Moulin-Joli, purchased in 1754, and developed to include a dairy and a cow barn in the garden scene in addition to the celebrated mill which gave the property its name.[47] Two years after Watelet's essay appeared, Le Rouge attempted a definition of the *ferme ornée*, but it applied to English models and seems, misguidedly, to describe a very general Brownian scene, where sheep and cattle roamed in the land outside the ha-ha, and hills were sometimes created and shaped.[48] The French moved into both agricultural improvement and what might be recognised as the *ferme ornée* only after 1775, by which time Thomas Whately's account of Woburn Farm and The Leasowes had been translated into French.

Watelet included a whole section on the *ferme ornée* in his Essay.[49] The house should command a view of what is both attractive and productive. The farm itself, the fields and vineyards are all part of the view, but varied by woods, streams and hillsides. The paths are gently sinuous, to admit variety, and lead through the farmland, sometimes alongside a hedge of flowering shrubs, sometimes beside spaced trees. The path deliberately takes in scenes of cowsheds, barns, granaries, orchards and beehives. There are areas for waterfowl and a herb garden. The overall intention was to secure peace of mind and find rest from the vanities and pursuits of the town.

Some in France adopted the *ferme ornée* as something very alien to the English concept, namely a quasi-theatrical 'playing at rusticity'.[50] Farm and 'hameau' (hamlet) were often indistinguishable, the principal examples being Chantilly (from 1775), Bellevue (1780-1) and, most famously, Marie-Antoinette's Hameau at the Petit Trianon of Versailles (c.1785-92). Structures which appeared to be rustic from the outside – barns, dairies, huts – would prove to have ballrooms or elaborate shell decoration inside. This is a long way from Woburn Farm. On the other hand, translations of English authors on husbandry and the new agriculture had appeared and been acted on, with the result that there were serious farm elements in some of the great gardens of the time – Ermenonville, Méréville, Le Raincy and Rambouillet.[51] Ermenonville, indeed, was known as the French Leasowes, though that had more to do with the literary dimension.

Elsewhere in Europe the term had particular application according to situation. At Altenstein, Thuringia, Germany, walks and plantings were made through agricultural land, and the term *ferme ornée* was used for that area, which was part of a much larger park. At Veltrusy, north of Prague, an island of pleasure ground contained arable plots which were integrated, 'joining ornamental and worked areas into a unified and artistic whole.'[52] And in Hungary the term was applied both to agricultural units within a landscape which were beautified and to a building (farmhouse) composed as a *cottage ornée*.

The *ferme ornée*, or parts of the idea, spread to America in the post-revolution years. Thomas Jefferson visited several landscape gardens in England in 1786, including The Leasowes, and returned home to plan his mountain garden at Monticello, Virginia. There he followed English ideas (such as those in Shenstone's writings) but also contemporary Virginia plantation practice.[53] It was divided up into areas, with ornamental flower gardens, shrubberies, orchards, vegetable gardens and finally fields and pasture laid out receding from the house. Half-way down the slope was the family burial ground.[54] From this layout it does not seem to have had much of the flavour of a *ferme ornée*, but from about 1808 Jefferson determined to integrate enclosures for farm animals with the ornamental gardens.[55]

Another American president, George Washington, read Batty Langley but seems to have been mainly interested in native trees and shrubs. He drew up plans for his 'home farm' at Mount Vernon, Virginia, where he experimented tirelessly with agricultural improvement but also sought out flowering trees and shrubs as he explored the vicinity.[56] There was a deer park, a family tomb half-way down the slope (as at Monticello), walled gardens for flowers and vegetables, and orchards.

One or two estates in South Carolina appear to have been influenced by Shenstone, such as Henry Laurens's Virgilian retreat of Mepkin.[57] Ralph Izard and his wife Alice developed The Elms, Goose Creek, from the mid-1790s, so that the kitchen gardens and the pleasure gardens were merged.[58] Dr Charles Drayton's naturalising of his father's garden at Drayton Hall[59] certainly had elements of the *ferme ornée* in its admixture of fields and gardens. Dr Drayton's papers contain references to Humphry Repton as well.[60]

The *ferme ornée* par excellence – indeed, perhaps the only pure example if we accept Whately – was Woburn Farm, near Chertsey, Surrey. Philip Southcote purchased the farm in 1735 and commenced work on ornamenting it more or less straight away. It was not therefore a conscious attempt to create a *ferme ornée* as such, since it predated the term, though Southcote might have been aware of Switzer's use of 'ornamental farm' from 1733. Authors who acclaimed it as the perfect type, such as Whately in 1770, did so with hindsight. Southcote (1697/8-1758) was a Catholic, so might have had an anti-Whig, anti-Protestant agenda, but in any case his work was in the spirit of the times, though he went further than anyone else. Joseph Spence, indeed, credited him with the invention of the *ferme ornée*.[61] Southcote knew William Kent and is said to have persuaded him to take up the planting of flowers in a natural way.[62] He was related to Lord Petre, the outstanding botanist and plantsman who died at twenty-nine, and this may have led to his interest in planting, especially with floral embellishments.

The property was relatively modest (which would have pleased Switzer), eventually reaching about 125 acres, of which 35 acres represented the pleasure grounds while the remainder comprised two-thirds pasture and one-third arable. Nonetheless the 'decoration' of colourful planting was continued through all parts by means of the principal structural device, a broad walk round the pasture and through the arable. The path was of sand in some places and gravel in others. Much of the walk was lined by a thick hedgerow ornamented by woodbine, jasmine and other flowering and scented creepers. Shrubs, firs and beds of flowers varied the walk, which was sometimes bare and sometimes cut through dense clumps of evergreens. Southcote was a pioneer in his use of colour so far from the house.[63]

The farm elements were omnipresent, and there were some complaints that the smell brought them uncomfortably close. The cattle, sheep and poultry were both visible and audible. A Gothic menagerie housed fowl that, initially at least, included Chinese and Indian cock pheasants. A number of buildings, including an octagon summerhouse attributed to Lord Burlington and a ruined chapel, graced the grounds, but the overall atmosphere and impression were rural English rather than the Italianate or classical feeling of William Kent's pictorial landscapes. Not that Southcote did not apply Kent's painterly approach, for each scene was composed with a foreground, a middle ground and a distance that changed as one moved from one part to another. Spence explained how this worked:

> In Mr Southcote's garden from the line that leads to the house, the foreground is the meadow, the mid-ground a winding stream with clumps of trees scattered about it and the background is the rising of the hill and the line of trees to the ruined church. These are all of moderate size and well-proportioned ... When you come to the summit of the hill, the foreground is the descent on the other side, the mid-ground is the menagerie, plantation, new building, Chertsey, etc., and the background is all the view extending from the Duke's new building on Shrub Hill [Fort Belvedere, overlooking Virginia Water] on one hand to Richmond Park on the other. In all this the parts are great, and the background much the greatest, which is a thing always to be wished for.[64]

The general planting of trees called on native species – ash, beech, elm, oak and weeping willow. Spence drew and scrutinised a small section of part of the walk, a sand path 5′ wide fenced off from one of the fields. The border on the other side of the walk was tiered in sections and in rows within each section. The first section was a 2.5′ wide border of flowers and shrubs – primroses, snowdrops, crocus, jonquils, hypia and pinks in the front; roses, stocks, wallflowers, carnations, lavender, scabious, marjoram, catchfly, sweet william and Canterbury bell in the middle row; and lilies, hollyhocks, golden rod, columbine, starwort, honesty, crown imperial, sunflower, peony and primrose-tree at the back. Behind the border was a 5′ wide plantation, again in three rows – first, bushes of rose, laurel, sweetbriar, holly, frutex and common broom; in the middle syringa, sweet willow, laburnum, lilac, whitethorn, honeysuckle and Spanish broom; and at the back trees – beech, black poplar, hornbeam, abele, alder, chestnut, hazel, crab apple. Behind everything was the original hedgerow.[65]

From Woburn we can see that Whately considered the essence of the *ferme ornée* to be that the farm should make its presence felt right through the estate as the visitor proceeds round; and, conversely, that the decorations of the pleasure ground, in terms of plantings or artefacts, are carried through the fields of the farm.

Not far from Woburn Farm was a property which certainly took some ideas of the *ferme ornée* into its composition, namely views of the garden and park from the farm, and views of the farm from the garden. This was Portmore Park, Weybridge, the seat of Lord Portmore. Held up as an exemplar of the mid-century pictorial garden by Richard Warner in later years,[66] it was an estate that had two rivers passing through it, the Thames and the Wey, with walks alongside the water. Robert FitzGerald commented, in his tour of Surrey gardens in the 1750s, that the terrace afforded noble views of extensive fields with oxen 'and many other fine objects',[67] while Henrietta Pye rhapsodised over the cascade, which was 'overshadowed with weeping Willows of extraordinary Beauty'. She brings farm and plantings of exotics together, with mention of flowers that provides a link with Woburn:

> The Trees are all extremely fine, and there is a grand collection of Flowers. Near one of the Rivers (and quite shaded with thick large Trees) stands a Farm, in which they greatly delight: It consists of a Parlour and a Chamber over it, which projects with a large bow Window, from whence the River, which runs close at the Roots of the Trees, resembles an Arm of the Sea, and forms the sweetest View that can be conceived. The whole Furniture and Appearance of [this] delightful Farm, can only be described by saying, it is most truly the *Simplex Munditiis*. There are also some Exotics of extraordinary Growth and Beauty, particularly the Tulip Tree in full Blow, the first that ever bloom'd in England. There is a fine Lawn to the back Front of the House.[68]

The *simplex munditiis* refers to Horace's theme of a natural yet elegant simplicity, where no artificial adornments are permitted to distort nature. This has been explicated by Mavis Batey as stemming from the image of the modest youth whose hair was neither unkempt nor falsely adorned but braided unostentatiously.[69]

Woburn Farm initiated keen interest in the genre, though very few were moved to emulate it. Even William Chambers, in *A Dissertation on Oriental Gardening* (1772), which has usually been taken to be an attack on Capability Brown in the guise of promoting supposed components of Chinese gardens, attributed some elements of the *ferme ornée* to the Chinese. Whether this was a dig at Southcote is not known, but Chambers's description might be taken to claim that China pre-empted Woburn:

> … introducing such plants, trees and buildings, into their design, as are not only beautiful, but also useful. Instead of lawns, they have meadows and fields, covered with sheep and other cattle;…of the buildings, some are barns for grain or hay; some stables for horses and oxen; some dairies, with their cow-houses and calf-pens; … others menageries for breeding poultry.[70]

While Switzer, Southcote and Spence promoted the idea of the *ferme ornée*, it was Thomas Whately who attempted to codify it and who is principally responsible for the understanding of it. In *Observations on Modern Gardening* (1770) he perceived the essence of a farm as simplicity, and also modest scale (as Switzer had). Whately opens his discussion by saying that, in the era of the formal garden, farm and garden elements were kept rigorously separate. The first step in combining them was (as we have seen with Addison, Bridgeman and Switzer) to open up views to the general countryside.[71] He makes an important distinction between the *ferme ornée* and what he calls the simpler, more rural kind of farm which postdates Woburn and is exemplified by The Leasowes. We shall return to this shortly, but Whately goes on to indicate that the *ferme ornée* is 'the means of bringing every rural circumstance within the verge of a garden.'[72] He says that the idea has often been put into effect but nowhere so completely and to such an extent as at Woburn Farm. The circuit walk 'is properly garden; all within it is farm; the whole lies on the two sides of a hill, and on a flat at the foot of it: the flat is divided into cornfields; the pastures occupy the hill; they are surrounded by the walk, and crossed by a communication carried along the brow, which is also richly dressed, and which divides them into two lawns, each completely encompassed with garden.'[73] Farm and garden run into each other: 'With the beauties which enliven a garden, are every where intermixed many properties of a farm.'[74]

Whately's conclusion, however, is that the *ferme ornée*, certainly as embodied at Woburn, loses sight of the simplicity that a farm ought to have: 'But though so many of the circumstances occur, the simplicity of a farm is wanting; that idea is lost in such a profusion of ornament; a rusticity of character cannot be preserved amidst all the elegant decorations which may be lavished on a garden.'[75] If Whately represents the feeling or taste of the 1760s-'70s, the *ferme ornée* had already had its day and its drawbacks exposed.

This brings us to the all-important question, was, or how far was, The Leasowes a *ferme ornée*? While fuller consideration of The Leasowes must wait till that section, this particular issue will be looked at now. Garden history has generally bracketed Woburn Farm and The Leasowes as the twin peaks of the *ferme ornée*, but contemporary perception was somewhat different. The greatly influential Whately distinguishes between the two properties, calling Woburn an ornamented farm and The Leasowes a 'pastoral farm' – he did not in fact consider it a *ferme ornée*. The marks of the pastoral farm were a simplicity lacking at Woburn and the inspiration of pastoral poetry, both of which (in Whately's view) characterised The Leasowes. Whately uses the word 'pastoral' in both senses, pasture and the classical literary. On simplicity at The Leasowes, he noted: 'It is literally a grazing farm lying round the house; and a walk, as unaffected and as unadorned as a common field path, is conducted through the several inclosures.'[76] Even if the farm did not pervade the walk as it did at Woburn, Whately's description of The Leasowes indicates that it kept coming into view: 'From the knole ... the beautiful farm of The Leasowes is included in the landscape. In other spots, plantations have been raised, or openings cut, on purpose to shut out, or let in, parts of it, at certain points of view.'[77] So, although the walk skirted the fields, their presence or concealment was carefully manipulated. Thomas Jefferson, going round in 1786, commented 'this is not even an ornamented farm. It is only a grazing farm with a path round it.'[78] But the wording indicates his debt to Whately (he took the *Observations* with him on his tours).

The principal contemporary account of The Leasowes was that written by Shenstone's friend and publisher Robert Dodsley, in an edition of Shenstone's works published a year after his death, although other hands almost certainly contributed to it.[79] It has to be admitted that there is little recognition of farm scenery, though a farmhouse is mentioned three or four times. But Dodsley uses the word 'farm' for the whole property, so that was very much at the heart of things, though Dodsley's concern was primarily with the circuit walk.

Shenstone himself had at least some perception of The Leasowes as a *ferme ornée*, if not an entirely serious one. In a letter to Richard Graves in August 1748 he claimed that he had adapted the term from *parque ornée*:

'The French have what they call a *parque ornée*; I suppose, approaching about as near to a garden as the park at Hagley. I give my place the title of a *ferme ornée*.'[80] But, as we have seen, he had not coined the term, which was not used by visitors by and large. It seems to have been mainly confined to Shenstone, Graves and Lady Luxborough, who in Dodsley's edition of Shenstone's works contributed (posthumously) some verses 'Written at a Ferme Ornee, near Birmingham', which is rather a coy way of putting it.[81] In 1758 Shenstone was still calling The Leasowes a *ferme ornée* in a letter to Graves,[82] but for more general purposes he seems to have abandoned the category since in his *Unconnected Thoughts on Gardening* he divides gardening into three types – kitchen-gardening, parterre gardening and landscape, or picturesque, gardening.[83] His usual term for The Leasowes was simply 'farm'. His own watercolours show how important the agricultural dimension was to him, physically and aesthetically, such as the inclusion of haystacks.

The plethora of descriptions of The Leasowes in the late eighteenth century dwell on the romantic nature of the changing scenes, the inscriptions and the scenery, particularly where it is striking or dramatic, as in Virgil's Grove. The forthright William Marshall, after his visit in 1785, expressed disappointment: 'For what is it? An ornamented farm? No such thing. What has farming to do with Temples, Statues, Vases, Mottos, Inscriptions, Mock Priories, and Artificial Cascades?'[84] Yet even where interest is focused elsewhere, the farm is still at the centre and colours the experience of going round the gardens. The reading of The Leasowes as a *ferme ornée* is part only of the story, though an essential one for its understanding: the other subtleties and complexities of this literary and cultural landscape will be explored later.

Perhaps because of the fame of Woburn Farm and The Leasowes, farm elements in other landscape gardens sometimes led to those gardens being described as *fermes ornées*. This has generally happened long after the event, sometimes in recent writings. In most of these cases, parts of the farm would be visible when going round the grounds, and might constitute an intended scene, but there would be no real integration nor was there the pervasive presence of the farm throughout. Such is the case at Enville, where the walk goes past Home Farm, Lyndon (where the house was gothicised) and across the Sheep Walk to the Shepherd's Lodge. There is a strong rural presence, therefore, and the sheep and cattle play an important part in the scene, along with harvest stooks, as Anthony Devis illustrates in his paintings, making the outward walk in some degree a *ferme ornée*. But the second half of the circuit – the woods, buildings, one of the cascades and pools – claim attention in a direction away from the agricultural. Joseph Heely made the contemporary judgment that it could be classified neither as a park nor as a farm: 'It partakes of all the principal divisions of gardening, and may be equally distinguished in the light of park, garden, farm and riding.'[85] Painshill, Surrey, too, has been called a *ferme ornée*, though the actual farm was on the other side of the main Portsmouth Road, and the term must have been applied simply on the strength of the presence of sheep grazing in the park.

Stowe, the greatest of eighteenth-century gardens, has sometimes been referred to as a *ferme ornée* because a terrace walk bounded the Home Park, where cattle grazed and there was a paddock for horses, while on the other side of the central vista there was Hawkwell Field, at first a pasture for cattle but later turned over to hay at the same time as it was adorned with the Lady's (Queen's) Temple and the Gothic Temple: 'Hawkwell Field marked yet another new development in the Stowe landscape in that it was laid out as a *ferme ornée*, with a hay field in the middle and a carriage drive round the perimeter from which there were ever-changing views to the different buildings and their beautifully contrived settings.'[86]

William Mavor, in his description of Blenheim, spoke of the *ferme ornée* as being combined with the park. What he describes, however, is simply a series of attractive agricultural scenes which become visible as one tours the grounds:

> In one quarter, the eye is delighted with the sight of waving corn, in another with green paddocks that invite the scythe: here a building dedicated to agricultural purposes… just peeps through the deep shade of surrounding trees; there the team rattles down a slope abrupt. On one side appears a herd of deer, on another a flock of sheep, and sometimes animals native and foreign graze in social peace. All is a picture of rural life in its most agreeable colours, in its happiest avocations: it presents cheerful activity, or tranquil repose – Arcadian scenes divested of fable, and real wealth without glitter.[87]

Rousham, Oxfordshire, has also had the same appellation, presumably

Three Great Eighteenth-Century Gardens

13. Hawkwell Field, Stowe looking up to the Gothic Temple designed by James Gibbs (1744-8) with later additions thought to be by Sanderson Miller

because the early part of the walk runs beside a ha-ha bounding a field for cattle (sometime a paddock). William Kent, the designer of the gardens who followed Bridgeman, built a Janus pavilion at a corner of this field which serves as a cowshed from the field but as a Gothic seat from the walk, with crenellation mirroring that of the house (fig. 14, page 58). Architecture has often been seen as contributing to the air of a *ferme ornée*, such as the Bantam Folly at Belsay, Northumberland (1757), a farm building next to a field. At Badminton, Gloucestershire, there are several barns with castellation, the largest being called Castle Barn. Also Gothic in style are the combined cowshed and dovecote at Exton Park, Rutland, and the dairy at Fawley Court, Buckinghamshire.

A late development of a related kind was the model farm. Particularly through the agency of Nathaniel Kent, working farms were designed by architects to incorporate the latest in agricultural technology and methods. Kent was responsible for the model farms at Windsor Great Park, for George III ('farmer George'), Holkham, Norfolk (for Lord Coke, the great agricultural pioneer), and Shugborough, where, as at Holkham, the buildings were designed by Samuel Wyatt. Although these examples were late eighteenth century, it appears that the Home Farm at Enville was a very early instance. The 4th Earl of Stamford was keenly interested in the agricultural side of his estate.

The *ferme ornée* stumbled on, though with diminishing vigour. The impetus had gone; the agricultural revolution placed an emphasis on

14. Rousham, Oxfordshire. Gothic Seat by William Kent masking a cow shed, late 1730s

farming not ornament; and farming and gardening were seen as separate activities, not suitable to be melded. The last word should be left to Whately, who saw that the two were ultimately incompatible and that the *ferme ornée* would disappear if it had not done so already: 'Though a farm and a garden agree in many particulars connected with extent, yet in *style* they are the two extremes. Both indeed are subjects of cultivation; but cultivation in the one is *husbandry,* and in the other *decoration*: the former is appropriated to *profit*, the latter to *pleasure*: fields profusely ornamented do not retain the appearance of a farm; and an apparent attention to produce, obliterates the idea of a garden.'[88] In other words, profit and pleasure can (and should) co-exist, but not be united.

3
Enville

٭

A SHENSTONIAN CASCADE, in full flow and fury; foaming and bellowing, as if the mountain were enraged: pouring down a river of water, as white as snow, and apparently so copious, as to render our situation alarming; lest the house [Boat House] and its contents should be hurried away with the torrent.[1]

ALTHOUGH THIS WAS WRITTEN SOME FORTY YEARS AFTER THEIR CREATION THE cascades at Enville still had the power to excite and astonish. This was just the beginning of a journey along gravel paths, over high rounded hills, across long ridges and into steep-sided valleys. New delights caught the eye at every turn and beckoned the visitor onwards with both intimate and far-reaching views together with a wonderful variety of buildings, seats and plantings. A walk around Enville stimulated the senses, from the breathtaking views from the Shepherd's Lodge on the Sheep Walk to the sensuousness of the serpentine path through the moss-carpeted shrubbery and the terror of the cascades.

The eighteenth-century grounds at Enville were created by Harry Grey, 4th Earl of Stamford, and, most probably, his highly intelligent wife Mary aided by Sanderson Miller, the gentleman architect from Radway in Warwickshire, and the poet William Shenstone. Their work was completed in the 1770s by Harry and Mary's eldest son George Harry, later the 5th Earl.

The Grey family and their circle

The Grey family trace their descent back to the time of the Norman Conquest when Fulbert was the chamberlain to Robert, Duke of Normandy. At Domesday, Anchitel de Grey held lands in Oxfordshire and it was his great, great grandson Henry who was granted the manor of Thurrock in Essex. The various branches of the Grey family are descended from him – Ruthin, Codnor, Sandiacre and Wilton as well as the Earls of Stamford.

The first major Grey estate was in Leicestershire. It was centred on

15. Engraving of Enville Hall in 1686. Robert Plot. *The Natural History of Staffordshire,* *Oxford: at the Theater*, 1686. [EA]

Bradgate Park, five miles north-west of Leicester, and came to the family by the marriage of Sir Edward Grey to Elizabeth Ferrers, who had inherited the estate in 1444 on the death of her grandfather, William, Lord Ferrers of Groby. Their son Sir John Grey married Elizabeth Woodville, who after Sir John's death at the Battle of St. Albans in 1460 married King Edward IV. The children of the Grey marriage subsequently held the titles of the Marquis of Dorset and Duke of Suffolk. Meanwhile it was Sir Edward's great-nephew who started the Enville line when the other moiety (or half share) of the manor of Enville was sold to another Sir Edward Grey. It was his son, Thomas, who built Enville Hall in the 1530s and became MP for Staffordshire. At Enville life was quiet and stable and the estate passed to his son John.

Peace did not prevail on the Leicestershire estate at Bradgate where there followed a period of family turmoil. Henry Grey's daughter was Lady Jane Grey who was executed in 1553 after her father tried unsuccessfully to install her as Queen of England. He was pardoned, but was then executed the following year for his involvement in the Wyatt rebellion. Two other brothers were also executed in the 1550s leaving the fourth son, John Grey of Pyrgo in Essex, as head of the family.

John Grey's son Henry was knighted in 1587 and created Baron Grey of Groby in 1603. He sold his estates in Essex and moved to Bradgate. His grandson Henry became the 2nd Baron Grey of Groby and in 1620 married Anne Cecil, the youngest daughter and co-heir of William Cecil, 3rd Earl of Exeter. Through his wife, Henry inherited the castle, borough and manor of Stamford and in 1628 was created Earl of Stamford. He was much involved in the Civil War and became a rather unsuccessful commander of the Parliamentary forces in Devon and Cornwall. His son, Thomas, was also a Parliamentarian and a regicide judge, his name being the second signature on the death warrant of Charles I. The Greys were, however, a family of divided loyalties. Henry Grey at Enville supported the King and maintained a garrison there for which he was declared a 'delinquent' by Cromwell and for a short time his lands were confiscated.

Thomas died before his father and so it was his son, another Thomas, who succeeded as the 2nd Earl of Stamford. The family once more became embroiled with royal intrigue and Thomas was imprisoned for his involvement with the Rye House Plot and Monmouth's rebellion. He supported the uprising of 1688 which brought William and Mary to the throne and was rewarded with several lucrative offices. He married the heiress Elizabeth Harvey who brought with her a fortune of £100,000. In spite of marrying twice he died childless, and so in 1720 his estates and the title passed to his cousin Harry Grey of Enville.

Harry Grey, 3rd Earl of Stamford, married Dorothy, daughter of Sir Nathan Wrighte, Lord Keeper of the Great Seal. Theirs was a stormy and tempestuous marriage, owing mainly to the eccentricities of the Earl which resulted in Dorothy living apart from him, though not before bearing him ten children of which the first three males died in infancy. The Earl suffered from various phobias and developed a fear of being seen by other people. His servants were required to enter and retreat from the room with their backs towards him. He also developed an aversion to lime mortar believing that it was injurious to his health. This prompted the building of a square enclosure with high walls about a quarter of a mile from the Hall, in which he pitched a tent in the centre and apparently lived there for some time.[2] The walls can still be seen both from the Kinver and the Stourbridge roads.

In 1735 at St. James's, Westminster, Harry and Dorothy's eldest son, also Harry, later to become the 4th Earl, married at the age of twenty. His wife was twelve years older than himself. Lady Mary Booth was the only daughter and sole heiress of George Booth, 2nd Earl of Warrington, who held large estates in Cheshire based at Dunham Massey and in Lancashire around Ashton-under-Lyne and Stalybridge. Harry had estates of his own and inherited not only the Staffordshire estate, but land and properties in Leicestershire, Lincolnshire, Derbyshire, Nottinghamshire and Warwickshire. The couple spent the first few years of their married life at Bradgate Park in Leicestershire, and their two eldest children George Harry and Mary were born there, but when the 3rd Earl died in 1739 they decided to move with their two children to the Staffordshire estate where there was a fine, large Tudor brick house with turrets and crow-stepped gables. At Bradgate the doors and windows were bricked up and the estate was subsequently managed as a deer park and farm. Both Harry and Mary were the product of unhappy and broken marriages; their arranged marriage and age difference does not seem to have caused any problems. They appear to have had a very contented life devoting themselves to their children, the embellishment of the grounds of Enville Hall and charitable works in the parish and surrounding area.

Harry, Lord Grey, had received a classical education and attended Queen's College, Cambridge. His library, where many of his books are annotated with his thoughts, shows he had a lively and interested mind ranging across a wide variety of topics from the classics and architecture to travel, philosophy and religion. His wife, Lady Mary, had been highly educated by her father, 2nd Earl of Warrington, in a manner to which only men of that age were accustomed.[3] She had a particular interest in all the sciences and medicine, plays and poetry. Both appear to have been fluent in French and Latin. Musicians and poets visited Enville Hall, and paintings were commissioned of their family and park. Lord Stamford enjoyed both hunting and coursing. The hounds were kennelled at Bradgate, but there were frequent movements of both horses and hounds between there and Enville. Racing was a great passion and he was a subscriber to 'the Races' at Bridgnorth, Knutsford and Northwich and to *The Sporting Kalendar* by John Pond from its first edition in 1751. He was very fond of betting on horses and events, such as the wager he had with Lord Gower 'upon Sir George Warren's Wedding' when he lost ten guineas. It would have been interesting to know the details of the bet! He also had a regular flutter on 'Lotterye Tickets' with some success.[4]

Altogether the Stamfords had five children, the last one John being born in May 1743. Later that year his sister Anne died aged two and a half but the rest survived into old age. Most of Lord and Lady Stamford's energies were put into bringing up their family and the improvement and consolidation of the estate. What they seem to have wanted most from their lives was a settled and contented home in pleasant surroundings. Although various family members became MPs, the 4th Earl does not seem to have sought high office either at Court or in Parliament. The epitaph on his memorial plaque in Enville Church probably sums him up: 'He was a kind father, an indulgent master, a warm friend; in every relation of life truly benevolent.' That does not mean to say that the Stamfords did not have strong opinions about things especially politics. This was a delicate situation as their daughter-in-law Henrietta's brother was William, 3rd Duke of Portland, whose life was dominated by politics and who was later to become Home Secretary under Pitt the Younger and was twice Prime Minister. On one occasion when William was first coming to stay at Enville she wrote a warning to him on the subject:

> though I must, my Dear Soul, give you a hint never to drop the least word upon any occasion whatever when you are here before the Grandees [Lord and Lady Stamford], for nothing ever was so hot and furious as they are, indeed, it puts me in a tremble if any stranger comes in for there are no bounds kept if the subject happens to be named.[5]

The Stamfords entertained a great deal, and Henrietta writes there was 'a good deal of company in the House with us'.[6] The Day Books record copious amounts of alcohol which was bought by the pipe or hogshead and then bottled at Enville. Oysters and lampreys together with eels and flounders were bought live and kept as store fish in the pools.[7] Game was plentiful and William Shenstone, who was a regular visitor, wrote almost complainingly whilst staying at the Hall that 'I am quite pampered with Snipes & Field-fare'.[8] Their wide circle of friends were drawn mainly from the same aristocratic social circle as themselves – Lord Gower at Trentham, the Lytteltons at Hagley, Viscount Torrington at Peover, Lord Dudley at Himley, Lord Egerton at Tatton. In addition to having visitors to stay they also travelled to stay with friends, as well as to their new house in Charles Street, London, to Dunham Massey, Cheshire, to Scarborough for sea-bathing and also to take the waters at Bath where they rented a house on South Parade. Their main pleasure, however, lay in their home.

When Lord Stamford inherited the Enville Estate it was very fragmented, with land and manors in most counties of the Midlands and only about 700 acres adjacent to Enville Hall. Within a few years he began to sell some of the outlying properties in order to raise money to buy land around the Manor of Enville.[9] It has often wrongly been said that it was money from his marriage to Mary that funded these purchases. Under the terms of the 2nd Earl of Warrington's will all the Cheshire and Lancashire estates were vested in two trustees, as women were not allowed to own property, although Mary managed the Dunham estate.[10] It was not until her death in 1772 that they passed to her son, by then the 5th Earl of Stamford.

Historical background

Enville lies about seven miles south-east of Bridgnorth on the Staffordshire, Shropshire and Worcestershire borders. The Hall is situated at the foot of rolling hills between the rivers Severn and Stour where the land rises to over 600 feet on top of the Sheep Walk. From here one can see to the Black Mountains in Wales, the Wrekin, the Malvern Hills and other ranges.

The designed landscape of Enville Hall Park lies within the Manor of Enville which forms the southern part of the parish of Enville. The Domesday Book records a considerable amount of woodland in the region,[11] and the Manor was within the Forest of Kinver which was held by the king for hunting. There was natural tree cover on the ridges with many oaks and beeches, and this forms the largest part of what is now the park. During the late thirteenth and into the fourteenth centuries the imposition of forest laws declined and groups of people started making small assarts or clearings within the forest in which they built dwellings and started to farm the land. The descendants of the first forest clearers became freeholders and later yeoman farmers; this has produced a very distinct pattern of land tenure and settlement.

Enville is situated on a geological fault line between hard and soft sandstones. The road between The Leasowes and Hagley to Enville crossed the soft sandstone which was being constantly eroded by the traffic. Lady Henrietta wrote that at Enville they were suffering 'great floods' as a result

Three Great Eighteenth-Century Gardens

col 1:
Lady Mary Booth, Wife of 4th Earl of Stamford by an unknown English artist,
c.1765. Dunham Massey. The Stamford Collection (The National Trust).
©NTPL/Fraser Marr

col 2:
Harry 4th Earl of Stamford by unknown English artist c.1765. Dunham Massey.
The Stamford Collection (The National Trust). ©NTPL/Fraser Marr

col 3: The Villa del Trebbio, lunette by Giusto Utens (1599)

col 4: Castle Barn, Badminton.
Castellated farm building designed by Thomas Wright (1750s)

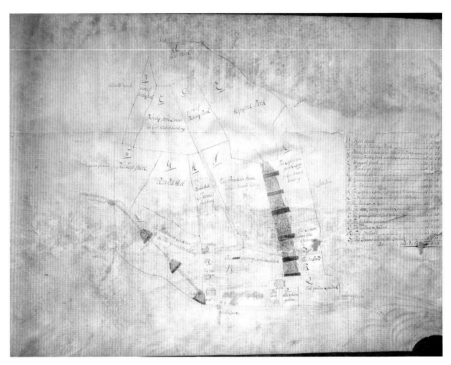

col. 5: Plan of Enville Estate – a later copy of a plan made c.1650 [EA]

col. 6: Enville Hall on the Estate Survey of 1688 by William Deeley [EA]

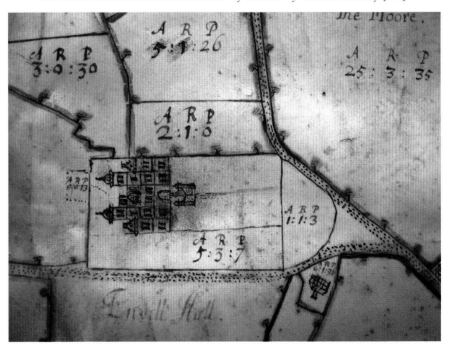

col 7: Enville, the view from the Doric Temple looking down the long dry valley towards the Black Country

col 8: Enville, the Rotunda and haymaking (detail) from a picture by Anthony Devis (c.1765). Private collection

col 9: The view from the Urn across the Temple Pool to Enville Hall and on to the tower of St. Mary's Church – a half-mile-long sightline. Peter Williams

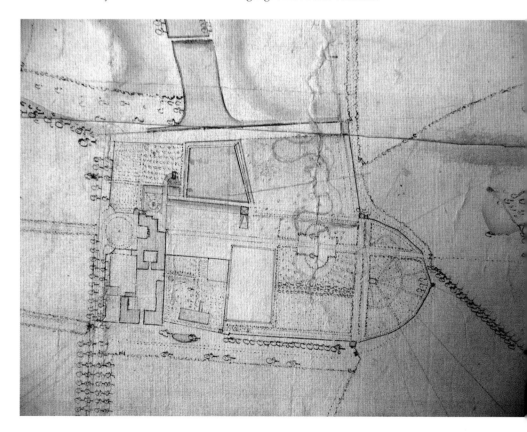

col 11: The Gothic Greenhouse at Enville by Sanderson Miller (1749-1750). Peter Williams

col 10: *Left*: the pleasure garden at Enville showing the formal layout with the Gothic Greenhouse tucked up in the top, right-hand corner of the garden. Detail from c.1750 Estate Survey [EA]

col 12: The interior of the Gothic Greenhouse at Enville. Peter Williams

col 13: A view taken from near the Gothic Seat at Enville looking northwards towards Wolverhampton c.1760. Watercolour by Anthony Devis. Private collection

col 15: *Right*: view over the Upper Pool to the Rotunda at Enville in a watercolour by Anthony Devis (c.1765). Private collection

16. Panoramic view of Enville showing the buildings in the landscape. Green Frog dinner service made for Catherine the Great. The State Hermitage Museum, St. Petersburg; photograph © The State Hermitage Museum

of the thawing snow followed by heavy rain which meant that it was impossible for any carriages to pass.[12] Of the three gardens it was the most distant and in bad weather almost isolated.

The earliest remains of human activity within the designed landscape of Enville Hall is the boundary ditch and bank of a deer park. It has not been possible to date it as no emparking licence has yet been found. It is shown on John Speed's Map of Staffordshire dated 1610, but by 1640 there were no deer in the park.[13] The Hall was built in the 1530s by Sir Thomas Grey on the eastern boundary of the deer park, with both the pleasure and kitchen gardens situated to the north of the Hall. In 1548 it was described as a 'park within a pale'.[14] The gardens enclosed an area of over six acres and were surrounded by a high brick wall, some of which still remains. The antiquary Sampson Erdewick describes it around 1600 as '[a goodly Manor] and a Park ... where Thomas Grey, late of Envilde [died 1559-60] built a very proper Brick House'.[15] The house was almost certainly on a new site, the old manor house being close to the parish church. The bricks were made from the local clay in the adjoining field. There were twenty-nine main rooms in the Hall which included a parlour, chapel and armoury.[16]

Seventeenth-century maps show an enclosed garden that ends in a bastion-shaped feature which looks north out over the Moors Pools and up to a small hill on top of which is the parish church of St. Mary's.[17] Bastions were popular garden features in the early eighteenth century such as those designed by Stephen Switzer at Grimsthorpe and Charles Bridgeman at Stowe. However, this is earlier and may have had an actual military purpose when during the Civil War Henry Grey maintained a Royalist garrison at Enville Hall.[18] By 1688 the garden had been extended westward by one field when the orchard and lowest pool were incorporated into the existing

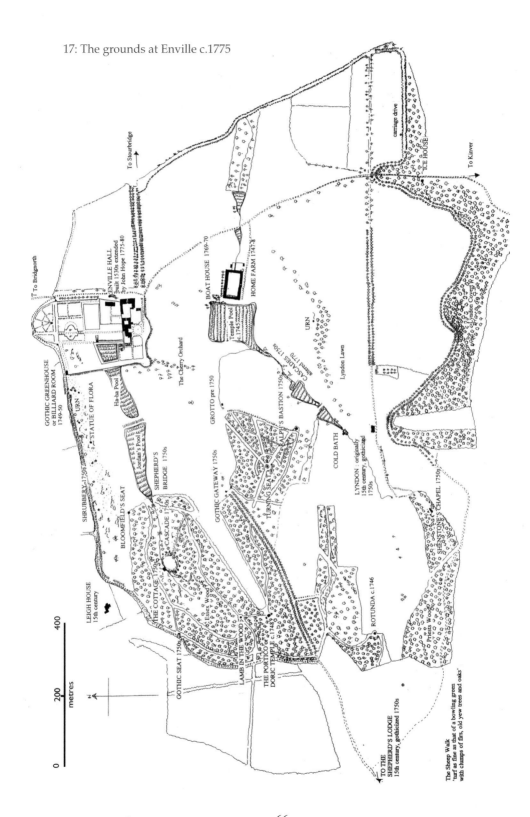

17: The grounds at Enville c.1775

To Stourbridge

To Bridgnorth

To Kinver

carriage drive

ICE HOUSE

ENVILLE HALL
built 1530s extended
by John Hope 1775-80

BOAT HOUSE 1769-70

HOME FARM 1747-8

Temple Pool
c.1745

URN

Lyndon Lawn

Fulton Coppice

GOTHIC GREENHOUSE
or BILLIARD ROOM
1749-50

URN

STATUE OF FLORA

The Cherry Orchard

Ha-ha Pool

SHRUBBERY c.1750s

Jordan's Pool

GROTTO pre 1750

RALPH'S BASTION 1750s

CASCADES 1750s
altered 1770

BLOOMFIELD'S SEAT

SHEPHERD'S
BRIDGE 1750s

GOTHIC GATEWAY 1750s

TURNING SEAT 1750s

COLD BATH

LYNDON - originally
15th century, gothicized
1750s

LEIGH HOUSE
15th century

THE COTTAGE 1750s

CASCADE 1750s

Essex Wood

SHENSTONE'S CHAPEL 1750s

GOTHIC SEAT 1750s

LAMB IN THE WOOD

THE PORTICO or
DORIC TEMPLE c.1748

ROTUNDA c.1746

Priests Wood

TO THE
SHEPHERD'S LODGE
15th century, gothicized 1750s

The Sheep Walk
'turf as fine as that of a bowling green
with clumps of firs, old yew trees and oaks'

metres

0   200   400

N

66
Three Great Eighteenth-Century Gardens

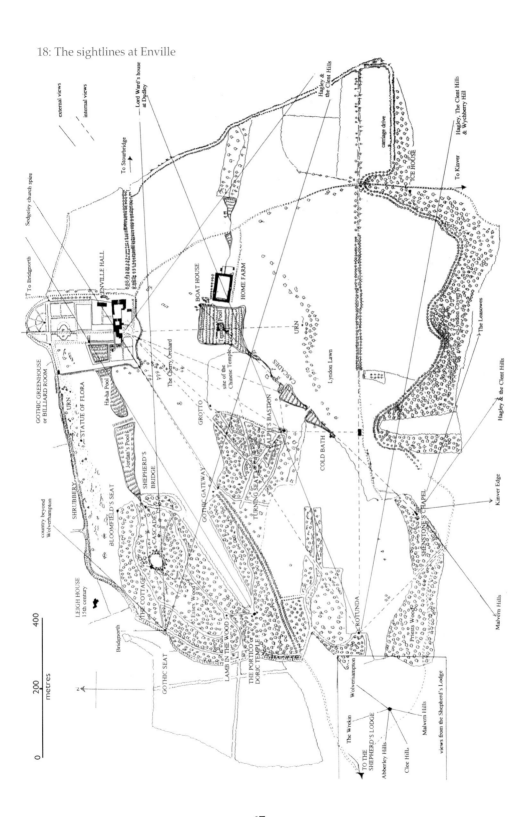

18: The sightlines at Enville

garden.[19] The western boundary now ran along the line of the ditch of the deer park, which at a later period was included to form part of the ha-ha.

In 1720 the title of Earl of Stamford passed to Harry Grey of Enville who became the 3rd Earl. There is little archival evidence about him apart from his rather eccentric behaviour. It seems unlikely that this self-centred man would have bothered with the landscaping of the park. So it is to his son, also Harry, that Enville owes the greater part of its fame as one of the trinity of West Midland gardens.

Over time opinions have changed as to the siting of the house at the foot of the hills as was the fashion of the sixteenth and seventeenth centuries. Robert Plot writing in 1686 thought this 'beautiful mansion is perhaps the best situate of any in the country',[20] whilst nearly a hundred years later Sulivan wrote in 1778, 'This house is unfortunately situated too low; it has neither prospect or airiness, and is, in fact, buried at the foot of a hill. Had the present possessor razed it entirely to the ground, and erected another on some more chosen spot, instead of the additions and improvements, which at considerable expense he is making, it would, perhaps, have been as little extravagant to his pocket in the end, and would most assuredly have rendered his residence more pleasing: he, however, knew best what he was about. It is only hard that the sins of the father should visit the children unto the third and fourth generation'.[21]

Early stages

It is not clear whether there was a grand plan at the beginning or whether the design gradually evolved. It is a garden where sight lines, patterns of light and shade, concealment and exposure, vast panoramic views and tightly manipulated ones are regularly contrasted. The green foliage is set against the red earth and the sweet scents of rose and honeysuckle fill the air. The sound of water gives different notes as it tumbles over a variety of rills and cascades mixed with the rustle of leaves and the notes of bird song. All these stimulants are extremely important to the enjoyment of the visitor. It is a garden for the senses.

It was not unusual for owners also to be the designers and there are numerous other examples such as Henry Hoare at Stourhead or the Aislabies at Studley Royal. Lord Stamford's close friendship with the Lytteltons and their group, including Sanderson Miller will also have been an influence. The fact that William Shenstone, Lord Lyttelton and Lord Stamford were all developing their parks at the same time and knew one another must have meant that ideas would have been exchanged.

Unfortunately Lord Stamford's bank accounts do not give details of whom he paid to construct the garden. No money would have been paid to either William Shenstone or Sanderson Miller as they were 'gentlemen', but his accounts show that he drew out large amounts of cash to 'himself' which would then be disbursed to the workmen. The amount rose rapidly from £210 in 1751 to £2699 15s 2d in 1755 and £2274 7s 6d in 1756 after which it declined to £415 in 1759. Bills at Enville were rarely paid on time and most were paid eighteen months to two years after the bills had been presented. This suggests that most of the money spent on landscaping was for work carried between 1753 and 1756.[22]

There are three periods to the development of the park and garden at Enville in the eighteenth century: before 1750: a formal landscape; 1750-1756: a more naturalistic view of landscape; 1769-1773: towards the Pictur-esque, the finishing touches.

A formal landscape

The new designed landscape at Enville was laid out to the north, south and west of the Hall and set within a productive agricultural landscape of small hedged fields and amongst wooded hills with streams in the valleys. The farmhouses, cottages and hovels were all made from the local materials of timber, clay for daub, tile and bricks, and thatch of either straw or heather. Paintings of the park by Anthony Devis in the mid-1760s show the harvest as well as grazing sheep and cattle.[23] Many early eighteenth-century books do not treat gardening as a separate occupation, but as part of the husbandry of the landscape.[24] The people who worked on the gardens at Enville were the same group of men and women who worked on the farm.[25] From this anonymous group of people we can identify one named gardener, Thomas Garnett, who was undoubtedly the head gardener. He was given a cottage on the estate and an annuity of £2 10s after his retirement in 1774.[26]

The Estate Survey of 1688 shows that the front of the house was surrounded by a wall with large gates at the southern entrance. From here one looked over a field called the Innage to the stables situated by a small pool and fed by a stream on which was once a watermill. This was the first area to be redesigned by the 4th Earl. The old stables were demolished and a new complex, including a brewhouse, was built adjoining the domestic services to the east of the Hall, probably to a design by William Baker of Audlem in Cheshire (1705-1771) who worked mainly on house improvements in Shropshire, Staffordshire and the adjoining counties. Howard Colvin describes him as 'a minor Georgian provincial architect'.[27] A dam was built on the north and east side of the old stable pool to create a large almost square sheet of water edged with bricks. In the centre of the pool a Chinese Temple was erected and connected to the west lawn by a Chinese bridge. It could be seen directly from the entrance to the Hall. The name 'Temple Pool' is marked on a plan of 1746 to show the lands owned by Thomas Shadwell.[28] The plan in the archives is a copy made in 1809 and it poses the question: is it an exact copy of the original or has the draughtsman adopted early nineteenth-century names on the plan? The plan names one of the tenants, a Mr Groves, and he appears on the Enville rent roll for 1747, the year after the Lyndon estate was purchased by Lord Stamford,[29] but he is not on the rent roll for 1809.[30] This indicates that the new map could be a correct copy of the 1746 plan, which would give the latest possible date for the construction of the Chinese Temple and Rotunda as 1746. Pococke describes the Temple thus '... on one side [of the house] is a piece of water, and in an island is a Chinese octagon building with a square at each end, to which there is a long bridge; the building stands on three arches'.[31] It was furnished with a table, chairs, pictures and fabrics, and was in all probability used for summer dining, relaxing and fishing. It was repaired and painted in 1761 as part of the celebrations for Lord Stamford's eldest son's 21st birthday on his return home from his Grand Tour.[32] Chinoiserie was beginning to go out of fashion, and a year after Lord Grey became the 5th Earl in 1768 the building was taken down as it did not fit in with his new plans for the garden.

The Estate Survey of c.1750 shows that the area around the Hall had been developed along the lines of the forest style of gardening as advocated by Stephen Switzer in his book *Ichnographia Rustica* published in three volumes in 1718.[33] This was a landscape style based on geometry with long straight avenues of trees and hedges. At Enville the formal Temple Pool was teamed up with geometric clumps of trees and a few garden buildings. The ideas behind the designs are similar to the landscape that Mary Booth had grown up with at Dunham Massey in Cheshire, where her father the 2nd Earl of Warrington started laying out his park of woods and radiating avenues from c.1712 and continued to do so for several decades.[34]

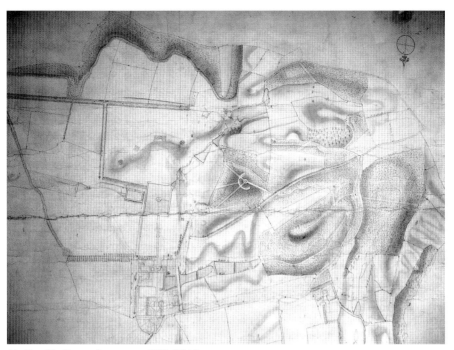

19. Enville Estate Survey c. 1750. [EA]

On a natural 'eminence' known as Round Hill that overlooked the Temple Pool a turning seat was built from which radiated four allées which were cut through the shrubs and trees that covered its slopes. Stylistically this pattern is known as a *patte d'oie* or goose foot and dates to the earlier part of the eighteenth century, but it remained quite fashionable in the 1740s. The long allées were linked by small paths which followed the contour of the hill and contained small seats in quiet seclusion. Turning seats were unusual garden structures. One was constructed for Queen Caroline, consort of George II in 1733 in Kensington Gardens as she 'improved the grounds by enlarging them towards the high road to Acton, so as to be able to make a lake in them. With the earth which was dug out for this purpose, was formed a hillock on which a covered seat was so arranged that it could be turned round according to the direction of the wind'.[35] That was designed by William Kent with four caryatid figures supporting the roof. By comparison, the Enville turning seat would have been of a much simpler design. It was approached high up from the Ash Walk by a path along a small ridge which was marked by yew trees. Only when one reached the seat was any view apparent. The seat was built of wood and was capable of being rotated either to keep their occupants facing the sun or out of the wind, or to enable

them to enjoy a change of views across the garden. At Enville the sitter had a choice of vistas either to the Hall, the Chinese Temple or to Lyndon farmhouse and also, more widely, over the countryside beyond.

The Grotto

At the corner of the base of Round Hill lie the remnants of a small grotto. This was a brick barrel-vaulted construction covered with lead on the roof and decorated with shells on the inside. The front was faced with quartzite and local industrial slag with its glassy blue bands.[36] These building materials were also used for the Grotto at Hagley. At the front two iron hinges indicate that there may have been a grill which protected a statue inside. The water was provided by a small stream which originated about twenty yards up the slope trickling through the grotto and spilling out into a small pool at the front, from where the water meandered across the lawn to the corner of the Temple Pool. The water-table in the eighteenth century was appreciably higher than it is today, so that now the grotto is virtually dry.

The Home Farm

On the eastern side of the Temple Pool lies the Home Farm. It is thought to have been designed by William Baker (1705-1771) who also designed the Stables. Baker's account book shows that he produced unspecified plans for the 4th Earl at this time.[37] The Farm is built of local brick and tile in Staffordshire vernacular, but seems to have owed its layout to the villa-farm architecture described by Andrea Palladio in *Quattro Libri dell'Architettura*

(1570) which was in the 4th Earl's library.[38] The plaque on the wall states that it was built between 1747 and 1748. The plan is roughly rectangular in shape with animal stalls, stables and sheds built around a courtyard in the centre of which were the muck yard and pig sties. Just outside the arched entrance were the cart and wagon sheds. It must have been one of the first model farms in the country.[39]

The Rotunda

The two classically-inspired buildings shown on the Estate Survey are the Rotunda and the Doric Portico. The Rotunda is built just below the brow of a steep, rounded hill and backed by trees. It is at the end of a long sight-line from the Kinver road which takes the eye along a tree-lined avenue to the farmhouse at Lyndon and thence up to the Rotunda just below the ridge. The field name 'Rotunda Piece' appears on the map of Shadwell's lands dated 1746 so it seems that it was built by that date. This pre-dates, by a couple of years, the Rotunda at Hagley (1748-9) which was similar in design. The base is a multi-faceted bastion built of brick and capped with local sandstone; on top of this were six Ionic stone columns with a wooden domed roof covered with lead and topped by a gilded ball. The interior of the dome was painted blue and the floor was paved with flagstones.[40] A seat provided a spot from which to enjoy the view 'from whence we look down upon blooming meads and corngrounds, amply diversified with trees and shrubs'.[41] On a clear day the vista extended over eight miles to the Wren's Nest at Dudley and along the skyline to Hagley and the Clent Hills.

The Doric Portico or Temple

At the head of the dry valley just over the ridge from the Rotunda was the Doric Portico which was later known as the Summerhouse. This has been attributed to a design by Sanderson Miller who recorded in his diary of 29 January 1749 'Drawing temple for Lord Stamford and writing to him'.[42] It is a single-storey building with a pediment supported on four square rusti-cated stone columns. Inside is a contemporary wooden seat. There is a great similarity between the design of this building and that of Pope's Seat (also known as the Doric Portico) at Hagley which was built about four or five years before, c.1745. Many of the buildings of this period at Enville have long sightlines which extend far out of the park to the countryside beyond. Here the view is centred on the spire of the church at Sedgley over eight

21. The Doric Portico with its original wooden seat which was built by 1750 and is attributed to Sanderson Miller

miles away. Heely writes:

> This building is well adapted to the place, standing on the verge of a wood that expands itself over the hills behind, and forming, as it sweeps down on either side of the valley, a deep concave of an open sloping lawn, shut in at a considerable distance by a detached airy grove.[43]

When the Doric Portico was first built the Industrial Revolution was in its infancy, but very soon afterwards the horizon must have been full of the billowing grey smoke and the glowing furnaces of the iron industry which was expanding on the other side of the river Stour around Dudley, in what later became known as the Black Country. Only in the last few decades has the Clean Air Act given the landscape back to the viewer.

A time of change

The period around 1750 marks a stylistic turning point not only in the design of the garden at Enville, but in many other gardens across the country as well. In 1748 Horace Walpole began the transformation of the small villa that he had bought at Twickenham into the building which we now know as Strawberry Hill. Ever the great propagandist, he wrote copiously extolling the virtues of the Gothic style of architecture. The eighteenth-century redis-covery of the Gothic style was not entirely new, and it could be argued that it had never really gone away. The revival of the style was linked with the emergent antiquarian interests in the British past evoking its heritage and the lives of its great rulers. Around 1720 a Gothic facade was erected at Shotover in Oxfordshire for Sir James Tyrrell, and a few years later a cottage embellished with castellations and entitled Alfred's Hall was built in Cirencester Park for Lord Bathurst. Batty Langley had published a successful Gothic pattern book in two parts entitled *Ancient Architecture Restored and Improved* in 1741 and 1742 which were then amalgamated into one volume in 1747. Lord Stamford had a copy of it in his library.[44] Other architects like Thomas Pritchard, Sanderson Miller and Henry Keene also endorsed the Gothic style. Formal, classical and exotic designs were slowly being phased out in favour of 'Gothic' buildings, though twenty miles from Enville in 1750 Lancelot Brown took up an early commission at Croome Court in Worcestershire working mainly in a classical style. In the landscape a wider, gentler approach to garden layout was becoming fash-ionable with sinuous lines reaching out into the far countryside. When this style developed a wilder edge it became known as 'the picturesque'. The popularity of the Grand Tour changed and developed many people's ideas of art, architecture and beauty and in particular encouraged an apprecia-tion of the idyllic Arcadian landscapes as depicted in paintings by artists such as Claude Lorrain (1600-1682) and Nicolas Poussin (1594-1665).[45] People started to appreciate the unadorned beauty of the landscape rather than wanting to have strict control over it, a view that was supported by Batty Langley: 'That all Gardens be grand, beautiful, and natural'.[46] There was a move away from the geometry and control of the previous decades towards a general softening of lines in order to accentuate the natural beauty of the landscape using carefully placed buildings and skilful plantings.

At Enville, 1750 is also a turning point and no further buildings were created in the classical or Chinese styles. In 1749 Sanderson Miller made his first visit,[47] followed the next year by William Shenstone.[48] On a cold, wet day in February 1750 Lord Stamford and some friends had visited The Leasowes and had invited Shenstone to view his 'improvements'.[49] This was the beginning of a friendship between the two men and the start of many visits that Shenstone made to Enville.

The pleasure garden in 1750

The estate survey of 1750 (fig. 19, page 71) shows a very different garden from the one that is there today although a few elements survive. The avenue to the Hall was set at right angles to the front of the Hall. It was entered from the Kinver to Bridgnorth road and was bounded by a double row of chestnut trees. The drive continued past the stables and beside a high brick wall which hid the domestic offices until one came to a carriage turning circle in front of the house, in the centre of which was a sundial.

To the west and north of the house was the walled formal garden. Closest to the Hall on the west was a small, neat parterre beyond which was a trapezoidal pool. A small canal flowed from the pool through the parterre turning at right angles to run underneath the house to the kitchens. Robert Plot describes how the water was diverted to a small overshot wheel at the back of the kitchen chimney in order to turn the spits in the kitchen.[50]

Along the eastern edge of the pool was a bank which terminated at the northern end with a small building, possibly a banqueting house, which could also be approached by a ramp. There was also a bowling green, hedged walks and a kitchen garden. Much of the area was laid to lawn, vwhich was ery labour-intensive to maintain and thus a subtle expression of wealth. A French visitor described how the grass was cut at Kew:

> At dusk the grass was rolled by a large heavy roller which flattens the ground and the grass. The grass is kept flat by the weight of the dew and next morning before it has time to evaporate the men with scythes cut the grass going against the direction in which it had been mowed the night before. This is done at least once a week.[51]

The northern end of the pleasure garden terminates in a bastion-shaped feature which projects into the field around the edge of which there appear to be small buildings or seats.[52]

The Gothic Greenhouse/Billiard Room/Summerhouse/Museum

The building which was created in 1750 is arguably Enville's most famous structure and the most disputed. Its design has been attributed to a number of different people as well as changing its name over time.[53] At first it was known as the Gothic Greenhouse but its role in the landscape at Enville today

Three Great Eighteenth-Century Gardens

is very different from when it was created. It is not that the building has moved but that the grounds around it have been so altered over the last 250 years as to create a very different feel of how we should view the building.

In the mid-eighteenth century the Gothic Greenhouse was tucked up in the far north-west corner of the grounds on an elevated site, its north and west sides literally being on the brick-walled boundaries. The first archival evidence for it is found in Sanderson Miller's diaries where he records that on 23 October 1749 whilst he was staying with the Lytteltons at Hagley he had 'Conversation &c. with Hitchcox [his stone mason] about Lord Stamford's green house'.[54] Two days later he writes that he is 'drawing Lord Stamford's green house' and again on the 26th and 30th. It is next mentioned on 23 November.[55] The building's construction must have been much talked about as William Shenstone wrote to Lady Luxborough on 4 February 1750 that Lord Stamford had been to see his walks and gave him 'many friendly Invitations to Enfield, where he is building a Gothick Greenhouse'.[56] In February and March Miller records that his mason Hitchcox has been at Lord Stamford's.[57] It was evidently still uppermost in Shenstone's mind when he wrote to Richard Jago that Lord Stamford is 'building a Gothic green-house by Mr Miller's direction, and intends to build castles, and God-knows-what. By all accounts, the place is well worth seeing when you come into the country'.[58] There are other mentions of the greenhouse in Miller's diaries, and then on 13 June 1750 he went to Enville with Miss Lyttelton in 'the Chair'. They lost their way and took two hours to cover the ten-mile journey. Nevertheless, Miller saw the new Greenhouse as well as the Chinese Temple and returned home in an hour and a half having given Lord Stamford's servant one shilling.[59] The following month Shenstone wrote to Lady Luxborough to see if she would consider 'a small Excursion to my Lord Stamford's' to see 'His Chinese house, Rotonde, Gothick Greenhouse &c'.[60] Regrettably there does not seem to be any written evidence that they made the journey or what their opinions were. In 1756 Bishop Pococke visited Enville and refers to the building as 'an elegant Gothick summer house of Mr Miller's design'.[61]

This delightful building is constructed of local sandstone with all but two small windows facing south as was directed for the construction of greenhouses in early eighteenth-century gardening books.[62] The south front has a central bay with two smaller ones on either side recessed under ogee arches and three round rose windows above a string course. Inside is elaborate

'Strawberry Hill'-styled Gothic plaster work with a fireplace, recessed niches and fan vaulting.

Various people have contested the attribution of the design of this building to Sanderson Miller citing Henry Keene and Thomas Farnolls Pritchard of Shrewsbury to be the more likely contenders, although there are also strong strains of the influence of Batty Langley in the design. Sanderson Miller's name is mentioned by too many different sources to be discounted and although Pococke refers to it as a summer-house there is no other building at Enville that he could have been describing. It would not be the only building to have had its name changed over time. Miller has been dismissed as an 'amateur gentleman architect' who was not capable of creating anything as innovative and delicate as Enville's Gothic Greenhouse. However, as Jennifer Meir has shown he was widely regarded as an architect of some worth creating not just garden structures but entire new mansions such as at Hagley.[63] There is no evidence that Pritchard was involved at Enville although he worked extensively in the area and in a broadly similar style.[64]

Stylistically some of the exterior decoration links with Miller's work at Radway which has similar low-relief panels, and at Lacock Abbey, Wiltshire, where he uses an almost identical string course. The overall design does not seem inconsistent with a greenhouse of this period when its chief purpose was a place to overwinter 'greens' or tender evergreen shrubs such as citrus away from the frost. The interior, if it was used as a greenhouse, most certainly would not have been elaborately decorated and would probably have been stuccoed and then lime washed. Soon after the Gothic Greenhouse was built other glasshouses and pits for pineapples and other exotics were being constructed in the garden. So this opened the way to a change of purpose for Miller's building.[65] By c.1755 the wall to the west of the Gothic Greenhouse had been demolished and replaced with a ha-ha which was bridged at this point to make an entrance into the shrubbery and the newly designed landscape beyond. By 1759 Edward Knight was describing it as the 'Gothic Room'[66] and the name was repeated in the Day Book of 1766 when repairs were carried out.[67] By 1770, the Day Book Accounts record that Joseph Willetts was paid one guinea for cleaning the Billiard Room grate.[68] It is therefore possible that during this period, just after the 5th Earl had inherited the title in 1768, the interior was considerably improved. The plain walls were embellished with elaborate plaster work decoration in keeping with its new use as a place to which members of the family could retire away from the formalities of life in the house, to play billiards and to sing, eat and drink. The alterations are unlikely to have been done to a design by Sanderson Miller who by 1756 was already suffering from debilitating headaches which reduced his capacity to work.[69]

Stylistically the interior, particularly the fan-vaulted ceiling, appears very similar to those executed to the designs of Henry Keene at Hartlebury, Worcestershire, the old ceiling in the Hall of University College, Oxford, which was destroyed in 1904 and the interior of Hartwell Church in Buckinghamshire. However, no archival evidence has yet been found to support this theory. Joseph Heely describes the building:

> This is a stately gothic edifice, extremely well executed, and does much honour to the designer. Its inside is richly and curiously adorned with stucco; the ceiling remarkably so. At one end in a niche is a bust of Homer: at the other end a Cicero. A billiard table and a small organ, are the furniture of this superb room; and you have from the windows a lively view, resulting from the garden, the lawn, and the woods ... Don't you think it is much to be regretted that this elegant building is visible from no other point in these grounds, than at the gothic gateway?[70]

Heely's complaint about its lack of visibility from the rest of the park reinforces the fact that it was originally designed to be viewed from a completely different point and is now to be found at the termination of the walk around the park rather than as an feature in an enclosed space.

Throughout the rest of the century and into the early part of the nineteenth the domestic accounts show a continual regime of care and repair although it became known as either the Old Billiard Room or the Gothic Room. By 1838 it had become a store room for the movable garden seats.[71]

In 1845 George Harry inherited the Stamford title as the 7th Earl at the age of eighteen years and the following year sees a plan for a new use for the Gothic Room as a Museum. Display cabinets were built and shells, fossils and curiosities purchased to be put on display.[72] At the end of 1854 a new room was added on the western side. This is now demolished, but the stone base can still be seen through the grass. The Museum was clearly not considered to be a building of much importance within the new Victorian gardens for it had become a convenient structure up against which to build a chimney so that 'the smoke from the furnaces which heated the great conservatory is conducted underground to an elegant tower at the north-east corner of the museum'.[73]

The Gothic Seat

There is one other Gothic structure in the grounds which was mentioned in the early writings of Edward Knight and Dr Pococke, but is not found in any account after 1760, and that is the Gothic Seat. Pococke writes:

> from this [the Gothic Greenhouse], there is a winding walk through shrubberies, which leads to a lawn, at the upper end of which is a Gothic seat which commands a fine view of the vale towards Bridgnorth, of the country beyond Woolverhampton, of Lord Ward's house, of Dudley Castle, Hagley and of the country to the south.[74]

An examination of the contours on a modern Ordnance Survey map shows that it could only have been situated in one place within the grounds from which one could have obtained all these views. That is from a point on a small ridge above Leigh House (see colour fig. 13) which lies just outside the deer park boundary and was the home of Lady Dorothy Grey, Lord Stamford's spinster sister. On this spot on the 1750 Estate Survey is a small red square which shows that something was built there. The Gothic Seat appears to be a good candidate. This is reinforced by the fact that a couple of yew trees, a device much used at Enville to mark out buildings in the landscape, are planted there. Also there is some evidence of brick and stone in the soil.

On 7 September 1754 John Ivory Talbot from Lacock in Wiltshire wrote to Sanderson Miller:

> At Enville we saw an Horrid Massacre of a fine Gothick design of yours, committed by the hands of some Shrewsbury man: we were very angry, and would not let the gardiner give us the particulars of the Misfortune.[75]

This letter has always been interpreted as referring to the Gothic Greenhouse, but it is more likely that it referred to the Gothic Seat. The finger of suspicion as to who the 'Shrewsbury man' was has usually been pointed at TF Pritchard, but there is no surviving archival evidence one way or another.

Towards a more naturalistic landscape

The Gothic Greenhouse was just the beginning of the extension of the landscape park to over 750 acres of the Stamford's Staffordshire estate. In 1759 Dr Richard Wilkes who was a doctor at Willenhall in Staffordshire wrote rather waspishly in his diary that:

> Harry, the present Earl of Stamford, having purchased several estates, so as to make the whole hill above the house and town his property; and having married the Lady Mary Booth, only daughter of the last Earl of Warrington of this name, by whom he had an immense fortune, has in a few years laid out many thousand pounds in making this hill beautiful. This he has done with so much art, and in so elegant a manner, that few places in England can rival, and none of the same compass of ground exceed it. Out-offices, barns and stables he has built, but not as yet, 1759, meddled with the house, which seems not a proper part of so delightful seat.[76]

Wilkes was wrong in one basic fact that has been put forward as a 'truth' ever since. Many people have interpreted this statement as implying that Lord Harry Grey had married Mary for her money. Lady Mary Booth was indeed a very rich woman, but under the terms of her marriage settlement her husband saw very little of it. The Earl of Warrington's marriage portion was to be £20,000 of which £16,000 was paid to the 3rd Earl of Stamford and £4,000 to Harry, Lord Grey. Harry was required to raise money from his estates for quarterly payments to his wife and any children who might be born.[77] As has been said, the Earl was a wealthy man in his own right.

About 1746 Lord Stamford bought several major properties in the parish of Enville which adjoined the land he already owned, notably the Shadwell land at Lyndon and Leigh House. In order to fund these purchases and give money to his brothers and sisters which should have been due to them had his father not had such substantial debts, he sold land and property in Derbyshire and Warwickshire and most notably the manor of Stamford.[78]

By the early 1750s Lord Stamford now had not only the money, but also the land to expand his grounds westwards up on to the woods and hills to the top of the Sheep Walk. An examination of the Estate Survey of c.1750 shows that someone has drawn faintly in pencil on it with long curving lines. Crosses were put through hedges on field boundaries and geometric clumps of trees on the skyline beyond the Temple Pool are linked to form a serpentine line of trees. Some of these new features are to be found on a

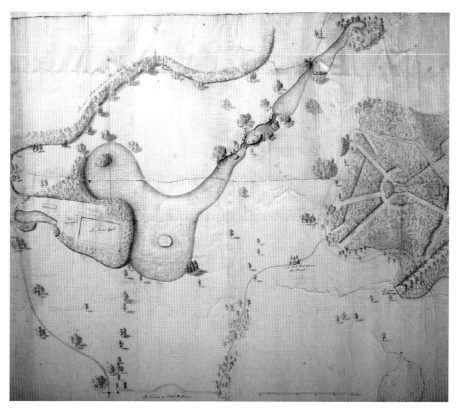

22. A proposed new design for the grounds at Enville (c.1752) showing a softening of the existing formal landscape around The Temple Pool and a serpentine row of trees made by linking up existing formal clumps. [EA]

recently discovered plan in ink and wash on which someone has written in twentieth-century handwriting 'A Plan for landscaping Enville Park – mid-18th century – possibly by William Shenstone'.[79] It has become known as 'The Shenstone Plan' although there is no actual evidence that it is by him and 'Capability' Brown has been suggested as a possible alternative designer.[80] This idea has probably arisen as Lord Stamford was one of the fourteen signatories on a petition to King George II, through the office of the Duke of Newcastle, for Brown's appointment as Royal Gardener. All the others who signed the petition had their grounds improved by Brown. However, there is no documentation in the Enville Archive or in Brown's bank accounts at Drummonds to substantiate this idea, nor did any of the many visitors mention him in their writings, including several who normally made a point of crediting Brown where they could and some who had spoken to Lord Stamford. So why did Lord Stamford sign the petition if Brown was not connected with Enville? It is possible that Brown did work for the Stamfords, but not at Enville. In 1758 Lady Stamford began to trans-form the Higher Park at her family home Dunham Massey in Cheshire in a style very similar to Brown's.[81]

What is not in doubt is that many of the ideas on both the Estate Survey and the 'Shenstone Plan' were implemented. The water level in the Temple Pool was raised to overflow the straight brick-lined edge of the original pool and create a softer appearance. Clumps of trees on the skyline were linked and an Urn (see: colour fig. 9) and Serpentine Seat were built there with a view straight across the Chinese Temple to the Hall and the tower of Enville Church beyond. Hedges were removed and a 'terras' and ha-ha created in the field called The Innage in front of the Hall. To the west of the Gothic Greenhouse the wall was demolished to be replaced by a ha-ha with a shrubbery beyond. During the first half of the 1750s work was being carried out all over the grounds, older buildings were being altered to the Gothic style and several new ones were being created.

There was no single circuit walk at Enville as at The Leasowes, and to a lesser extent at Hagley where there was a main walk with small variations. At Enville the grounds could be viewed from a number of differing start points, but the route that seems to have been used by most visitors started from the front of the Hall by the Stables and crossed the large field known as the Innage. The pathway is slightly raised above the rest of the field and affords views to what were the open heathlands on the left and the deer park with its ancient pollarded oaks on the right. To the front is a bank above which would originally have appeared the roof of the Chinese Temple. The walk continued between the walls of the Home Farm and the Temple Pool then turned along the south side of the pool until it reached the base of The Cascades.

The Cascades and Boat House

Where the Cascades are today was shown on the c.1750 Estate Survey as a series of small pools linked by a stream. A watermill is recorded at Lyndon in the sixteenth century, but probably dates from a much earlier period.

On a wet day in February 1750 Lord Stamford and three friends had visited The Leasowes to look at the walks there. William Shenstone recorded in a letter to Lady Luxborough that 'he was much struck with Virgils Grove, & particularly ye Cascade you were us'd to admire; gave it ye Preference to ye Rock Work &c.: at Hagley, & said obliging Things'.[82]

How much of the development of the Enville watercourse can be attributed to Shenstone is open to question. The c.1753 'Shenstone Plan' shows an enlargement of the pools with water gushing through rocks in a naturalistic design and it appears that this work was carried out as shown in two of the paintings of the landscape park by Anthony Devis (1729-1816)[83] – see colour fig. 14.

The tree-lined Cascades run for about a quarter of a mile through a series of pools and drops which flow into the south-west corner of the Temple Pool. They are thrown into contrast with the smooth 'lawns' on either side which are grazed by cattle and sheep. The water source is a spring and a series of small dams were built to impound the water. A local ironmaster, Edward Knight, who lived nearby at Wolverley, Worcestershire, spent much of his leisure times visiting notable gardens such as Hestercombe in Somerset, and cryptically noted at Enville in 1759, 'View down the water to the Chinese Temple, Temples view of Water, Cascades and Woods'.[84] The view both up and down the Cascades was one of the key elements of their design. From the Chinese Temple the eye was drawn up the length of the Cascades. At first the view passed along a small chasm to a modest cascade, then through a rock arch and along a raked rill where the bricks were laid unevenly so that the water jumped and glistened over them to another cascade above which appears yet another cascade. Each one was set slightly off-centre to the next and finally towering above all was a small brick chapel with large 'Early English Gothic' doors. From here the visitor would have looked back down the tumbling water to the Chinese Temple in the middle of its pool.

There is much in the design which reflects Shenstone's gardening ideas as laid out in his *Unconnected Thoughts on Gardening*:

> VARIETY ... as the eye, passing from one form or color, to a form or color of a different kind, finds a degree of novelty in it's present object which affords immediate satisfaction. .... THE eye should always look rather down upon water: Customary nature makes his requisite. .... WHEN a building, or other object has been once viewed from its proper point, the foot should never travel to it by the same path, which the eye has travelled over before. Lose the object, and draw nigh, obliquely.[85]

The Cascades lasted in their original form for only about 16 years. When the 4th Earl died in 1768, his son George Harry became the 5th Earl of Stamford. He decided that something more dramatic should be created in line with the newly fashionable taste for the picturesque with its emphasis on the wild and dramatic. The biggest casualty of this redevelopment was the Chinese Temple which was taken down in 1769 so that nothing should impair the view of the Cascades.[86] To replace it as a viewing point a Boat House was built facing diagonally across the Temple Pool opposite the Cascades. Meanwhile the Cascades were 'improved' by building dams with sluices to retain the water in the two largest pools. When the Serpentine Pool at the foot of the second cascade was drained and cleared out, one of the stones at the base was found to have the date 1770 carved on it.

The Boat House, a gem of rococo design, was built in the early months of 1770, probably to an earlier design by Sanderson Miller. It consisted of a stone arched base under which boats could float and with a door leading out onto the path at the opposite end; this 'room' was painted in bright blues and greens which reflected in the water.[87] Above this was a decorated octagonal room approached by a side door. On the exterior wall facing the pool were three arched bays of a Gothic design with a string course similar to that on the Gothic Greenhouse.

Visitors would have walked across the open expanses of the Innage with only a view of a grassy bank and trees. As they climbed the stone steps up the bank any forward view out onto the Temple Pool was shut off by the plantings of evergreens. On passing through the door at the top of the steps they would then find themselves in the octagonal room of the Boat House. This room was painted in two tones of Adam green and was decorated with gilded swags, festoons and medallions made from *papier mâché* by Watson and Kinder.[88] On the pool side there was a large painted glass window which deliberately obscured the view out. Whilst the visitors were admiring the interior, a servant was dispatched to run about quarter of a mile up the hill to release the sluices on the holding pools. At the sound of the torrent the windows were slid open to reveal the view of the water gushing down the Cascades causing waves to flow across the Temple Pool. This was gardening as theatre. In the 1970s a large branch broke off from a nearby beech and entirely demolished this enchanting pavilion.

After viewing this spectacular cascade the visitor left the Boat House through a door opposite the entrance and down some stone steps which led out onto the gravel path. From the light and excitement of the Boat House one was then plunged into the gloom of a box and holly tunnel, catching only glimpses of the Temple Pool and the Gothic Gateway on the

23. The Cascades: the brick rill

right. At the end of the Pool one burst out into the light of the open field with views of an urn on top of a small hill on one side and of the Hall reflected in the Pool on the other. The walk continued along the southern end of the pool to a small promontory at the end of the Cascades where there is a small wicket gate. This is the entrance to a path which runs upstream along the edge of the Cascades through a tunnel of box trees. Again the view is shielded and the visitor is enticed by the sound of water gurgling and splashing over the rocks until the hedge finishes and one is rewarded with a close-up view of the first drop as water flows under a rock arch and bounces down the face of a cascade into the chasm beyond. The path climbed gently beside the raked brick rill where the water ripples and sparkles in the light as it flows from the Serpentine Pool which is at the bottom of a drop from a large cascade faced with heavy iron-rich industrial slag. Most of the pieces of slag are bowl-shaped and some are set at right angles to the face of the cascade so that they catch the water and cause it to spray out. In contrast to the noise of the water the dell was planted with calming sweet-smelling shrubs including roses and honeysuckle. A bench surrounded by a 'flowery ground'[89] was situated here from which to admire the view of the cascade. The eye was then drawn over the pool and across the sheep-grazed lawn up to a large yew tree surrounded by a white high-backed wooden seat on top of a brick and stone bastion. This feature is known as Ralph's Bastion and the date of 1753 is carved into the yew (see

24. The Temple Pool, Boat House and Enville Hall. Pen and wash by E. Barber, (1800). Private collection

25. The Boat House. Reproduced by permission of English Heritage, NMR AA58/269

26. The Boat House, interior. Reproduced by permission of English Heritage, NMR AA58/271

fig. 28, opposite). To reach it the visitor had to cross the watery rill by a single plank adding yet another note of excitement to the walk.[90] Heely enthuses that:

> Nothing can be more engaging than the walk from the seat, to the outside of this romantic spot ... the impetuous torrent of one cascade rushing down a chasm near your foot ... another seen at a distance through the trees; pouring over rocks its whitened foam; and as you stand on my favourite plank, looking down the sloping channel edged with laurels, the boat house over the broad lake, will hold you long in admiration of its beauty, and picturesque situation ... turning to the cascade behind you, and then to it's troubled waters below, you have other feelings ... it is true, nothing was ever better formed to create surprise, and pleasure; but at the same time one cannot help be affected by a sort of terror, standing in the midst of an incessant roar of water, and seeing it break with such restless fury ... I declare I considered myself as a victim devoted to its rage, and expected every moment, upon some sudden burst, to be washed without any kind of ceremony, down the torrent into the dreary hollow below.[91]

Ralph's Bastion was situated at one end of the Hornbeam Walk which ran along the eastern boundary of the old deer park to the grotto at the other end. The name is presumably taken from successive lords of the manor of Enville in the fourteenth century. This is comparable to the use of the old name of 'Mowbray' which was used for two of the garden buildings at Hackfall, North Yorkshire. The bastion was designed as a viewpoint to reinforce in the mind of the visitor places which they had already seen and to tempt them on to new pleasures, for over the top of a stone-stepped cascade could be seen the newly gothicised farmhouse at Lyndon. This view of the castellated farmhouse at Lyndon and Ralph's Bastion created a medieval effect.

The Cold Bath

The route to Lyndon, however, was not straight but took a detour through a small copse in which there was a 'commodious' cold bath.[92] Cold baths were considered to be good for one's health and are found in many gardens of this period. It is situated near the head of the watercourse which forms the cascades and was the last of the 5th Earl's improvements. The cold bath

27. Lyndon after its alterations to create a Gothic Farmhouse, and the seat known as Ralph's Bastion. Pen and wash, artist unknown (c.1760). Private collection

28. Ralph's Bastion: ?RAF'S ASTION 1753 carved into the trunk of the yew around which the seat is built

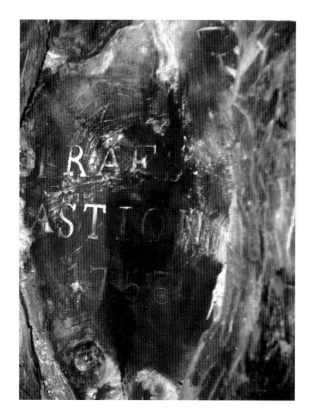

29. View from the Kinver Road to Lyndon before it was remodelled in the Gothic style with the Rotunda on the hill beyond. Pen-and-ink drawing by Thomas Robins. Thomas Robins drawing no. 131 V&A Images Museum No 1308:125-2001

was built of brick and stone in 1773 beside the Upper Pool at Lyndon Spout by a local man, John Guest, who worked for the estate. This was the source of an icily cold spring. The estate accounts also mention sizeable payments to the blacksmith and glazier so it is possible that there may have been some sort of shelter built over or around the bath.[93] The water from the cold bath then flowed into a large horseshoe-shaped pool edged in brick. Bathers could reach this pool by a flight of stone steps. Little is known about the way in which cold baths were used but pieces of fine porcelain have been found in the mud of the horseshoe pool which suggests that people were taking refreshments here.

Lyndon

From the Cold Bath the walker would ascend a small slope to the farm-house at Lyndon. This had been the home of the Shadwell family from at least the fifteenth century and comprised a farmhouse with several cottages and outbuildings with just over fifty-eight acres of land.[94] Part of the estate lay along the southern boundary of the Enville estate whilst some parcels of land were surrounded by Lord Stamford's fields; thus its purchase in 1746 enabled Lord Stamford to consolidate his own holdings.

The Estate Survey c.1750[95] shows Lyndon House as an L-shaped

30. Lyndon before it was demolished in the 1960s

building. It was depicted by Thomas Robins as having a central tower (fig. 29, page 90).[96] Before Lord Stamford's purchase a long avenue of trees had been planted connecting the house to the Kinver Road. The Survey also shows a pencil cross has been put through both the house and some of the other surrounding buildings. During the 1750s the house was either demolished or a wing removed to leave a rectangular structure. A late-eighteenth-century watercolour (fig. 27, page 89) shows that it has been gothicised with a castellated roof line and so it became an interesting feature in its own right. Heely wrote, in 1777, that it formed 'a scene entirely pastoral; composed of a farm-house, fold, fields of rich herbage, stored with cattle ... tasting the smell of the dairy.'[97] This area can be truly said to have the flavour of a *ferme ornée*.

Shenstone's Chapel

All the time since leaving the Temple Pool the visitor would have been slowly ascending. Shortly after quitting Lyndon one could see the Rotunda situated in the distance across a dry valley on another steep convex hill. Past the deer park boundary with its ancient field maples a stiff climb was required to reach a small chapel in Priest Wood. Before entering the visitor would pause to admire the panoramic view from which both Hagley and

The Leasowes could be seen. In the distance were the Malvern and Clent Hills with Kinver Edge and St. Peter's Church in the mid-ground. The wood is mainly of beech and oak, but around the Chapel is a horseshoe-shaped planting of yew trees which appear to have been shredded in order to produce a long clean trunk with a canopy of yew branches.

The building in the wood is now known as Shenstone's Chapel although it was originally built c.1753 and only later dedicated to the memory of William Shenstone after his death from a putrid fever in 1763. It is a gothic-style building made of bricks and covered with pinky beige harling or pebble dash, with a tiled roof. Many of the bricks date from the sixteenth and seventeenth century, but it is unclear whether they are the base of an older building, or whether they may have come from buildings which were demolished at the nearby settlement of Lyndon. The Chapel consists of a nave and cylindrical west tower in which are set three pointed windows. At the east end are a pair of full-height double doors which originally contained stained or painted glass 'casting a dim religious light'.[98] On the north and south side of the small nave are identical panelled and studded doors. In the outside walls are two cupboards with shelves and a cavity below the door height. Their use has been the subject of much debate though the most plausible seems to have been for storing food and drink. The bottom cavity could have been used to contain ice, which would have been brought from the ice house via the carriage drive so that the victuals were kept cool on the shelves above. Although Joseph Heely describes the chapel as 'being closely embraced by a gloomy, impenetrable wilderness of thicket and wood, accompanied by a solemn dead silence that naturally links the mind to ferocious meditation',[99] there is no evidence that it was ever used as a religious building. It was more probably a place to take refreshments and enjoy either the wider view of the countryside or gaze down upon the Cascades to either the Chinese Temple, or later the Boat House.

The Sheep Walk and the Shepherd's Lodge
From Shenstone's Chapel the path continues more gently upwards through the wood and follows the line of the narrow ridge with the land dropping away on either side. About half way along there is a diagonal cut through the trees so that the visitor was able to see the Rotunda on one side and Kinver Church on the other. At the end of the wood the path leads out onto the wide open expanse of the Sheep Walk. This is an area of summer sheep

31. Shenstone's Chapel, interior view. Reproduced by permission of English Heritage, NMR AA58/281

32. The Shepherd's Lodge. The Green Frog Service made for Catherine the Great : The State Hermitage Museum, St. Petersburg, photograph © The State Hermitage Museum

pasture with closely cropped grass and a dew pond. At Enville the name Sheep Walk does not appear to have been used until the mid-eighteenth century; before that it was known simply as 'the hills'. From here at over 200 metres high there are wide-ranging views for almost 360 degrees, from the Wrekin, Abberley and Clee Hills, to the Black Mountains round to the Malvern and finally to the Clent Hills. A walk of about half a mile across this ridge brings the visitor to the Shepherd's Lodge. It is situated near the highest point on what was a main routeway from the River Severn at Arley, through No Man's Green, across the Sheep Walk, through the park at Enville and out onto the heathland towards the market towns of Wolverhampton and Stourbridge. The Shepherd's Lodge may originally have been a warrener's or a hunting lodge. All that remains today are tall brick walls that appear to be late-fifteenth century in origin.

The Lodge is marked on an estate map of 1688 as a two-storey building with a barn beside it and surrounded by hedged fields.[100] Edward Knight who visited in 1759 called it the Shepherd's House.[101] By this time the hedges had been removed and the building altered to provide a permanent home

33. The Gothic Gateway and two pavilions with seats on either side. In front are iron railings and gates to keep out the sheep. Peter Williams

for the shepherd and his family as well as a place for the Earl's family and friends to visit. Apart from looking after the sheep the occupants also kept chickens and pigeons. Coal, or more probably charcoal, was regularly taken up by carrier as it must have been a bitterly cold place to live all year round.

During the 1750s the Lodge was gothicised with a crenellated roof line and pointed arched windows.[102] The front door, which faced south-east, was sheltered by a portico (fig. 32, page 93). The exterior was painted white and the roof covered with lead.[103] Inside the rooms were rather more exotically decorated. The walls in one parlour were covered with silhouettes of the Earl's family and friends, whilst another was decorated with prints of landscapes, houses and gardens, possibly by Kip and Knyff or the now fashionable Woollett and Sullivan.[104] The prints were paid for in 1761 and cost three shillings.[105] The staircase was 'plaistered' with old songs, maps and Christmas carols. William Marshall in 1796 writes of there being 'a lounging room and an observatory'.[106]

The Gothic Gateway

The Shepherd's Lodge was literally the high point of the tour of the grounds and there were a variety of ways that could be taken to return to the Hall. The most straightforward was to walk along the main track called the Ash Walk which entered Essex Wood at the Welch Gate and ran in a straight line through the ancient oak woodland. At the other end the visitor emerged through a tall castellated gate, known as the Gothic Gateway, onto a hill top looking down to Enville Hall and with a distant view of Sedgley church spire. The gateway is meant to be viewed from the other side and here it is revealed as an eyecatcher on top of its hill backed by dark woodland (fig. 33, page 94). It was built c.1752 probably to a design by Sanderson Miller out of the local red sandstone. In the centre is a tall carriage arch with an imitation portcullis at the top and gates below, while on either side are crenellated walls which terminated with a pavilion and set slightly obliquely. Each pavilion contained seats, one looking out over the Temple Pool, the other over Jordan's and in front was a low iron fence to keep the sheep out. From here the visitor could go straight back to the Hall or else walk along a short high ridge, pausing to look up the long dry valley to the Doric Temple and then drop steeply down to a series of pools.

Jordan's and Ha-ha Pools
The map of c.1650 shows that there was a series of six pools and cascades subsequently to be known as Jordan's Pool and the Ha-ha Pool, which was itself later renamed the Seahorse Pool. The Jordans, like the lords of the manor, Ralph, had been important members of the Enville community in the Middle Ages, so their names lived on in the landscape (fig. 34, page 96). The land just to the south of the pools is known as Brick Kiln Piece and it is probable that the pools were originally formed when the clay was dug for brickmaking during the building of the Hall in the 1530s and then subsequently used or enlarged as ornamental features. The pools were kept stocked with fish such as tench, perch, gudgeon, flounders and eels.[107]

By c.1750 the Estate Survey shows that the original six pools and cascades had been altered to become three main pools.[108] Jordan's Pool now had a dam at the eastern end and appears on the survey to be divided not by cascades, but by narrow banks, possibly of turf, across which one could walk. The lower pool originally known as the Ha-ha Pool was divided in two by a similar turf bridge. One of these turf bridges survives to cross the stream just before it flows into Jordan's Pool. Upstream of this bridge a lost circular pond linked Jordan's Pool with the landscape around its head and where a rather eccentric building known as the Cottage was erected; downstream was a small cascade made from industrial slag, similar in construction to the lower part of the main cascades. The water flowed beneath a bridge which appeared to have two small turrets at each end and then

34. View over Jordan's Pool to the Gothic Gateway. Pen and wash, artist unknown (c.1760s). Private collection

dropped down over six feet gushing into the pool below. This scene would have been viewed from a wooden rustic bridge known as the Shepherd's Bridge and also from the dam of Jordan's Pool. The Ha-ha Pool is of a similar design. It was given this name because the dam boundary at the eastern end used the ha-ha as part of its construction, which in turn had used part of the deer park boundary ditch. In 1759 Edward Knight records the 'new water' which indicates that the turf bridges of the two pools were removed.[109] This idea is supported by Devis's painting of the Shepherd's Bridge in the mid-1760s which shows no sign of any division in Jordan's Pool.[110]

The accounts show that the pools needed constant maintenance with repairs to the dams, dredging of silt, making new sluices and puddling the clay on the base of the pools to prevent leakage.[111] One of the problems with the pools at Enville has been how to keep the water levels at an optimum height. This was solved in the early 1760s by making a very long brick-lined culvert, known as the Navigation. It ran partly underground from the Batch Pool around the edge of a hill to Jordan's Pool to provide a water top-up system. The accounts for 28 June 1766 show that Mr Beswick was paid £170 'for bringing the water from the Batch Pool to Jordan's Pool and another £24 for making the pool below The Cottage'; however, the workmen were paid for this from May 1763 indicating when work would have begun.[112] Another culvert was made to link Jordan's Pool to the Temple Pool passing

35. The Cottage, a photograph taken c.1860. The original heather roof has been replaced by lead. [EA]

36. The Cottage, a drawing taken from the sketchbook of Katharine Grey of Groby and George Harry Grey (1836). [EA]

through the Cherry Orchard, any surplus being taken through the Home Farm and out to the pools on the eastern boundary.

The Cottage

Having crossed the head of Jordan's Pool by the Shepherd's Bridge the visitor then turned left away from the Hall and after a short walk beside a stream came across a large circular lawn surrounded by larches. Beside the lawn was a rustic three-roomed cottage constructed of randomly laid stones and bricks (figs. 35 and 36, page 97). The windows had pointed Gothic arches and were filled with coloured glass. The roof was thatched with heather. On either side of the habitable part of the cottage were aviaries filled with ornamental birds such as guinea fowl and silver and Chinese pheasants.[113] The Cottage was occasionally referred to as 'The Hermitage' although there is no evidence that it ever was used as such.

In Osvald Sirén's book is a photograph of a small building at Enville with the caption 'The bark-covered Hermitage'. He describes it as 'a little octagonal pavilion covered on the outside with pine bark and provided with a conical roof of thatch and leaded windows of stained glass'.[114] Nothing of this building survives although the remains of some leaded lights were found beneath the azalea bushes near the Ha-ha Pool.

The Cottage is first mentioned in 1756 as a 'pheasantry and hermitage for the keeper of the fowl'.[115] Accounts show that hemp and canary seed were regularly sent to the Cottage, along with 'Nuts for Squirells',[116] and that the house was occupied by a series of female inhabitants. Although visitors admired the Cottage there was some criticism as to its use as a menagerie. Joseph Heely expressed the opinion of many visitors.

> Whether it be the name, or the simplicity that commonly surrounds the dwellings of indigence ... or rather, whether it be from the insinuating effusions of the muse, that true happiness is only to be found in a sequestered rural life, is of little consequence ... a cottage, properly situated within the precincts of *a riding*, or in such extensive grounds as these, is an object that always excites pleasure, and impresses on the mind extreme soothing; and no one, in my opinion; has a juster claim from situation, to be admired, than this, so delightfully environed by the loveliest of woody hills, and twining valleys: nothing can be more retired, nothing more cheerful, though solitude itself ... Believe me, this humble thatched cot, its little circular sloping lawn in front, and the graceful clustering trees, that verge the area, and form

37. The Shrubbery as shown on the Green Frog dinner service made for Catherine the Great. The State Hermitage Museum, St. Petersburg; photograph © The State Hermitage Museum

a perfect canopy over the building, have greater powers to charm the eye of taste, than the most magnificent temple, loaded with all the finery art can give.

But what think you of a menegere of extraneous birds? – it is true, there is a pleasure in contemplating the variegated plumage, and different forms of creatures brought from distant climes; but, that such a costly ornament as a menegere, should be brought to grace a cottage of all places, is not only a very singular circumstance, bur admits of the strongest doubts of its eligibility. Perhaps you will be ready to excuse it when you are sensible that an indigent family is maintained, and placed here, through charitable motives, merely to be attentive to the wants of fowls – this speaks benevolence only; it does not invalidate the objection in regard to the locality of the object. The proper place for a menegere, I should think, is a gay garden, among fine objects: and quite in character, if placed as wings to a green-house, or to a pinery; as it may be said that the birds bear some relation to the various exotic plants, natives of the very climes they themselves come from.[117]

From the Cottage visitors retraced their tracks walking gently downhill towards Jordan's Pool. Once out of the wood a large undulating lawn, known as 'The Parks', rolled away in front down towards the shrubbery which was one of the most fashionable new features to be found in a mid-eighteenth-century garden. *The Oxford English Dictionary* credits William Shenstone as the originator of the term 'shrubbery', when in 1748 he entered into a long correspondence with Lady Luxborough over the modelling of her shrubbery.[118] At Enville the shrubbery was planted by 1756 with a variety of fragrant shrubs, larches, and with beeches close to the deer park boundary ditch and bank (fig. 37, page 99).[119] It probably included a range of 'exotics' which would have been introduced into England from north-east America. A serpentine path wove through the plantings and from here one could see a large vase embossed with figures and a statue of Flora, the classical goddess of flowers, with a wreath of roses in her hair and holding a nosegay of jessamine and woodbine.[120] As Heely expressed it:

> I now lingered through the pleasant shady bowers of an elegant and extensive shrubbery ... I trod on soft moss-grown carpets ... wherever I turned, nature looked pleased with her silky dress ... I thought she hovered on every parterre, on every groupe of trees, and on every smooth-shorn lawn.[121]

As with the other two gardens Enville has little statuary. Although there are several urns and vases in the grounds Flora is the only statue that is known about.

The walk now finished by the Gothic Greenhouse and the more formal pleasure gardens to the north of the Hall. For visitors who were unable to walk far in the very extensive grounds, a carriage drive had been made around the eastern edge of the park and up on to the top of the Sheep Walk, returning home via the Ash Walk and Gothic Gateway.[122]

Little changed in the park at Enville until the late 1840s. Botanical collections rather than landscape alterations were the chief horticultural preoccupations of the family. The garden buildings were maintained and painted and the paths gravelled, but tastes were changing and in the late 1840s the young new 7th Earl of Stamford and Warrington decided to design a pleasure garden of over eighty acres. He created an enormous conservatory and massive fountains with impressive bedding plants which would rival the best in the country. Fortunately most of the work was carried out to the north and west of the Hall and the eighteenth-century gardens were left largely untouched.

4

Hagley

✳

Lyttelton and his circle

GEORGE LYTTELTON, THE PRIME SHAPER OF THE LANDSCAPE AT HAGLEY (THOUGH
not the only one), was born into a family circle that grew to include the
Temples of Stowe (Lord Cobham), the Grenvilles of Wotton and the Pitts
(who included a Prime Minister, garden advisers and architects), thus
giving him close connections with those who not only had power and
authority in the political world but who were in the vanguard of the 'new'
naturalistic landscaping. The burgeoning of Hagley as a landscape park of
great beauty and fame must accordingly be seen in the context of this
extraordinary family nexus.

Lyttelton (1709-73), who will be referred to throughout by his surname
to distinguish him from the other Lytteltons, who will be given their first
names, was educated at Eton and Christ Church, which he left when only
just nineteen. He was precocious in study and in writing, concentrating on
the classics and literature, perhaps making up intellectually for the physical
robustness he may have lacked, for his constitution was never strong.[1]
Satirists and cartoonists latched on to his thin and scrawny appearance:

> Who's dat who ride astride de Pony,
> So long, so lank, so lean and bony?
> O he be de great orator Little-Tony.[2]

In his life he had to endure many tribulations. His first marriage was happy
but cut tragically short when his wife Lucy died soon after childbirth; his
second marriage was unhappy; and his son Thomas was not merely a
disappointment but a source of considerable upset and aggravation. He
sought and found consolation in religion, and also in working on the varied
beauties of the park. He had some pretensions as a writer, and his *Observations on the Conversion and Apostleship of St Paul* was not only translated into

French and German but ran to several editions right up to 1911. In the realm of poetry, his *Monody* after Lucy's death is probably his best-known production. For Lucy he also composed a prayer to Venus in her temple at Stowe.[3] He was, too, responsible for some of the inscriptions at both Hagley and Stowe.

Despite his uncertain health (which did not incapacitate him as it did his father), Lyttelton was a great traveller. After Oxford he went on the customary Grand Tour in 1728, but it entailed a lengthy stay in France, almost a year and a half, before he proceeded to Italy, returning home in 1730. Whether this had any effect on the later landscaping is hard to say, but it might have given him a love of classical architecture and also a taste for ruins, although his were to be Gothic rather than classical. For the next twenty years he visited a number of estates, such as Cliveden, Buckinghamshire, Cirencester Park, Gloucestershire, and Castle Hill, Devon, usually for political reasons, but then, from 1751, he toured properties widely through the land and commented on them, in the manner of a Gilpin or a Walpole, though most of the visits came too late for the gardens to have had an impact on what was going on at Hagley.

Lyttelton's circle was both political and literary. The political links were mainly based around family, but owed much too to his own career. Unlike his father (Sir Thomas, a staunch Whig), Lyttelton, who entered Parliament as MP for Okehampton in 1735, was soon drawn into the Whig Opposition that centred round Lord Cobham at Stowe from 1733. Frederick, Prince of Wales, was the figurehead of this Whig Opposition, and Lyttelton joined his staff in the mid-1730s as equerry, becoming Frederick's secretary in 1737. Although there was a later falling out with Frederick and also with William Pitt (by 1756),[4] Lyttelton's connections were of enormous importance when it came to gardening, since many of the Whig Opposition were engaged in the new landscape movement, and those closest to Lyttelton were instrumental in creating the greatest garden of them all, Stowe.

In the course of Lyttelton's work for the Prince he would have encountered others who were also on the staff, such as Charles Hamilton of Painshill, a great designer and plantsman. The two shared an interest in woodland and in such species as cedars of Lebanon and in North American imports. Lyttelton would also have come across William Kent, pioneer of the pictorial circuit garden, who was active at Stowe and who also built the White House for the Prince at Kew.

102

Three Great Eighteenth-Century Gardens

Lyttelton's literary acquaintances include Alexander Pope, James Thomson and Shenstone, each of whom wrote about or cultivated their own gardens and those of others. Pope and Shenstone were theorisers and advisers as well as practitioners, and Lyttelton could have gained much from Pope in particular. So, from the point of view of family connections, the gardens he knew and visited, and the people he conversed with, Lyttelton had an enviable position when it came to working on his own landscape.

The creators of Hagley

While Lyttelton is normally accorded principal credit for creating and embellishing the landscape at Hagley, there were others who, in varying degrees, must be recognised for their input. Principal of these is Sir Thomas Lyttelton, his father (1686-1751). Although a steady Whig who continued to support Sir Robert Walpole after the breakaway by Lord Cobham in 1733, Sir Thomas, through his marriage with Christian Temple, a sister of Lord Cobham, must have been well acquainted with the exciting developments at Stowe and decided to update his park. During the time of Sir Thomas, the set of four rustic buildings in Hermitage Wood was probably constructed, the cascades and pools set in train and the Rotunda, Thomson's Seat and the Ruined Castle erected. These altered the face of the park dramatically, and Sir Thomas claims the credit in a memorandum:

> In the year of 1747 I built the Castle and also the Cottage the same year part of the plantations upon the Hill were made the rest in the following year, I also bought about the same time of Mr Cox the piece of course Land near the park together with the little Image on the top of the Hill for both wch I paid sixty Guineas. The former was Copyhold the latter freehold in 1748 I built the Rotundo and in 1749 the half Octagon Seat [Thomson's Seat] and made the Haha over against it. Mr Miller Architect of the Castle Mr John Pitt of the Rotundo & Octagon.[5]

Taken at face value, this sounds as if we should recognise Sir Thomas rather than Lyttelton as the 'onlie begetter' of the major works at Hagley. However, even though Sir Thomas was the owner and therefore had overall responsibility, he was far from well and indeed had suffered ill health since his retirement from Parliament in 1741.[6] So for the last ten years of his life, during which time the park was really coming into shape, his may have been the notional rather than the actual guiding hand, even though he writes in proprietorial terms. Furthermore, Lyttelton's recorded connection with Stowe and the Cobham circle, and his close involvement with the Prince of Wales, make it far more likely that he rather than his father was the creative force. And that would certainly have been true of any developments after 1751.

Three of the Pitt family made significant contributions. William Pitt the Elder (Lord Chatham), who was involved in a great many garden designs,[7] gave advice and contrived some 'considerable new improvements' in concert with Lyttelton.[8] He was responsible for some of the plantations and attending to the sylvan backdrops to buildings such as the Rotunda.[9] Rose Mary Davis claims that he was consulted at every step in the period from 1748.[10] John Pitt of Encombe, Dorset, a distant relative, was the architect who was brought in to design both the rotunda and Thomson's Seat, a small pavilion with a flat back and the front half of an octagon. Thomas Pitt, nephew to Lyttelton and who became Lord Camelford, designed the Palladian Bridge a few years later.

The greatest of the architects brought in was, of course, Sanderson Miller. Not only did he design Hagley Hall but several of the service buildings such as the dairy and greenhouse, together with a cottage and the Ruined Castle. The other architect to be involved was James Stuart, to create the Temple of Theseus. Each of these architects brought his own experience and sensibilities to bear on what he designed, giving a colouring that, however subtly, steered the buildings in his direction. Thus, the Ruined Castle, while a crucial landmark at Hagley, is also emphatically a Miller production.

But the most significant organiser of the landscape may have been Molly West (c.1704-86), daughter of Richard West and Maria (née Temple), another sister of Lord Cobham. Molly West was therefore cousin to Lyttelton. She spent much time at Hagley, and looked after, in particular, the plantings when Lyttelton was away. She attended to practical matters and discussed plantings and timber management with William Pitt.[11]

Alexander Pope completes the list of advisers. In a letter of 2 August 1739, he wrote to Ralph Allen, the squire of Prior Park, who supplied the Bath stone for the Prince's Column at Hagley, to say that he had 'designed three buildings'.[12] It has been surmised[13] that this trio – if executed – is likely to be part of the set of four buildings in Hermitage Wood, all of a rustic nature, though there is no definite evidence. A further candidate is Pope's

Three Great Eighteenth-Century Gardens

Seat, though there is some uncertainty about whether the Seat went up before Pope's death (1744) or was built to commemorate him after it. But, just as he had co-designed many of the developments at Cirencester Park with Lord Bathurst, Pope must have given a great deal of advice to Lyttelton, including possible building designs.

The nature of Hagley

What sort of garden or park was Hagley? While having much in common with Enville and The Leasowes, it had its own character, adapted to the topography and reflecting the thoughts, personality and circumstances of its owner. In contrast to Enville, it was very much a literary garden (though differently so from The Leasowes); a political garden; a Whig Opposition garden; an elegiac garden; and, like the other two, an expansive and outward-looking garden. Garden, is, perhaps, not such an appropriate term, for it was often referred to as a park, and Shenstone for one contrasted his own 'farm' to the 'park' at Hagley. This may well stem from the fact that there had been a park at Hagley from the time of Edward III and that the eighteenth-century landscaping was accordingly carried out within the setting of an existing park. Thomas Whately considered that it was possible to unite the character of a park, grazed by deer and sheep, with that of a garden, and that this was demonstrated here: 'The excellencies both of a park and of a garden are thus happily blended at Hagley, where the scenes are equally elegant and noble.'[14] The gravel paths across the glens, through the woods and along the sides of the lawns, all leading to the 'principal scenes', combined with the number and style of the buildings and the high state of maintenance, made Whately conclude that the whole park had the air of a garden.[15]

The house is set quite low within the property, with views upwards and outwards, though it itself commands views downwards beyond the estate. Before it appears a ring of hills, some wooded, some lawn, usually with a building on top. There was no lake – and indeed no place for one – but water played an important part in cascades and pools at different levels, fed from springs in the hills, and issuing down two narrow valleys. Some commented that the water was deficient and did not run too freely.

The name Hagley means a woodland clearing where haws grow. The Old English *haga* means a yard or a haw (hawthorn or hedge). The 'ley' suffix, a clearing, might also relate to 'leag' (=locus, a residence). In the Domesday book (1086) the place is called 'Hageleia'. In the first chapter it was indicated that the land was principally a deer park, and this is what

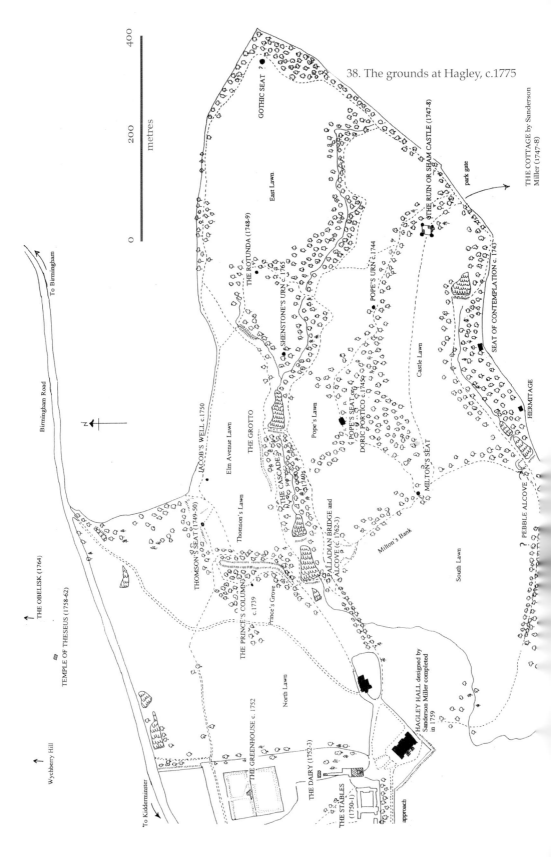

38. The grounds at Hagley, c.1775

To Birmingham

Birmingham Road

To Kidderminster

Wychberry Hill

THE OBELISK (1764)

TEMPLE OF THESEUS (1758–62)

JACOB'S WELL c.1750

Elm Avenue Lawn

East Lawn

THE ROTUNDA (1748–9)

SHENSTONE'S URN c.1765

GOTHIC SEAT ?

THE COTTAGE by Sanderson Miller (1747–8)

park gate

9 THE RUIN OR SHAM CASTLE (1747–8)

POPE'S URN c.1744

SEAT OF CONTEMPLATION c.1743

Castle Lawn

HERMITAGE

THE GROTTO

THE CASCADE

c.1749?

THOMSON'S SEAT (1749–50)

Thomson's Lawn

Pope's Lawn

POPE'S SEAT or
DORIC PORTICO c.1749

MILTON'S SEAT

PALLADIAN BRIDGE and
ALCOVE (c. 1762–3)

Milton's Bank

PEBBLE ALCOVE ?

THE PRINCE'S COLUMN
c.1739

Prince's Grove

South Lawn

North Lawn

THE GREENHOUSE c.1752

THE DAIRY (1752–3)

THE STABLES
(1750–1)

HAGLEY HALL designed by
Sanderson Miller completed
in 1759

approach

metres

N

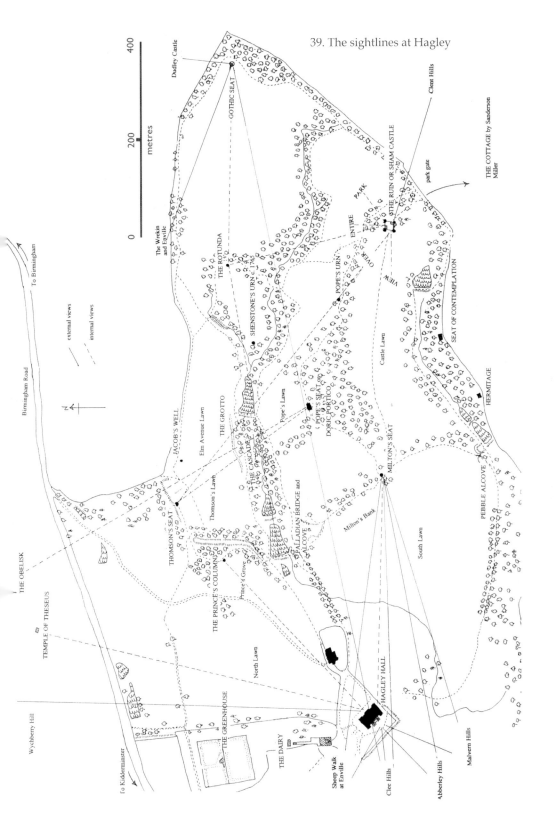

39. The sightlines at Hagley

0   200   400
metres

external views
internal views

N

To Birmingham

Birmingham Road

To Kiddermunster

THE OBELISK

Wychberry Hill

TEMPLE OF THESEUS

THE GREENHOUSE

THE DAIRY

Dudley Castle

GOTHIC SEAT

Clent Hills

THE COTTAGE by Sanderson Miller

park gate

THE RUIN OR SHAM CASTLE

PARK

ENTIRE

OVER

VIEW

SEAT OF CONTEMPLATION

The Wrekin and Enville

THE ROTUNDA

SHENSTONE'S URN c. 1765

POPE'S URN

Castle Lawn

HERMITAGE

JACOB'S WELL

Elm Avenue Lawn

THE GROTTO

Pope's Lawn

POPE'S SEAT

DORIC PORTICO

PEBBLE ALCOVE

THOMSON'S SEAT

Thomson's Lawn

THE CASCADE

PALLADIAN BRIDGE and ALCOVE

Milton's Bank

MILTON'S SEAT

South Lawn

THE PRINCE'S COLUMN

Prince's Grove

North Lawn

HAGLEY HALL

Sheep Walk at Enville

Clee Hills

Abberley Hills

Malvern Hills

107
Hagley

the Lytteltons inherited in the eighteenth century.

Whately considered that the chief glory of Hagley consisted in its continual contrast of wood and lawn, in varying sizes and forms, with a range of openings: 'some stretch out into lengthened glades; some widen every way; they are distinguished by buildings, by prospects, and often by the style only of the plantations around them'[16] (colour fig. 22).

Lyttelton first met Pope around 1731, when the former was only twenty-two, and the poet may well have been responsible for steering him in the direction of creating a literary landscape. Pope was also in the vanguard of the new 'naturalistic' approach to garden design, even if his limited acreage at Twickenham did not permit the sort of landscaping which proved possible at Hagley. As at Cirencester Park, where Pope also worked on a large scale, he welcomed the chance to help plan an expansive estate. He drew three buildings c.1739, which may or may not have been executed.

From Pope Lyttelton could have learned much about the layout and the planting of a large estate, exploiting the *genius loci*, and the ornamentation of a landscape by buildings that are spread out over a substantial area. From Pope, too, there would have come a sense of reverence for the classics and for classical learning, evinced in the erection of classical temples and seats and inscriptions from Latin authors. Perhaps the ring of hills would have provided a faint echo of the hills round Rome. Above all Pope would have instilled the idea of a metaphysical landscape, one which appealed not only to the eye and the other senses but to the mind.

James Thomson, whose poem *The Seasons*, first published in 1730, was one of the most popular of all eighteenth-century poems, and who revised it to incorporate a section on Hagley (published 1744), was another who contributed at a number of levels to the way in which the park was developed. He was a visitor to Hagley, and doubtless discussed garden-making with Lyttelton; he wrote about it; he is commemorated by Thomson's Seat; and above all he introduced a new dimension to thinking about and reacting to the landscape. That dimension was the imagination.

In the first chapter of this book there was some discussion about the role of the imagination, especially from the time of Joseph Addison. With Thomson it is taken further and made more explicit by tying it to a particular landscape so as to shed light on responding to that landscape. Thomson's words, in his revised version of *Spring*, indicate the play between the mind and the eye and how the physical scenes provoke and promote thoughts of various kinds. And not only thoughts – the opening lines are concerned also with feelings:

THESE are the Sacred Feelings of thy Heart,
Thy Heart inform'd by Reason's purest Ray,
O LYTTELTON, the Friend! thy Passions thus
And Meditations vary, as at large,
Courting the Muse, thro' HAGLEY-PARK you stray,
Thy British Tempe! There along the Dale,
With Woods o'er-hung, and shag'd with mossy Rocks,
Whence on each hand the gushing Waters play,
And down the rough Cascade white-dashing fall,
Or gleam in lengthen'd Vista thro' the Trees,
You silent steal; or sit beneath the Shade
Of solemn Oaks, that tuft the swelling Mounts
Thrown graceful round by Nature's careless Hand,
And pensive listen to the various Voice
Of rural Peace: the Herds, the Flocks, the Birds,
The hollow-whispering Breeze, the Plaint of Rills,
That, purling down amid the twisted Roots
Which creep around, their dewy Murmurs shake
  On the sooth'd Ear. From these abstracted oft,
You wander through the Philosophic World;
Where in bright Train continual Wonders rise,
Or to the curious or the pious Eye.
And oft, conducted by Historic Truth,
You tread the long Extent of backward Time:
Planning, with warm Benevolence of Mind,
And honest Zeal unwarp'd by Party-Rage,
Britannia's Weal; how from the venal Gulph
To raise her Virtue, and her Arts revive.
Or, turning thence thy View, these graver Thoughts
The Muses charm: while, with sure Taste refin'd,
You draw th'inspiring Breath of antient Song;
Till nobly rises, emulous, thy own.
Perhaps thy lov'd LUCINDA shares thy Walk,
With Soul to thine attun'd. Then Nature all
Wears to the Lover's Eye a Look of Love;
And all the Tumult of a guilty World,
Tost by ungenerous Passions, sinks away.

The tender Heart is animated Peace; ....
Meantime you gain the Height, from whose fair Brow
The bursting Prospect spreads immense around;
And snatch'd o'er Hill and Dale, and Wood and Lawn,
And verdant Field, and darkening Heath between,
And Villages embosom'd soft in Trees,
And spiry Towns by dusky Columns mark'd
Of rising Smoak, your Eye excursive roams:
Wide-stretching from the Hall, in whose kind Haunt
The *Hospitable Genius* harbours still,
To where the broken Landskip, by Degrees,
Ascending, roughens into ridgy Hills;
O'er which the Cambrian Mountains, like far Clouds
That skirt the blue Horizon, doubtful, rise.[17]

Part of Lyttelton's supposed reaction to the scenes around him as he strolls through his park is directed to the objects themselves, which provide a sense of 'rural peace'; but they also serve to launch him on to a completely different plane – 'You wander through the Philosophic World'. This leads to backward-looking reflections that inform Lyttelton's current political opportunities to plan '*Britannia's* Weal'. Thomson manages to pack a lot into this walk – history, rural contentment, the state of Britain and its arts, love and seeing the landscape with a lover's eye. We then return in a coda to the landscape itself, though with the comment that the hall stands as a reminder of Lyttelton's hospitable spirit.

The literary nature of Hagley is manifested in several ways. While it does not have the sheer number of inscriptions as were to be encountered at The Leasowes, nonetheless classical authors were invoked to give a sense of Arcadia and the ancient world of pastoral. The inscriptions were painted on wooden tablets. Hagley also contains prominent architectural tributes to the literary giants who knew and loved it, viz. Pope and Thomson, and one from the preceding century, John Milton. There was also an urn raised after Shenstone's death. The fact that the park can be 'read' in terms of a sequence of associationist features is also literary. Finally, the Seat of Contemplation suggests a mixture of contemplating the view and meditation. It may also be an echo of the earlier Temple of Contemplation at Stowe. The Hermitage nearby carries a similar meaning.

A rather sycophantic poem by the Rev Meadowcroft on the completion of the new Hall alludes to the park as a Mount Parnassus, graced by Apollo and the Muses and thus a source of inspiration:

Here Pallas dwells: she built these stately towers
On classic ground, and near Parnassian hills;
She formed these smiling lawns, these solemn bowers,
These ever murmuring streams, and ever tinkling rills;
Delighted with her Lyttelton's domains
Where sit the Muses, and Apollo reigns.[18]

Describing the water as ever-active was, however, somewhat optimistic.

Hagley is also to some degree an elegiac garden. The main period of work on the gardens in the later 1740s followed the death of Lyttelton's beloved first wife Lucy, and may be seen in terms of solace and indirect memorial, just as Stourhead was largely created following the death of Henry Hoare's wife. A further burst of activity followed the departure of Lyttelton's second wife, who left him after several vexed years together. The elegiac quality shows itself also in the buildings of meditation and retreat mentioned above. Some of the buildings are memorials – Pope died in 1744, Thomson in 1748 and Shenstone in 1763 – so they have a flavour of sadness.

Lyttelton himself closely identified the landscape with Lucy, and his *Monody* on her death demonstrates her love for the park and how she gave lustre to it. It also conveys a sense of the park as a place of retreat:

In vain I look around
O'er all the well-known ground,
My Lucy's wonted footsteps to descry;
Where oft we us'd to walk,
Where oft in tender talk
We saw the summer sun go down the sky;
Not by yon fountain's side,
Nor where its waters glide
Along the valley, can she now be found
In all the wide-stretch'd prospect's ample bound
No more my mournful eye

Can sight of her espy,
But the sad sacred earth where her dear relics lie.

O shades of Hagley, where is now your boast?
Your bright inhabitant is lost.
You she preferr'd to all the gay resorts
Where female vanity might wish to shine,
The pomp of cities and the pride of courts.
Her modest beauties shun'd the public eye;
To your sequester'd dales
And flow'r-embroider'd vales
From an admiring world she chose to fly.[19]

It is a political garden in that Lyttelton's position and loyalties are conspic-
uous. The most overt sign of this is, of course, the Column to Frederick,
Prince of Wales (colour fig. 23), Lyttelton's employer. While it was not
Lyttelton's idea (it was a gift from Frederick), it stands in a prominent position – more so now than at first. Frederick was the rallying point for the
Whig Opposition of the day, and their clarion call of 'Liberty' was often
expressed in Gothic garden architecture. Apart from the Gothic Seat, the
most striking Gothic presence in Hagley park was the Ruined Castle, which
dominates all the other buildings.

One of the characteristics of Hagley represents a Whig Opposition garden in other, less concrete,
ways. Lyttelton was in a circle of friends, relatives and colleagues who were
involved in the new, naturalistic gardening and which became associated
particularly with the great Whig landowners such as Lord Cobham at
Stowe. So the whole approach to reshaping his land would have been
coloured by fashion and the ideas circulating within Lyttelton's sphere. This
would have included such elements as planting and design on a large scale.

One of the characteristics of Hagley was its contrast of scenes and
moods as one went around the park. Heely expressed it thus: 'Hagley has
a pre-eminence over most of the pleasure grounds I am acquainted with
... it not only affords a multiplicity of scenes, but every one rises somewhat
different in character, though all of them perfectly relative; and what adds
still more to its glory, is, that you always conclude the present can never
be rivalled by another, till another appears, and, with its beauty and unexpected novelty, effaces the impression the former has made upon you.'[20]

To experience the different scenes in sequence was, accordingly, highly desirable.

The natural appearance of the grounds, together with their diversity, was commented on by many, such as John Parnell on his visit in 1770:

> But the great Beauty of Hagley is the great Diversity of the ground in View all gently swelling or Rising pretty steep with Valleys between the Hills well coverd with fine old Wood & the Vales Either Dressd finely in Little Lawns or waterd by Little streams in one part thrown down in four or five very Pretty cascades and forming Basons between them which in some points of View Appear one Peice of water in all they are made to Resemble nature much as possible.[21]

The views obtainable from vantage points in the park were wide-ranging. Distant mountains contrasted with 'the busy town of Stourbridge', mineral mining, 'the smoke of Worcester, the churches in Birmingham' and what would progressively become an industrialised landscape.[22]

George Mason, in weighing up the respective qualities of a number of estates, praised Painshill for 'creative genius' but attributed 'correctest fancy' to Hagley.[23] This appears to chime with Horace Walpole's conclusion that 'There is extreme taste in the park',[24] for the word fancy in the eighteenth century embraced ideas of imagination, taste and inventiveness. Arthur Young adds further corroboration, saying that Lyttelton had disposed the grounds 'with the utmost taste.'[25]

A description of Hagley

It might seem that the best circuit to follow, for descriptive purposes, would be that described by Joseph Heely. However, he does not follow the usual clockwise route, and so what follows is a composite based on several contemporary descriptions. There was no distinct set circuit, and indeed it is impossible to encompass all the 'incidents' in the park on a single path – there will be a certain amount of retracing one's steps. This is because there is a principal thrust north-east from the house which takes in the Palladian Bridge, cascades, grotto and rotunda (see plan), but there are features to be found on the slopes to either side. For the purposes of this account, the sequence will be: the western part, the central part and the eastern part. The present tense is used, as if the park were being seen by an eighteenth-century visitor.

North of the Hall lie the service buildings, stables, dairy, greenhouse and kitchen gardens, (colour figs. 24 and 25) all dating from the period 1747-53. They are beautified by a shrubbery with winding paths which contains varied evergreens and a profusion of colourful plants and is bounded by large luxuriant limes and other trees, which also serve to screen the service buildings when viewed from out in the park. The stables (1747), the greenhouse (c.1752) and the dairy (c.1752) were all designed by Sanderson Miller. It seems that the shrubbery is to be admired at the start of the walk rather than at the end as was the case with Shenstone's shrubbery adjoining his house. That is because the walk begins at the Hall, while at The Leasowes it finishes at Shenstone's house.

Immediately facing the Hall, to the north-east, is a slope which leads up to the Column to Frederick, Prince of Wales. The Column is built of Bath stone, and was originally erected c.1739 in a less prominent position, on the lawn below Pope's Seat. It may be, as Michael Cousins suggests, that Sir Thomas, not being of the Prince's party, did not wish it to have too much prominence.[26] It was transferred to its present position in 1751, a move that did not please Shenstone.[27] It is backed by pines on the crown of the hill, with elm and beech sweeping down the sides. This idea, with varying trees, was a common device to set off a building or other feature (favoured particularly by William Kent in his painterly approach to garden design and found also at Enville). The Prince had died in 1751, as did Sir Thomas, which presumably prompted the move of the Column. Frederick himself stands on top of the Column in Roman attire, an echo of the way in which his forebears were portrayed (cf the equestrian statue of George I as a Roman emperor at Stowe) and an indication of an Augustan cast of thinking.

On the left of the column, a falling lawn leads the eye down and then up to Wychbury Hill, the next port of call. Striking up and across to the north-west from the Column, over the Birmingham road, the visitor reaches the Temple of Theseus (1758-62) – colour fig. 26. Like the Column, it is backed by trees, in this case 'Scotch firs' (presumably Scots pines) and elms. It was a present from Admiral Smith and cost £300. The Temple has traditionally been hailed as the first Greek revival building in Europe, but this has to be qualified in some such terms as the first *significant* building of that kind. For James 'Athenian' Stuart, the designer of the Temple, had already (in 1756) been responsible for a Grecian Doric portico at The Grove, near

Three Great Eighteenth-Century Gardens

Watford, Hertfordshire,[28] though that probably did not last long and certainly caused no architectural stir. The Temple of Theseus, inspired by the Theseion at Athens, though it is only a portico, took up to four years to complete, so its usual attributed date of erection (1758) is only the start date. In 1761 the building was still unfinished,[29] which means that another early example of Greek revival had already appeared. That was the Temple of the Winds at West Wycombe, Buckinghamshire (1759), a heavily rococo version of its Athens original probably by John Donowell working from drawings by Stuart's Greek project partner, Nicholas Revett.[30] There may even be a much earlier example of a Grecian building in a garde: Vanbrugh's rotunda at Stowe (1720), said to have been modelled on the Temple of Venus at Cnidos.[31]

Lyttelton may not have fully appreciated what he was pioneering, since the 'Grecian gusto' did not spread at Hagley in the way that it did at West Wycombe or Shugborough, Staffordshire. How he came to know Stuart is uncertain, though Sanderson Miller may well have known of Stuart, and Miller had overall supervision of the construction of the building. The Greek revival came largely out of the Society of Dilettanti, founded by Sir Francis Dashwood of West Wycombe, among others, which subscribed to publishing the findings of Stuart and Revett arising from their tours of Greece in the 1750s and sponsored a subsequent expedition to Asia Minor. Dashwood, like Stuart, was also a member of the Society of Antiquaries, of which Lyttelton's brother Charles, a member from 1746, became President 1765-8.[32] It may be, therefore, that Charles was the link between Lyttelton and Stuart, though Richard Grenville was a member of the Dilettanti from 1736.

Behind the Temple, on a further swell out on Wychbury Hill, stands the Obelisk. Constructed of sandstone ashlar and brick, the Obelisk was raised in 1764 for Sir Richard Lyttelton. This is, by contrast, in the middle of an open lawn and sheep-walk, with the Wychbury wood and its old oaks running behind it. Further out still is an open hexagon temple in a grove (now gone), with columns made from trunks of oak trees. This rustic construction has a primitive sort of cornice and frieze of wood.[33] By 1770 it served as a cattle shed.[34] In character it resembles the buildings in Hermitage Wood.

Returning back towards the centre of the landscape, the visitor encoun-ters Thomson's Seat, an arched stone pavilion. It commemorated the poet after his death and was designed by John Pitt, going up in 1749-50 under the supervision of Sanderson Miller. In the middle of the nineteenth century it was demolished by a falling tree. The seat was often called octagonal,

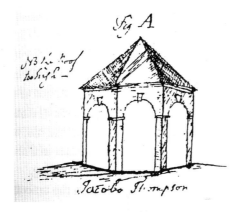

40. Thomson's Seat. A sketch
by Sir John Parnell: *Journal of a
tour thro' Wales and England
Anno. 1769*: LSE Libraries MS
Coll Misc 38

though the ground plan shows five sides of an octagon plus a blank wall closing off the back (fig. 40, above and colour fig. 19). Lyttelton paid tribute to his friend with this memorial, inscribed:

Ingenio immortali
JACOBI THOMSON
Poetae Sublimis
Viri boni
Aediculum hanc in secessu quem vivus dilexit
Post mortem ejus constructam
Dicat dedicatque
GEORGIUS LYTTELTON

[To the immortal genius of JAMES THOMSON. A sublime poet; A good man; This small temple (built after his death) in that recess Which when living he delighted in; Is consecrated and dedicated By GEORGE LYTTELTON]

The view south-east across the landscape from Thomson's Seat (which was about to make its appearance) is depicted in the engraving by Vivares after Thomas Smith, 1749 (fig. 41, opposite). Three features appear from left to right in the engraving: the Sham Castle, Pope's Seat and a small anonymous seat. Thomson and Pope are thus linked by this cross-axis. Heely rhapsodised about the view: 'For variety ... for almost every principal feature that distinguishes the beauty of landscape, perhaps not one place in the whole park, holds the eye so much in pleasure as this ... the favourite one of the ingenious and descriptive *Thomson*.'[35] What is most striking is the richness and density of planting, with the two Seats picked out by virtue of the clearings in front of them, and the Sham Castle rising above the trees

41. A View of Hagley Park. Engraving by F Vivares after Thomas Smith (1749)

42. Jacob's Well

43. The Palladian Bridge by Rev Thomas Streatfield (c.1820). Conway Library, The Courtauld Institute of Art, London image no. 607/4(16A)

in true Miltonic fashion ('Embosom'd high in tufted trees'). The cascade valley is hidden in the front row of trees.

The final feature on this western side is what Heely termed 'a whimsical well', Jacob's Well, which was there by 1751. The well head consists of a small stone arch surmounted by a tiny opening in the pediment, possibly for a bell. It is medieval in style. 'O ye wells bless ye the Lord' is carved on one side. It is a very rare example of a biblical feature in an English landscape garden and may reflect Lyttelton's own religious frame of mind.

The central section starts with an upward walk from the church through a steep hollow surrounded by bare rocks and disordered trees with roots exposed. In Thomas Maurice's poem on Hagley (1776) the wildness is described thus:

> To that lone Dell, beneath the deep'ned shade,
> Where down the valley bursts the rude cascade;
> Whose rugged sides – with hoary moss o'er grown,
> Deck'd with huge fragments of romantic stone,
> Grotesque and wild – with verdure never bloom,
> But o'er the senses shed a grateful [pleasing] gloom:[36]

The path leads, by complete contrast, to an arcadian scene marked by arrival at the Palladian Bridge and Alcove. They were built 1762-3, incorporating an earlier 'rustick seat of bricks ... in the form of a Venetian window'.[37] The bridge (fig. 43, opposite) is a somewhat truncated version, with only four columns, of the bridges at Wilton (1737), Stowe (1739) and Prior Park (1755), and was probably designed by William Pitt's and Lyttelton's nephew Thomas Pitt (Lord Camelford). It stands near the foot of the series of cascades and pools, with one further steep descent and small cascade below it, so it is founded on an embankment. The rear wall, above the small lowest pool, is filled in, which constitutes the 'alcove' as described by visitors including Heely. The idea of a solid wall along the 'unimportant' side of the colonnade came, doubtless, from Stowe, where the bridge had originally had such a wall, decorated with a relief that was later transferred to another building. The Alcove was destroyed by a falling tree c.1840.

Wicker chairs stand inside the Alcove, which bears the inscription:

Viridantia Tempe, Tempe, quae sylvae cingunt super impendentes
(Catullus, *Carmina*, 64, ll. 285-6)

[Verdurous Tempe, Tempe which overhanging woods engirdle]

Tempe was the wooded valley in Thessaly leading to Mount Olympus. It was often used as a type or symbol of beautiful scenery, as was Arcadia. This is just one of a number of inscriptions to be found as one walks up the valley of the cascades, all in praise of their surroundings. Not that the view from the Palladian Bridge up the valley needed such aid: 'No vista surely has ever held to the eye with such advantage to please!'[38] Thomas Maurice rhapsodised about the view in the prose account which preceded his poem: 'Never before did the hand of art model, or the eye of fancy behold, a scene so ravishing. The grand cascade tumbling from one rock to another down the embosomed vale. The richness of the woods, and the distant *Rotunda* that terminates the swelling vista, at once fill the mind with astonishment and pleasure'[39] (colour fig. 28).

It was described by Whately as 'a perfect opera scene',[40] with its perspective and the trees on each side acting as the wings in a stage set. Operas such as Handel's *Rinaldo* included scenes of enchanted gardens. Whately's comment also indicates the theatrical nature of much garden-making at the time, the composition of three-dimensional tableaux with the illusion of the perspective found in a theatre. This view, up to the rotunda, is shown in an engraving of c.1750 (fig. 44, opposite). It represents the heart of the design of the park, the principal beauty. The cascade valley dates from the 1740s, and the view developed as the trees grew and arched over, to create a framed vista.[41] Within the naturalistic park this constituted a set-piece garden scene, which was even a little formal, with straight edges to the banks.

Further up the valley, on the left of the water, is an area of rocks with seats and recesses. In the largest of the alcoves an inscription reads:

> Ego laudo ruris amoeni
> Rivos, et musco circumlita saxa nemusque. (Horace, *Epistles*, I, 10, ll. 6-7)

> [I praise the brooks of the pleasant countryside, its rocks overgrown
> with moss, and its groves]

On the other (right hand) side of the water, there is an inscription on a bench around an old oak deep in a glen:

> Libet jacere modo sub antiqua ilice
> Modo in tenaci gramine:
> Labuntur altis interim ripis aquae
> Queruntur in silvis aves;
> Fontesque lymphis obstrepunt manantibus
> Somnos quo invitet leves. (Horace, *Epodes*, II, ll. 23-8)
> [It is pleasing to lie now under an ancient ilex, now on the matted
> grass. Meanwhile the waters glide between high banks, birds twitter
> in the woods, springs chatter with the flowing of waters, thereby
> inducing gentle sleep]

There is some uncertainty about whether the above bench and inscription actually replaced another bench on the same spot or very close to it, with an inscription in similar vein:

> Hic gelidi fontes, hic mollia prata, Lycori,
> Hic nemus, hic ipso tecum consumerer aevo. (Virgil, *Eclogues*, 10, ll. 42-3)

44. A View of the Rotunda looking over the Cascades, James Mason after Thomas Smith (c.1750). Bodleian Library, University of Oxford, Gough Maps, vol. 11, f. 37. B view b

> [Here are cool springs, here soft meadows, Lycoris, here groves; and
> here, with you, I would never be wearied except by age itself]

Robert Williams has drawn attention to how Thomson, in his section on Hagley quoted earlier, seems to have been inspired as much by the inscriptions as by the scene itself.[42] Winding through a wood of oaks in the cascade valley, still on the eastern side, the visitor is confronted with a screen on a bench under a large oak which bears the following quotation:

> Inter cuncta leges, et per cunctabere doctos,
> Qua ratione queas traducere leniter oevum,
> Quid minuat curas, quid te tibi reddat amicum,
> Quid puri tranquillet, honos an dulce lucellum,
> An secretum iter, et fallentis semita vitae.
> (Horace, *Epistles*, I, 18, ll. 95-102, but omitting ll. 97-9)

> [As well as all this (lines preceding the quotation, which give advice
> on moral choices), you should read and take time to consult the
> learned and to find by what plan you may pass your days in peace;
> what will diminish care; what make you at ease with yourself; what

will bring you the tranquillity of singlemindedness – public office or a modest profit, or a hidden progress and a way of living unnoticed]

The missing three lines are presumably omitted for reasons of space.

The cascades were varied in strength and dramatic effect, and, as we know, did not always flow with sufficient force. The water would swirl round mossy stones and burnt cinders,[43] moss and cinders (burnt industrial slag) being also a feature of the rocky dell and grotto on the west of the water. Shenstone too used cinders in his cascades at The Leasowes.

Towards the top of the water sequence, and to the left of it, stands the grotto, in a set scene entered by a gate. Initially characterised by a grove of 'gloomy yews', which casts a feeling of darkness and retreat, this area opens up into 'Arcadian felicity ... fairy land' (Heely). The banks are covered with moss, shrubs and sweet-scented flowers, and the surroundings are dominated by tall trees. The grotto itself is a niche or cave composed of 'cinder-studded rocks', made from a blue-grey glassy slag. It dates from c.1740. There has been some confusion with another grotto planned for Lyttelton's second wife Elizabeth, but Michael Cousins has shown that this grotto was never constructed in the park and is in fact identifiable with the one in the basement of the house.[44]

In a park not overpopulated by statues, a particular point is made of providing a figure of the Venus de Medici in its own rustic arched niche, in a thicket of trees and shrubs near the grotto. This may have inspired Shenstone to place the same representation of Venus in his (equally unstatued) garden, in an ornamental shrubbery. George Mason speaks of a statue looking as if it were about to dart across a grove,[45] but that cannot have been either Venus or Apollo, which existed at one time at Hagley, since both figures are static.

Beyond the water is Shenstone's Urn (colour fig. 27), placed there c.1765 after his death. Given the uneasy relations between the Lytteltons and Shenstone, it was a graceful gesture on Lyttelton's part to erect the urn with this inscription:

To the Memory of
WILLIAM SHENSTONE, ESQ.
In whose Verses
Were all the natural Graces
And in whose Manners

Was all the amiable Simplicity
Of Pastoral Poetry
With the sweet Tenderness
Of the Elegiac.

The urn has now been moved to near the Hall.

Further up the hill, crowning the view up the valley, is the rotunda (1748-9), designed by John Pitt and constructed under the supervision of Sanderson Miller at a cost of £151[46] (colour figs. 29 and 30). It has a two-stepped circular platform with eight Ionic columns supporting a domed roof. It is seen to best advantage from below, being invisible from other parts of the park. With its ball finial it resembles the rotunda at Stowe.

East from the rotunda, in a corner of a wild part of the park stretching in the direction of the Clent hills, is a white Gothic Seat, probably by Miller, affording views of the Castle, the hills and the distant country. This area is overgrown with fern, and won Whately's approval: 'The wildness is an acceptable relief in the midst of so much elegance and improvement as reign in the neighbouring lawns.'[47] The Seat, described as 'one of the prettiest *Gothic* alcoves imaginable,'[48] has four fluted columns and three seats. It has long since disappeared.

The south-eastern section includes the building for which Hagley is best known, the Ruined Castle (1747-8), designed by Sanderson Miller (colour fig. 31). It consists of a square walled keep with four corner turrets in various stages of dilapidation. One of the towers is more or less intact. Originally large stones were left lying about as if fallen from the crumbling ruin, but by Heely's visit in 1777 they had been removed, though the ivy growing up the walls preserved the fiction of antiquity. The appearance of a medieval castle was carried out realistically, causing Horace Walpole on a visit in 1753 to comment that 'it has the true rust of the barons' wars',[49] though he knew perfectly well it had only gone up five years before. Ivy and other vegetation on the walls enhanced the effect, but if one looked too closely the whiteness and smoothness of the mortar gave the game away.[50] Some elements may in fact have been genuine: the windows are said to have come from the old Halesowen Abbey. Although this story appears to date from no earlier than 1868,[51] it was common practice at the time to recycle genuine medieval fragments when building a mock ruin, for example the Ruined Chapel at Mount Edgcumbe or (allegedly) Shenstone's

Ruined Priory. Alfred's Hall at Cirencester Park used elements from the demolished church at Sapperton. It also had stones and fragments lying around. Pope's three drawings of 1739 might have included the initial idea for the Castle, since it has so much in common with Alfred's Hall. Lyttelton knew Alfred's Hall himself, having seen it in 1738, and with Pope's encouragement might at that early stage have conceived a fancy for something similar.[52] Even inside the habitable parts of the Castle there was an attempt to present the medieval – Henry Keene and Miller together designed eight Gothic chairs for a room at the top of the tower, which could well be the chairs purchased by Lord Stamford from Hagley in 1768.[53]

The 'courtyard' within the keep is a farmyard, and the three ruined turrets are used, respectively, as a coal store (or 'turf house', possibly referring to turf as peat, i.e. for fuel), a hen house and a cow house.

The Castle is both associationist and iconic. As a purportedly medieval construction it gives a sense of dynasty stretching back, and by the architecture it signifies a period of England's past that was seized on by the Whig Opposition as exemplifying traditional virtues and liberties that had been lost in the (to them) corrupt Walpole administration. In this way it links with the Gothic Temple at Stowe, which bears an unmistakeable political

The Ruin

46. The Ruined Castle, a sketch by Sir John Parnell from *Journal of a tour thro' Wales and England Anno. 1769*. LSE Libraries MS Coll Misc 38

message. But visually too the Castle would have struck a chord when viewed across woods so that it appears to be rising from among the trees. This evokes the well-known line about a castle in Milton's *L'Allegro*, 'Embosom'd high in tufted trees', which Repton later adopted as an icon and illustrated in the trade card with which he set up his practice. Views of the Gothic Tower at Painshill, for example, would often show it breast-high in woods.

Having the Castle within the park blended with the distant view of the ruined Dudley Castle and also added to the sense that the whole region was historical, with generations of families who had inhabited these old monuments.

The Castle is prominent and visible from many parts of the park. It commands, immediately below it, an extensive lawn, which the visitor now proceeds across in a south-westerly direction, reaching the second valley with pools, streams and cascades, echoing the earlier one but not so dramatically. Having crossed the stream and climbed the steep bank on the other side, one reaches the Seat of Contemplation (c.1743). This is a curving seat within an alcove decorated with sheep bones. In a small niche is an owl, and the ceiling is adorned with a star composed of shells of various colours. The sharp pointed finials are reminiscent of the grotto at Stowe. An inscription reads 'Sedes Contemplationis. Omnia Vanitas' [Seat of Contemplation. All is vanity], written in snail-shells split in two. This seat is partly for meditation and partly for the setting, 'retired, solitary and serene' yet 'in the midst of sylvan beauty.'[54]

Continuing down in a south-westerly direction, still along the boundary, the visitor comes across the Hermitage (c.1739), linked conceptually with

47. The Seat of Contemplation, a
sketch by Sir John Parnell from
*Journal of a tour thro' Wales and
England Anno 1769.* LSE Libraries
MS Coll Misc 38

the Seat of Contemplation. The Hermitage is set in a dark corner, surrounded
by horse chestnuts, and is reached via the hermit's fountain, covered with
an old tree trunk. A rail and gate of rough stakes stand before it. The
Hermitage is a rough construction, a square with two rooms, composed from
tree stumps, trunks and roots, with the interstices filled with earth and moss
of different colours. The floor is paved with small pebbles. A couch is in the
first room, which contains the familiar lines (slightly adapted) from Milton's
Il Penseroso:

> And may at last my weary age
> Find out the peaceful hermitage;
> The hairy gown and mossy cell,
> Where I may sit and rightly spell
> Of every star that heaven doth shew,
> And every herb that dips the dew:
> Till old experience do attain
> To something like prophetic strain.
> These pleasures melancholy give,
> And I with these will chuse to live.

This reference to Milton is not only appropriate to the meditative life of a
hermit but forms a counterpoint to the other side of the poet as expressed in
Milton's Seat and Milton's Bank. A parody on the use of these lines in the
Hermitage, much more *L'Allegro* than *Il Penseroso*, was written by J Giles:

48. The Hermitage, a sketch by
Sir John Parnell from *Journal of
a tour thro' Wales and England
Anno 1769.* LSE Libraries MS
Coll Misc 38

> May I, while health and strength remains,
>
> And blood flows warm within my veins;
>
> Find out some virgin, soft and kind,
>
> Who is to social joy inclin'd;
>
> A nymph who can for me forego,
>
> The fop, the fribble, and the beau;
>
> From noise and show, content can be,
>
> To live at home with love and me:
>
> Such pleasure, Love and Hymen give,
>
> And such a life I wish to live.[55]

Just below the Hermitage is a root house made of stumps of wood, built against a bank and turfed over. There is extensive use of moss, which is stuck on the interior and on the top. The seat itself is of sticks.

At the southern tip the Pebble Alcove, 'a sort of cell' (Heely), is encountered, but no detailed descriptions survive, other than Bishop Pococke's observation that the pebbles formed various patterns – a cross, beads and ornaments of pots and flowers.[56] The idea of a pebble alcove was not new, and Lyttelton would have been well acquainted with that at Stowe. This quartet of buildings in Hermitage Wood has proved difficult to date, since there is no documentary evidence of their origins. It may be that some were by Pope, which would date them to c.1739, but although he drew designs for three buildings they may well not have been implemented: Pope had a history of drawing excitedly without necessarily any execution. In 1734 Lord Bathurst described Pope as 'every day drawing me a plan for some new building or other, and then is violently angry that it is not set up the next morning.'[57]

The visitor now climbs the path north from the alcove, with the south lawn on the left and the castle lawn on the right, affording a climactic view of the ruin. The path leads through a grove of oaks and then along an old walk of elms and sycamores before a slight dip signals arrival at Milton's Seat, with its contrasting scenery of the 'splendid and sublime' (see colour fig. 32). Visual details are lacking, as indeed is the date, though it was in place by the mid-1750s. On it are lines from Milton's great epic *Paradise Lost*:

> These are thy glorious works, parent of good!
> Almighty! thine this universal frame,
> Thus wond'rous fair; thyself how wond'rous then!
> Unspeakable, who sit'st above the heavens,
> To us invisible, or dimly seen
> In these thy lowest works; yet these declare
> Thy goodness beyond thought, and power divine.

Visitors were entranced by the panorama. William Toldervy proclaimed it:

> The most amazing View you ever beheld. It looks towards the West, having the House at some Distance below, which from hence affords a grand Appearance. Over this, the Eye is enticed to a prodigious Variety of Lawns, Towns, and Villages, quite to the *Clee-Hills* already mentioned, and beyond them to the Mountains in many Counties of *Wales*. On the Right, beyond the Village of *Hagley*, the View continues to the *Wrekin*, and then over a fine Country to the Mountains of *Denbigh* and *Montgomery* Shires. On the South is a Wood, and beyond that the lofty Hill of *Clent* (on Part of which this Park is formed) obstructs the View that Way.[58]

The majestic lawn sweeping down from the Seat leads to the Hall, with a background of the Shropshire hills and other parts of the park, including Thomson's Seat, the Temple of Theseus and the Obelisk. Enville is discernible from this vantage point, one of the finest in the park.

Continuing the clockwise circuit of this part of the park, Milton's Seat is succeeded by Pope's Seat, probably dating from c.1745, in other words just after his death. This consists of a Doric portico with rusticated bands on the four columns, in the manner of the Portico at Enville. It is inscribed 'Quieti & Musis' [To Quiet and the Muses]. It stands above a sloping lawn (Pope's

col 14: The Lower Cascades at Enville in a watercolour by Anthony Devis (c.1765). The water falls in three cascades into the Temple Pool. In the trees above the Cascades there is a dark, arched feature – the end doors of Shenstone's Chapel. Private collection

col 16: Shenstone's Chapel in Priest Wood, Enville. It was built in the 1750s and dedicated to Shenstone after his death in 1763

col 17: The Shepherd's Bridge, Enville, at the head of Jordan's Pool. Anthony Devis, watercolour, c.1765. Private collection

col 18: A view of the park at
Hagley. Unknown artist.
Estate of Priscilla Mitchell

col 19: Thomson's Seat at Hagley,
designed by John Pitt (1749-50).
Unknown artist.
Estate of Priscilla Mitchell

col 20: The pools
above the Palladian
Bridge at Hagley.
Unknown artist.
Estate of Priscilla
Mitchell

col 21: The Rotunda at Hagley
designed by John Pitt (1748-49).
Unknown artist.
Estate of Priscilla Mitchell

col 22: Hagley: a view of the park

col 23: Hagley: column of Frederick, Prince of Wales in Roman habit c.1739. Moved to its present site in 1751

col 24: The Dairy at Hagley designed by Sanderson Miller (1752-3)

col 25: The Greenhouse at Hagley designed by Sanderson Miller (1752)

col 26: The Temple of Theseus at Hagley designed by James 'Athenian' Stuart (1758-62)

col 27: Shenstone's Urn at Hagley which has been moved from its original place between two streams to a site by the Hall

28: The pools above the Palladian Bridge at Hagley looking up towards the Rotunda

col 29: The Rotunda at Hagley

Lawn) bordered by trees. The path swings round to the east to reach Pope's Urn, c.1744. Fig. 49 (page 130) shows David Parkes's watercolour of the urn, with its double mask, possibly of Satire and Philosophy. It is inscribed:

ALEXANDRO POPE

Poetarum anglicanorum

Elegantissimo dulcissimoque

Vitiorum castigatori acerrimo

Sapientia doctori suavissimo

Sacra esto Ann. Dom. 1744

[Sacred to the memory of ALEXANDER POPE. The most elegant and harmonious of English poets; The severest satirist of vice, And the most agreeable teacher of wisdom. In the year 1744]

According to Whately, the urn was chosen by Pope for that particular location, with the inscription added in his memory.[59]

To the south-east, on the top of Clent Hill, Lyttelton placed four upright stones in the manner of a 'Druid Temple', a kind of Stonehenge which became popular later in the century. This may, in fact, be the earliest example, which was soon copied by a neighbour, Sir Samuel Hellier, at the Woodhouse, Wombourne. Like the Ruined Castle it was intended to convey a (spurious) historicity to the site, perhaps to complement the genuine Iron Age fort on Wychbury Hill opposite. As has been mentioned, there was also considerable antiquarian interest in Druids at the time, expressed in gardens by Thomas Wright among others, with his Druid's Cell at Stoke Park, Bristol. A further association was with Ossian, the figure of legend exaggerated by the contemporary poet Macpherson, for the stones were referred to as Ossian's Tomb.[60]

Connections with Stowe

As the greatest and most famous of all eighteenth-century gardens, Stowe was bound to exert some influence or inspiration. What made this all the more inevitable were the close family links with the Temples at Stowe. Apart from the Lyttelton-Temple connections there was strong input from the Pitt family (who were also connected by marriage). Although Stowe was still being developed and added to in the late 1730s and 1740s, when

49. Pope's Urn, a watercolour by David Parkes. Shropshire RO ref. 6001/154

50. The base of Pope's Urn today

Three Great Eighteenth-Century Gardens

Hagley was coming into shape, the influences noted below are all examples where Stowe came first. All concern architecture.

The two properties had a great deal in common in the matter of buildings and indeed the approach to their design. Sometimes there were specific architectural similarities; sometimes just a generic correspondence. An example of the latter is the grotto. At Stowe the grotto was a commanding feature, a piece of architecture that was modified at least twice during the century, with a central chamber and wings. The grotto at Hagley was a very slight affair, in contrast, little more than a primitive, rustic niche. Another example would be the Seat of Contemplation, at Hagley a simple rustic seat with shell decoration and at Stowe a formal classical pavilion.

The connection might be a particular element of architectural style. Thus, the rusticated bands on the 'guglio' (obelisk fountain) at Stowe are replicated in the rusticated bands on the columns of Pope's Seat at Hagley, and the sharp finials of the grotto find reflection in those of the Seat of Contemplation.

In one instance there is an identical copy, and that is the figure of the Venus de Medici. The statue appeared at Stowe in Vanbrugh's rotunda and at Hagley, in its own niche near the grotto. The purpose and positioning were, however, very different. At Stowe, Venus was on prominent display in an iconographical scheme of carnal love: at Hagley she is, rather, a symbol of beauty, modesty and retirement, as she is, indeed, at The Leasowes.

Inscriptions were another shared feature. Stowe carried a great many, and Lyttelton might well have been impressed by an approach to garden design which took into account the importance of engaging the mind as well as the eye, and of using inscriptions to evoke or enhance the associations that would contribute to the garden experience as a whole. He was himself responsible for some of the inscriptions at Stowe.

There were several features that could have acknowledged Stowe as their source. One is the rotunda – John Pitt's dome at Hagley is flatter than Vanbrugh's steep dome at Stowe, though the latter was subsequently made shallower by Borra in the 1760s (perhaps the dome shows influence going the other way for once). But the idea of an open building with columns supporting a dome is very similar (and common to a great many gardens, it should be said). Another is the column – the pillar supporting Frederick at Hagley resembles that supporting his father George II at Stowe, where the columnar idea was varied by a quadruple fluted column topped by

Queen Caroline and by a rostral column, decorated with maritime devices, dedicated to one of the Grenville family. Finally there was the very elaborate tower column raised by Lady Cobham in commemoration of her husband in 1747.

The Palladian Bridge, with alcove or screen wall, was clearly a case of Lyttelton using Stowe as a model, though in simplified form. There were also Pebble Alcoves at both estates, though that at Hagley was far less solid and elaborate than its Stowe inspiration.

The Obelisk was another feature in common. At Hagley it was remote, perched on Wychbury Hill; at Stowe there were several in more visible positions, ranging from the small memorial to the clergyman Robin Coucher to the above-mentioned guglio and the squat, half-pyramid, half-obelisk monument to William Congreve. The guglio was demolished and its stonework recycled to form an obelisk to commemorate General Wolfe after his death in 1759.

The Hermitage at Hagley accords by name with that at Stowe, but not architecturally. In that regard it is actually closer to another construction at Stowe, namely St. Augustine's Cave, as a simple, primitive work of moss and tree roots.

There are also possible connections with another Cobham-Grenville estate, that of Wotton, Buckinghamshire. In this case, however, although Sanderson Miller was involved, there is unlikely to have been influence or copying, since most of the Wotton works come from the late 1750s and thus postdate much of Hagley. Similar edifices include a grotto (late 1750s), a rotunda and a Palladian bridge of wood, recreated in recent times, though dissimilar in design.

Traffic of design worked the other way as well. Lyttelton was invited to provide an elegy, inscribed on one side of the base of the Grenville column at Stowe, to commemorate his cousin. It is said that the inscriptions on the Temple of British Worthies, including the mock-heroic tribute to a greyhound on the back of the temple, were also written by Lyttelton.[61] He featured as one of the busts set in the Temple of Friendship in 1739. And there was some commuting between Hagley and Stowe in terms of those who advised on architecture. Sanderson Miller, though figuring little at Stowe, claimed to have worked on a finishing of Gibbs's Gothic Temple, or the Temple of Liberty.[62] If, as seems probable, Miller added the crocketed pinnacles to the angles of the highest tower, and was possibly responsible too for the lanterns on top of the lower towers, then he was certainly steering the temple in a more 'Gothick' direction. Thomas Pitt, fresh from designing the Palladian Bridge at Hagley, composed the huge Corinthian Arch, 60 feet in height, at Stowe (1764), commanding the distant view from the south front of the house. He may also have rebuilt the Doric Arch (1768), designed the altered Nelson's Seat c.1773, and modified the Temple of Friendship and Queen's Temple in 1776.[63]

Against the possible influences noted above, however, must be balanced an acknowledgment that the two sites of Stowe and Hagley are very different and that in landscape terms there is little in common.

The plantings

Hagley was an amply wooded park. For the most part, native timber was grown, some of it surviving from previous generations. There were plentiful oaks and horse chestnuts; Scots pines were used as backing to buildings; and wych elm had a strong presence, often in clumps, together with ash and sycamore. Beech was grown, but not as prominently as one might expect. Limes were used for lining avenues, or singly. The approach to the house was along an avenue lined with a double row of elm, lime and horse chestnut. Most avenues would have trees of one species, but to have three was by no means uncommon. Colour figs. 18 and 22 show the general dominance of timber in a view across the park.

Yew and the darker evergreens were used for the effect of seclusion. Shrubs were planted on the stony banks of the cascades, while roses, woodbine and other shrubs were mixed with annuals to give regular flowering on the gentler slopes. Groups of laurel contrasted with open lawn. One of the seats was placed in a knot of old and crooked alders. Whately mentions a clearing among the larger trees filled by coppiced wood, nut, hawthorn and hornbeam, which act as an understorey.[64]

It was not so much dendrological interest but design that marked out the powerful yet subtle use of timber in the park. Again, it is Whately who is most perceptive on this subject, spending a considerable proportion of his long description of Hagley on the effect of the plantings.[65] He is particularly eloquent on light and shade, for example 'The several lawns are separated by the finest trees, which sometimes grow in airy groves, chequered with gleams of light, and open to every breeze; but more frequently, whose great branches meeting or crossing each other, cast a deep impenetrable shade. Large boughs feathering down often intercept the sight ... '[66]

One of Lyttelton's design trademarks was the triangular clump. In a letter of c.1751 he wrote that the best of his cedars should be planted with two Silesian larches as a trio between the castle and the lodge pool, and a set of three New England pines (*Pinus strobus*) close to the pool. In each case it was left to Molly West to decide precisely where these clumps should go. Another triangular clump, of one scarlet oak (probably *Quercus rubra* rather than *Q. coccinea*) and two Carolina cherries (*Prunus virginiana*), was suggested for Molly West to place.[67]

The source for much of the timber was Archibald Campbell, 3rd Duke of Argyll, the most famous 'treemonger' of his time. After the death of Lord Petre in 1742, Argyll's garden and nursery at Whitton, Middlesex, contained the greatest private collection in the country. Argyll himself received seeds from North America via Peter Collinson, and Lyttelton's American holdings were augmented after his brother William Henry became Governor of South Carolina. There are records of despatch of seeds from William Henry to Lyttelton in 1758-9, including magnolias (probably *Magnolia grandiflora*, *M. acuminata* and *M. virginiana*), red acacia (*Robinia hispida*) and purple-berried bay (*Laurus sp.*).[68] Among other species, obtained from Argyll or elsewhere, were silver firs (*Abies alba*) and pinasters (*Pinus pinaster*).

The plantings extended to shrubs and herbaceous plants. The shrubbery was praised, and roses and honeysuckle were grown out in the grotto area. There was a flower garden and also a kitchen garden, where the gardener achieved prodigious feats with exotic fruits. Nicknamed the 'hobbed [=hotbed] Conjuror', he produced melons, peaches, nectarines and gourds, along with pineapples.[69]

Thomas Lyttelton on Hagley

Lyttelton left no comprehensive statement of his scheme for landscaping Hagley. However, there is an extraordinary attack on the park in the letters of his son Thomas. A collection of the letters was published in 1780,[70] a year after Thomas's death, and the most relevant appeared in the *Westminster Magazine* for May 1780 as a piece entitled *On the Taste in Modern Gardening* ('From Letters by the late Lord Lyttelton'). In particular Thomas deplores the mid-century fashion for pictorial building-studded gardening before focussing his shafts on Hagley itself:

The system of modern gardening, in spite of Fashion and Mr. Brown, is a very foolish one. The huddling together every species of building into a park or garden, is ridiculous. The environs of a magnificent house should partake, in some degree, of the necessary formality of the building they surround. This was Kent's opinion; and, where his designs have escaped the destruction of modern refinement, there is an easy grandeur, which is at once striking and delightful.

Fine woods are beautiful objects, and their beauty approaches nearer to magnificence, as the mass of foliage becomes more visible; but to dot them with little white edifices, infringes on their greatness, and, by such divisions and subdivisions, destroys their due effect. The verdure of British swells was not made for Grecian temples: a flock of sheep and a shepherd's hut are better adapted to it. Our climate is not suited to the deities of Italy and Greece; and in an hard winter I feel for the shuddering divinities. At H - there is a temple of Theseus, commonly called by the gardener the Temple of Perseus, which stares you in the face wherever you go; while the Temple of God, commonly called by the gardener the Parish Church, is so industriously hid by trees from without, that the pious matron can hardly read her prayer-book within.

This was an evident preference of strange gods, and, in my opinion, a very blasphemous improvement. – where nature is grand, improve her grandeur, not by adding extraneous decorations, but by removing obstructions. Where a scene is, in itself, lovely, very little is necessary to give it all due advantage, especially if it be laid into park, which undergoes no variety of cultivation.

STOWE is, in my opinion, a most detestable place; and has in every part of it the air of a Golgotha: a princely one I must acknowledge, but in no part of it could I ever lose that gloomy idea. My own park possesses many and very rare beauties; but, from the design of making it classical, it has been charged with many false and unsuitable ornaments. A classical park, or a classical garden, is as ridiculous an expression as a classical plum-pudding, or a classical sirloin of beef. It is an unworthy action to strip the classics of their heroes, gods, and goddesses, to grow green amid the fogs of our unclassical climate.[71]

Thomas Lyttelton, in favouring a grander, less fussy style of gardening, rebels against the style of his father, for what partly, at least, he gives as religious reasons. His tastes happened to accord with those of another celebrated designer, Charles Hamilton, turning to such a style in practice after retirement from Painshill in 1773. Hamilton created his own town garden in Bath and advised at Bowood and Fonthill.[72] The Rev Richard Warner, a curate and follower of William Gilpin, seized on both Hagley and Painshill as examples of bad taste, praising Hamilton for his later 'conversion'. In the case of Hagley, he wrote in 1802:

> The land rises majestically behind the house, but is utterly spoiled by those artificial decorations which the fashion of the day sixty years ago considered as additions the most elegant and appropriate; and which attached to Hagley-park almost the exclusive character of taste in the design, disposition and ornament of pleasure-grounds. These decorations are – a temple; a Gothic ruin; an obelisk; a pillar; a Palladian bridge; two or three trumpery grottos; and as many bits of water of diminutive size and accurate mathematical forms;[73]

It seems likely that Warner had read Thomas Lyttelton, either in the *Westminster Magazine* or in the edition of Lyttelton's letters. If so, Warner would have found a soul mate peddling his own ideas against artifice, which accorded to some extent with those of the proponents of the Picturesque, Sir Uvedale Price and Richard Payne Knight.

5

The Leasowes

✳

William Shenstone and his milieu

IF EVER A GARDEN EXPRESSED ITS OWNER'S SPIRIT, IT WAS THE LEASOWES. IN ALL kinds of ways it reflected the mind, opinions, personality and circumstances of the man who created it. William Shenstone (1714-63) inherited an estate purchased by his grandfather William which was a run-of-the-mill farm, nothing more, and developed it into a landscape garden which won world renown. The whole creation, and the process of creating it, were determined by his vision though circumscribed by his situation. The estate was pronounced 'Lezzoes' at the time.

Shenstone was the son of Ann Penn of Harborough and a farmer, Thomas Shenstone, of The Leasowes, 'a plain uneducated country gentleman.'[1] William's first schooling was with Sarah Lloyd, later immortalised in Shenstone's most well-known poem, the Spenserian pastiche *The Schoolmistress*. Then he attended Solihull Grammar School, where one of his lasting friendships was made, with Richard Jago (1715-81), who was to become a fellow poet and was ordained. Jago shared Shenstone's interests and wrote the topographical poem *Edge Hill*. He also contributed to Dodsley's *Miscellany* which Shenstone helped to edit.

In May 1732 Shenstone was admitted to Pembroke College, Oxford. He intended to read medicine, though Dodsley said it was for the church,[2] but in the event he read mathematics, logic, moral philosophy and science. He also studied literature. Though shy, he seems to have enjoyed himself, talking and drinking till all hours, and cultivated a number of friends who, in their own way, would colour the garden he would go on to make. Chief of these was Richard Graves (1715-1804), a man of wide-ranging interests. He was a poet and novelist who later took Holy Orders and became rector at Claverton, near Bath, but his enthusiasms encompassed archaeology, numismatics, modern and ancient literature and landscape gardening.

Shenstone's school friend Jago was up at University College at the same time as Shenstone was at Pembroke, so they kept in touch. Another Oxford friend was Anthony Whistler (1714-54), an author who wrote *The Shuttlecock*

(1742) and, like Jago, contributed to Dodsley's *Miscellany*. Shenstone, Graves and Whistler together constituted 'the dangerous triumvirate', which lasted till Whistler's death. Other acquaintances, who are mentioned in Shenstone's correspondence later, were Robert Binnel (died 1763), who was to become rector of Newport, Shropshire, and George Whitefield, publisher of *Whitefield's Journal*.

An older figure whom Shenstone met at Oxford was the poet William Somervile (1675-1742), also spelled Somerville. He lived at Edstone, near Henley-in-Arden, was one of the 'Warwickshire coterie' and, *inter alia*, wrote *The Chace* (1735), *Hobbinol* (1740) and *Field Sports* (1742). From all this we can see that Shenstone's Oxford circle was composed of those of like mind, all of whom would take up literature and were of the same class, the gentry.

Thomas Shenstone died in 1724, when William was only ten, and his grandfather in 1726. Although he inherited the estate, he was of course in no position to run it, so it was managed by his uncle, the Rev Thomas Dolman (d 1745). After Oxford, which he left without taking a degree, he took up residence at Harborough, the home of his mother's family, which was in the parish of Hagley. His mother herself had died in 1732. Some time between 1736 and 1739 he moved to The Leasowes but lodged initially with distant relative Shenstones, tenants on the estate.[3] It is thought that he took up residence proper around 1743 and began to administer the property on a modest income of £300 p.a. from his mother's estate. It was only in later years that he was encouraged to publish his poetry and thereby derive a little additional revenue, and the lack of funds clearly limited the scope of what he could do at The Leasowes. There he stayed till his death in 1763, writing (mostly not very successfully) but above all working on his greatest composition, the landscape itself. His beloved brother Joseph lived there with him until Joseph's death in 1751.

In the 1730s he often visited the Graves family at Mickleton, which, as mentioned previously, might have inspired him to create something similar at The Leasowes. Mickleton was owned by Richard Graves's older brother Morgan, who lived there with his sister Mary. Shenstone fell for Mary, but nothing seems to have come of it. He continued to visit Mickleton in the 1740s and was attracted to Utrecia Smith (c.1726-46), literary daughter of the vicar of Mickleton. However, she had her sights set elsewhere and longed for Richard Graves to marry her. He did not do so, and she allegedly died of a broken heart. The following year Graves was forced to marry the pregnant Lucy Bartholomew.

These were not Shenstone's only forays into love, although it is likely that the attachments were mostly if not entirely romantic and sentimental rather than physical. In 1743 he was greatly smitten by a Miss Carter of Cheltenham, but any possible flowering of the relationship may have been hindered by his lack of money and a sense that she was above his station.[4] She herself seems not to have been unwilling: 'Mr. Shenstone was never married, but acknowledged it was his own fault, that he did not accept the hand of the lady whom he so tenderly loved and whose charms he has so affectingly sung in his pastoral ballad, which is among the most admired of all his poems.'[5] Miss Carter remained Shenstone's muse and was the Delia in his elegies and songs. A much later attachment was to his cousin Maria Dolman (1733-54), who, although nearly twenty years younger than Shenstone, inspired enormous warmth and tenderness in him.

There were, however, rumours that Shenstone's path was not always celibate, though they may well have been just rumours. One was that he slept with his maid,[6] presumably Mary Cutler, an educated woman who later became his housekeeper, following Mary Arnold in that role. Another story was that his long and close relationship with the fifteen years older Lady Luxborough (1699-1756) might not have remained platonic.[7]

Henrietta, Lady Luxborough, plays a part of considerable importance not only in Shenstone's life but in the gardening sphere. She was the daughter of Viscount St. John and his French wife Angelica and married Robert Knight, a Whig MP, in 1727. However, after a scandal involving another man, she was banished by Knight to live at Barrells, Ullenhall, Warwickshire around 1736. There she became a neighbour of William Somervile and Richard Jago, and a friend of Richard Graves as well as of Shenstone. She began to lay out an attractive garden at Barrells, seeking advice from Shenstone as well as giving him moral support for his activities at The Leasowes. Both were on a limited income, both could afford only cheap improvements – and both were peeved at the amount the Lytteltons were able to spend on the grounds at Hagley.[8] They corresponded regularly from 1742, and exchanged not only ideas but practical assistance: Shenstone would send over his gardener and handyman Thomas Jackson, 'trusty Tom', to help her. She would act as sounding-board for some of his schemes, and in turn he would proffer suggestions as to how she might, for instance, erect a screen in her garden. Her legal adviser and secretary, Captain Outing, frequently accompanied her and figures prominently in Shenstone's letters.

Furthermore, Lady Luxborough had her own circle of friends and acquaintances, which would have rubbed off on Shenstone at one remove. These included the novelist Samuel Richardson, Ralph Allen of Prior Park,

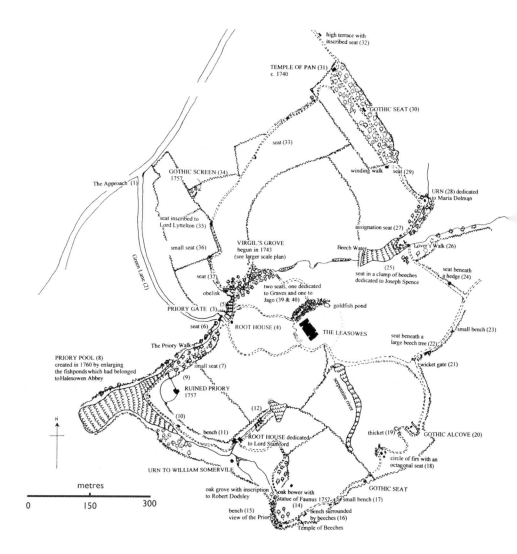

51. The Leasowes during Shenstone's time

the Methodist Lady Huntingdon, Dr Oliver the Bath physician and William Hoare of Bath, the portrait painter. Her great friend was Frances Thynne, Countess of Hertford and later Duchess of Somerset, to whom Shenstone dedicated his ode *Rural Elegance*.

Lady Luxborough was, too, acquainted with the two early *fermes ornées*, Dawley and Riskins.[9] This may well have had implications both for her own garden at Barrells (though she described it as a *ferme negligée*)[10] and The

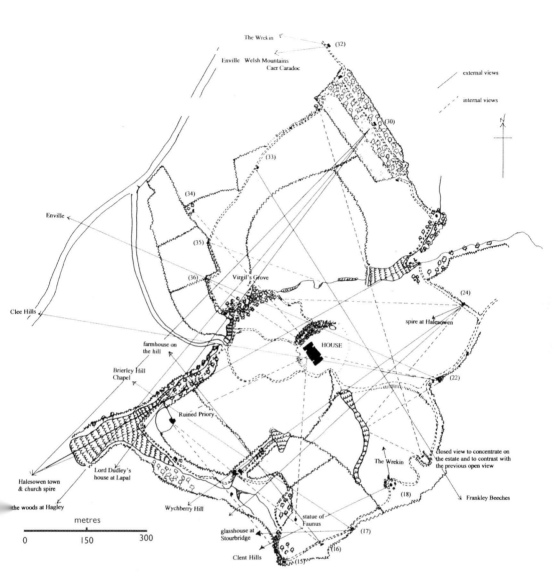

The Wrekin

Enville Welsh Mountains
Caer Caradoc

external views

internal views

N

(32)

(30)

(33)

(34)

Enville

(35)

(36)

Virgil's Grove

(24)

Clee Hills

spire at Halesowen

farmhouse on
the hill

HOUSE

Brierley Hill
Chapel

(22)

Ruined Priory

closed view to concentrate on
the estate and to contrast with
the previous open view

The Wrekin

Halesowen town
& church spire

Lord Dudley's
house at Lapal

(18)

Frankley Beeches

the woods at Hagley

Wychberry Hill

statue of
Faunus

metres

glasshouse at
Stourbridge

(17)

0   150   300

(16)

Clent Hills

(15)

52. Sightlines at The Leasowes

Leasowes. Barrells consisted of a pleasure garden and groves round the
house, with fields further away, beyond the ha-ha. This was the pattern of
most gardens, and in design was opposite to The Leasowes. Yet, although
it was far from being a *ferme ornée* itself, the views of and over the fields
were always highly prized.

If Shenstone was able to try his ideas sometimes on Lady Luxborough,
there was help much closer at hand. An extremely tall (six feet six inches)

53. The Leasowes from *The Works in Verse and Prose of William Shenstone, Vol II* (1765 edition)

athletic young man, James Woodhouse (1735-1820), who lived two miles away, used to come over to consult Shenstone's library. Although much younger than Shenstone he won his confidence and Shenstone asked him to assist in laying out The Leasowes,[11] though since that did not occur till 1759 it can only have been in regard to some late alterations. Woodhouse, a sometime cobbler, who became land steward to Lord Lyttelton, was knowledgeable about shrubs and wrote a detailed account of them and of the various other beauties of The Leasowes in verse (see later). His collected poems appeared in 1764.

Another adviser was William Pitt, Lord Chatham, who had considerable input at Hagley and who often rode over from there to The Leasowes. He is said to have advised on Shenstone's summerhouses and walks.[12] He even offered to lay out £200 of his own money for improvements, though Shenstone refused, according to Graves: 'This, however, Mr Shenstone considered as a species of dalliance with his *mistress*, to which he could not submit.'[13]

Indolent and melancholy in temperament, Shenstone was not as much of a high-flyer as he might have been, especially in his poetry, nor was he ambitious: 'he chose rather to amuse himself in culling flowers at the foot of the mount, than to take the trouble of climbing the more arduous steeps of PARNASSUS.'[14] He has been dismissed as not just a minor poet but a mediocre one, yet at a time when there were in any case few poets of stature Dodsley thought well of him: 'In the tenderness of elegiac poetry he hath not been excelled; in the simplicity of pastoral, one may venture to say he had very few equals.'[15] And at Hagley he was commemorated in company with Pope, Thomson and Milton.

Shenstone sometimes ventured into Birmingham, and there he would have met John Baskerville (1706-1775), printer and typographer, the inventor of Baskerville type. He published an edition of Virgil and also Dodsley's *Select Fables* (1761), and much of their correspondence is on

54. Elements of Taste, from *The Works in Verse and Prose of William Shenstone, Vol II* (1764)

55. Shenstone and Apollo, from *The Works in Verse and Prose of William Shenstone, Vol II* (1764)

matters literary. Shenstone is said to have advised Baskerville on his garden at Easy Hill in the 1750s.[16] Another acquaintance was Matthew Boulton (1728-1809), engineer, industrialist and entrepreneur who in 1762 founded the Soho Manufactory and Mint two miles north of Birmingham and later created a notable landscape garden round it. Shenstone corresponded with him concerning the obtaining of an electrical apparatus for a friend, John Scott Hylton (1725-1784), and indeed Shenstone seems to have been interested in electricity since at least 1747, though he admitted it taxed his brain.[17] Hylton himself was a neighbour of Shenstone, living at Lapall House, Halesowen, corresponded with him and edited some of Richard Jago's poetry.

Matthew Boulton employed a friend and neighbour of Shenstone, Amos Green (1753-1807), in painting trays and other hardware. Green specialised in portraying flowers, fruit and birds. Later on Boulton would hold meetings at his house with fellow innovators of the Industrial Revolution – James Watt, Joseph Priestley, Erasmus Darwin and others – and discuss science and philosophy. They would meet monthly, on the night of the full moon to light their way home, and became known accordingly as the Lunar Society.

Shenstone's scientific interests came together with his pictorial view of landscape in regard to the Claude glass and the *camera obscura*. The former, a convex glass to shrink actual landscape into a small picture, was something which Shenstone explained to Lady Luxborough that he was going to have fitted up by a local joiner – he also hoped to use it to view perspective prints.[18] In the same letter he mentions a *camera obscura* owned by Lady Luxborough, a small box which by lenses and mirrors would project a miniature image of the scene viewed on to an inner wall of the box.

Thomas Hull (1728-1808) was a versatile man of the theatre who also fancied himself as a literary figure. He was an actor at Covent Garden for 48 years, actor manager of the King's Theatre, Birmingham, and an undistinguished playwright. He also edited and published *Select Letters* in 1778, including some from Shenstone, Whistler and Dodsley. Shenstone's letters to Hull are usually about plays and how they could be improved, though one refers to a visit paid by Hull to The Leasowes.[19]

Of all Shenstone's contacts, the one who looms largest in a professional sense is Robert Dodsley (1703-1764), publisher, bookseller and author. At first a footman, he wrote a poem in 1729 called *Servitude* and later a satirical play, *The Toy Shop*. He even saw himself as a rival to Garrick as a playwright, and thought that Garrick had attempted to spoil one of Dodsley's opening nights by putting on a play of his own. He published works by

Three Great Eighteenth-Century Gardens

some of the leading writers of the day such as Goldsmith and Pope, and urged Shenstone to publish his poems. Shenstone helped to edit the six volumes of Dodsley's *Miscellanies*. Dodsley became a close friend and wrote a short and flattering account of Shenstone's life in his edition of Shenstone's works a year after the latter's death. His publishing business was conducted with his brother Joseph at Pall Mall.

One of Shenstone's most literary correspondents was Thomas Percy (1729-1811), a poet who became Bishop of Dromore, Ireland. He co-edited with Shenstone the *Reliques of Ancient English Poetry* which was published in 1765. Of the twenty-six letters that Shenstone wrote to him in the period 1758-63, most deal with literary subjects.

In the sphere of architecture and design, Shenstone's most important connection was with Sanderson Miller. Although Miller worked at both Enville and Hagley, there is no evidence that Shenstone used him in that capacity, though he was a friend and visited The Leasowes. Perhaps there was informal and unrecorded advice given, particularly on the Gothic features. The two Gothic Seats, the Alcove and the Ruined Priory all look as if there could have been input from Miller.

There were considerable dealings with the local aristocracy, especially with the Lytteltons at Hagley and Lord Stamford at Enville. Sir Thomas and Lady Christian Lyttelton were known to Shenstone, though there was more frequent contact with, and knowledge of, George Lyttelton, the prime mover in the works at Hagley. But Shenstone mentions several others of the family – Charles, Sir Edward, Sir Richard and William, to whom he wrote a letter of recommendation on behalf of Amos Green.[20] Admiral Smith was also a visitor to The Leasowes. There is no question that Hagley, and the Lytteltons, were a constant presence in Shenstone's mind – a physical presence too, since he could not avoid seeing the estate and what was going on there. Irritation, envy, admiration and emulation all fed into Shenstone's view of his wealthy neighbours. And, whether he liked it or not, the Lytteltons' opening up of distant views from the park must have had some effect on Shenstone's cultivation of similar kinds of views at The Leasowes.

Shenstone's involvement with the 4th Earl and Countess of Stamford has, of course, been noted in relation to what he did at Enville, such as his work on the shrubbery. There may have been a reciprocal effect, especially the shaping of the cascades at Enville, which might have helped him continue creating and improving the cascades at The Leasowes. The chronology is that the cascades in Virgil's Grove were developed in the 1740s; involvement at Enville was during the 1750s; and the later large

56. The Ruined Priory in an engraving by D Jenkins, *The Modern Universal Traveller* (1779)

cascade at The Leasowes dates from around 1757.

Ferdinando Dudley Lea, Lord Dudley (died 1757), had a distant family connection and was a close friend of Shenstone, becoming a dining and drinking companion. He lived at The Grange, Halesowen, which Shenstone visited frequently, and in turn Dudley came over to The Leasowes.

From the letters Shenstone's preoccupations – literature and the creation of The Leasowes – surface more often than other subjects, which tend towards gossip or who had just died. His circle of friends and acquaintances promotes those two concerns and shares them. Many of his correspondents were relatively local, so he saw them as well as writing to them. Nothing is ever created in a vacuum, and this applies distinctly to The Leasowes, though the vision was filtered through Shenstone's individual mind.

Shenstone on gardens

Shenstone set out his opinions on gardens and layout in a piece called *Unconnected Thoughts on Gardening*, which were exactly that. This miscellany of observations and short comments did not appear in his lifetime but was published by Dodsley in the 1764 edition of his works. They do not add up to a coherent philosophy of garden design, but many can be seen as pointing in the same direction, and some also show that they were implemented at The Leasowes and Enville.

The piece opens with a division of gardens into three categories – parterre, kitchen and landscape. It is announced that the focus of the

Thoughts is to be 'landskip, or picturesque-gardening'. While considerable discussion could be generated on the subject of 'picturesque', it is clear that what Shenstone means by this is a garden that forms a number of pictures, or views, that an artist would find suitable for depicting. He states the aim of such a garden, which is to provide the pleasures of the imagination and to produce agreeable sensations: 'It consists in pleasing the imagination by scenes of grandeur, beauty, or variety. Convenience merely has no share here.'[21] How different from his successor Humphry Repton, who, ever the pragmatist, tempered his ideas to suit the convenience of his client. The importance of the imagination has already been mentioned and will be discussed further. Shenstone divides individual garden scenes into the beautiful, the sublime and the melancholy or pensive. Variety is the principal component of beauty, while simplicity is essential to grandeur.[22]

Shenstone follows Vanbrugh and Pope in comparing the art of the landscape gardener with that of the painter: 'I think the landskip painter is the gardiner's best designer.'[23] He uses the term 'landskip' to refer to home scenery and 'prospect' to refer to distant scenery, such as hills on the horizon. This latter was sometimes called 'offskip' by contemporaries.

There are various principles that Shenstone follows in order to further the overall idea of the naturalistic garden. Straight lines and avenues are to be avoided, and variety is crucial. Angles and heights are necessary for appreciating the features in a garden: 'The eye should always look rather down upon water.'[24] This was certainly true of The Leasowes, which relied heavily on views from above. The water itself should look natural – an irregular lake or a winding stream.

In order to maintain variety and surprise, a building should never be approached on foot the same way as the eye has reached it: 'Lose the object, and draw nigh, obliquely.'[25] Variety might also be found in ruined structures (The Leasowes had two), since they display irregularity of surface. Trees have personalities:

> Oaks are in all respects the perfect image of the manly character: In former times, I should have said, and in present times I think I am authorized to say, the British one ... a large, branching, aged oak, is perhaps the most venerable of all inanimate objects.[26]

This, presumably written during the Seven Years' War, conforms to the 'Hearts of Oak' patriotism that was so widespread at the time.

Shenstone makes strategic use of urns for commemorative purposes. He has definite thoughts on their manufacture and placing: 'URNS are more solemn, if large and plain; more beautiful, if less and ornamented. Solemnity is perhaps their point, and the situation of them should still cooperate with it.'[27]

The overall effect should be pictorial: 'Concerning scenes, the more uncommon they appear, the better, provided they form a picture.'[28] Nature was paramount, though buildings or other products of art were admissible if they delighted the mind. Indeed Shenstone claims that buildings are necessary to complete a 'rural scene'. There could also be much art in arranging the perspective of a scene:

> To distance a building, plant as near as you can to it, two or three circles of different coloured greens – Ever-greens are best for all such purposes ... The consequence will be that the imagination immediately allows a space betwixt these circles and another betwixt the house and them.[29]

This echoes Pope's prescription for distancing by planting, though he accomplished it by lines rather than circles. At The Leasowes there was one major circle of firs (which might pre-date Shenstone) and that tree was also used as backing to features such as the Gothic Screen.

I Ie wonders why lead statues are not more popular in modern gardens. They are well suited to a garden or landscape: Shenstone himself, however, had only the one in the gardens, the *Piping Faun*,[30] and a second, *Venus*, in the shrubbery.

To sum up, Shenstone wants nature to look natural; the scenes in a garden to form pictures; the views to be as varied as possible; and buildings or monuments to be appropriate in size, positioning and style. At The Leasowes he spent twenty years doing precisely that.

Shenstone visited and commented on a number of other gardens, which help to illuminate his thinking and his practice at The Leasowes. As with his early knowledge of Mickleton and Warlies, it may also be a case of other estates influencing him.

The estate he was most familiar with was that at Hagley. His letters speak of several visits and constant monitoring of the developments there – often, as we have seen, with some envy of the money Lyttelton was able to spend on his park.[31] But there was also response to what went on at Hagley – for example, the Ruined Priory answering the Ruined Castle. From the chart in chapter one it will be remembered that Hagley and The

Leasowes had many features in common, so it is important to look at the dates to see if there was any possible influence one way or the other.

Shenstone observed the improvements at Hagley with the eye of a designer: 'They are going to build a Rotund to terminate the Visto at *Hagley*; I think there is a little Hill joining the Park, that would suit one better, tho' it will be very pretty where it is',[32] though he baulked at the cost of £200. When the Castle was going up, Shenstone accorded it slightly reserved praise: 'There is no great Art or Variety in ye Ruin, but the Situation gives it a charming Effect. The chief tower is *allowedly* about 10 Feet too low.'[33] But Shenstone was not averse to taking advantage of the Castle as an eye-catcher from The Leasowes, after the removal of a few trees: 'I believe it may be rendered a considerable object here.'[34]

He also went round the perimeter of the park, and thought that the views from the heights of Wychbury wood exceeded the views obtainable within the park.[35] As a self-professed expert on urns he commented disparagingly on the fluting used on an urn at Hagley, which was 'Abominable'. He was asked by Sanderson Miller if he approved of the re-siting of the column to the Prince of Wales: he did not, and had to fight an internal battle between politeness and sincerity.[36]

By 1750 Shenstone was in touch with the Stamfords, who came over to see The Leasowes and invited him in return to Enville. There is little mention of Enville in his letters, which is surprising given his substantial input there.

Included in his copious correspondence with Lady Luxborough are a number of comments praising her garden at Barrells, where her small-scale delights 'exceed ye scenery of Stowe.'[37] He spends much time advising her on plantings, shrubberies, gates, urns and inscriptions, based on his own experience.

Other estates visited included Basildon Park, Berkshire, where he described Lady Fane's shell grotto as 'a very beautiful disposition of the finest collection of shells I ever saw'[38] – too elaborate for Shenstone to emulate. He saw Sanderson Miller's house and grounds at Radway Grange in January 1750 and gave an unusually full description of what he termed Miller's 'farm', thereby equating it with his own. The trees – elderly ash – were 'detestable' and ought to be replaced. A cascade with a stone basin flowed only occasionally and was a 'juvenile Performance, & only retain'd because it *is* there & has cost him money.'[39] The landscape view was extensive, and one climbed up a hill among coppice, as at The Leasowes, until one came to a 'hanging lawn' surrounded by wood. The appearance was

'*Forest-like*', and the end of a stable made to look like a door with pediment acted as an eye-catcher – this scene pleased Shenstone greatly. Miller's famous tower itself did not appeal to him. He also visited Admiral Smith at Rockingham Hall, Messrs Vernon at Harbury and Clare at Clent, Lord Ward at Henley and Lord Plymouth at Hewell Grange, where Shenstone wished he had been consulted before Plymouth started planning the water effects:

> That Side ought apparently either to have been cover'd with water, at any given expence, for near an 100 yards lower; or it ought to have been thrown into a broad Serpentine River, the fens drain'd; & the ground slop'd down to it, from about the Present hahah. The stream is sufficient for any sort of purpose. The *Cascades* might have been *display'd*, or the stoppages where they *were*, conceal'd wth aquatick Plants.[40]

Introduction to The Leasowes

We have seen that the estate was basically a pasture farm, through which a circuit walk was fashioned. The question of its being considered a *ferme ornée* has already been discussed, but the farm was undoubtedly at the heart of the property (see Shenstone's watercolour, colour fig. 32). Physically this was the case, and the idea of having a farm was present too, though for scenic and landscape purposes the important views were generally not the agricultural ones. What counted were the internal views of set scenes such as Virgil's Grove and the outward views of the hills in the middle distance and the mountains in the far distance. Near and middle distance could sometimes be combined, as in the view of Beech Water with Halesowen church and steeple behind it.

John Parnell, writing about a tour made in 1770, spoke of how skilfully Shenstone divided his estate, creating an enclosed farm which nonetheless preserved 'all the Beauty of an Extensive Lawn ... What a cheap and at the same time charming species of Improvement is this surrounding walk sometimes thro' open meads or cornfields without any Expence but a little coarse gravel and sometimes Entring little Inclosures of coppice or other woodland where at the same time flowering Shrubs may be Introducd.'[41]

The idea of the circuit is paramount. There was a correct way to go round (anticlockwise), with the individual 'incidents', as the eighteenth century liked to call them, being experienced in sequence. The effect was both cumulative and contrasting. The sequence was not just visual, for Shenstone contrived to stimulate emotional and mental responses in his visitors. The mood was thereby varied, from cheerful to elegiac, and an overall atmosphere of pastoral retreat established.

Shenstone insisted that the circuit should be properly followed:

> It is said of the elegant Mr Shenstone, that nothing created in his mind
> greater vexation than the perverseness or malice of those who passed
> thro' the walks of The Leasowes in a contrary direction to that which
> he originally designed.[42]

This evidently came to the notice of the impressionable Sir Samuel Hellier twelve miles away at the Woodhouse, Wombourne, who wrote to his steward John Rogers in July 1767 to say that if the gardener was away he (Rogers) or someone else should 'shew the wood and take People round the right way it being show'd wrong Distroys all the Effect'.[43]

The means by which Shenstone achieved his effects were largely literary. Inscriptions, in Latin or English, abounded, and verses were also left by visitors to augment the sense of a literary garden. The inscriptions were to be found carved on wooden seats or benches, on urns and inside huts or root houses, which is where the verses written by visitors were sometimes left. The literary allusions were often backed, or enhanced, by plantings in order to produce the desired emotional effect.

Shenstone explained that his method of displaying verses was a very simple and cheap one: 'I paste some writing Paper on a strip of Deal, & so print with a Pen. This serves in Root-houses, & under Cover.'[44] Some of the verses left by visitors were printed by Dodsley at the end of his description of The Leasowes (1764).

Inscriptions gave The Leasowes its own character, although it was far from being the only such garden. Nor were they universally acclaimed. Thomas Whately, having conceded that they were justly admired, starts to undermine their use: 'the elegance of the poetry, and the aptness of the quotations, atone for their length and number' before delivering the crushing verdict, 'in general, inscriptions please no more than once.'[45] He distinguishes, however, between commemorative inscriptions, which are necessary to make the urn or monument intelligible, and the more common ones, which describe the scenes they refer to, 'but those beauties and those effects must be very faint, which stand in need of the assistance.'[46]

The inscriptions were taken from both ancient and modern sources, the latter usually composed by Shenstone himself, once in a (deliberately) old-fashioned Spenserian style.[47] Indeed he looked to Spenser for quotations but could not find what he wanted.[48] Virgil furnished the material for twelve inscriptions in all, and Horace, that author of rural retirement, some others. Whately commented that to use classical and native British traditions and quotations was perfectly acceptable provided that they were kept apart: their presence in the same spot would jar,[49] by raising different sets of associations. At The Leasowes they were not always separate. Robert Williams has emphasised the pastoral and Arcadian nature of the Virgilian inscriptions,[50] but they must be balanced against the medieval English.

The use of (in particular) Latin inscriptions was undoubtedly snobbish and elitist, cutting Shenstone off from many who came to visit. He spoke of 'the *large crowd* of the vulgar ... [who] *gape, stupent* and *stare* much more. But one would chuse to please a few *friends* of taste before mob or gentry, the great vulgar or the small; because therein one gratifies both one's social passions and one's pride, that is one's self-love.'[51] So, although Shenstone sought fame through his garden, true appreciation of it was limited to the few. Inscriptions in English were, however, preferred to Latin for the Gothic constructions, as was only fitting.

It is often thought that there was a dearth of buildings at The Leasowes, attributable in part to Shenstone's impecunious state and also to the pastoral simplicity he wished to achieve. However, the buildings totalled twelve, or thirteen if one includes the Gothic Screen, which is a not inconsiderable number. Admittedly some of the buildings were slight and ephemeral, and the only substantial construction was the Ruined Priory, but the architecture was eloquent of what Shenstone wished to express just as was the case at Enville or Hagley. Basically the architecture fell into two categories, rustic and Gothic, with classical conspicuously absent (though it appeared in the urns and the obelisk). The rustic works included the three root houses, the Hermitage, the summerhouse, the quasi-grotto in Virgil's Grove and the Temple of Pan (though that might be counted as rustic/classical), while Gothic was evident in the Ruined Priory, the Priory Gate and wall, two Gothic Seats, the Gothic Alcove and the Gothic Screen.

'Rustic' is here used rather loosely to cover constructions that were simple to put up or were composed of such materials as could readily come to hand – tree roots, branches, rocks. This applied also to the multitudinous seats and benches, many of which were simply slabs of wood laid across tree stumps. Such constructions sorted well with Shenstone's view of nature unspoiled and with amplifying the feeling of a rural scene. Nature did, however, need a helping hand: William Pitt is reputed to have commented that 'Nature has done everything for you, Mr Shenstone', to which the reply was, 'But I hope I have done something for Nature too by displaying her beauties to the best advantage.'[52] This exchange is very similar to one found in Graves' novel *Columella* (see below) and there may have been some confusion.

Shenstone's attitude to Gothic was more complex. He disliked its ornamentation – 'Nor do we view with pleasure the laboured carvings and futile diligence of Gothic artists.'[53] And, although he erected six Gothic structures, he had some ambivalent feelings towards doing so: 'I shall never, I believe, be entirely partial to Goths … but I think … I could sketch out some charming Gothic temples and Gothic benches for garden-seats.'[54] Sometimes it was a result of the expense of the stonework – after having two pinnacles made for the Gothic Alcove and having received the bill he exclaimed 'The Devil take all Gothicism!'[55] But in the event Gothic proved necessary for his evocation of a scene that was rooted in the national past, the world of Puck and Oberon. So, for all that so many of his inscriptions evinced the classical world of pastoral, the tangible and visible manifestations of Gothic gave a more physical sense of an English past. Rivalry, too, may have played some part, for he wrote to Lady Luxborough in June 1749 that he proposed to build a Gothic hermit's seat 'at sight of which all the Pitts & the Miller's Castles in ye World shall bow their Heads abash'd',[56] in jocular rather than hostile vein.

It is significant that The Leasowes was originally in Shropshire, for this colours Shenstone's thinking and design, which tends on the whole to point westwards, to the Shropshire hills and to the Welsh mountains, although closer views to Staffordshire and Worcestershire are present too. The goblet with its Wrekin inscription indicates the tendency.

The terrain was of considerable help to Shenstone. The enormous slope afforded spectacular views from the long terrace at the top, and allowed for variety of plantings at different levels. The natural water in Mucklow hill provided the sources for the range of effects that were created – pools, streams, cascades. Some pools and streams were already there, but they were moulded, harnessed and tightened into a series of aqueous beauties that comprised major attractions of the place.

In order to achieve the appearance of rural simplicity, Shenstone relied on native timber – mostly oak and beech, together with fir, pine, mountain ash (rowan), cherry, birch, alder, hornbeam, yew, larch, ash, horse chestnut, lime, plane, elm, osier and sallow (broad-leaved willow). He did not avail himself of the exotics that were by then available. For variety and sometimes underplanting he grew small trees and bushes – hazel, dogwood, hawthorn, crabtree, elder – in addition to flowering shrubs (frutex, laburnum, eglantine, honeysuckle) and flowers,[57] though all tended to be indigenous, including woodland flowers.

The circuit was constructed so as to reach the climax in Virgil's Grove, clearly a site invested with great meaning by Shenstone. It confers on The Leasowes the character of an elegiac garden, where the final feeling is one of meditation and sadness at mortality and the fleeting nature of Arcadia.

Evolution and description

The history of the site, and how Shenstone developed it, has been ably told by John Riely and by Christopher Gallagher,[58] so it will just be summarised here. Shenstone inherited the estate from his father, and it had been used in the past both for arable and meadow (the word 'leasow' meant pasture or meadow, or, as a verb, to pasture – *OED* definitions). Even though he took up formal residence around 1743, it seems that he started some work c.1740, cutting a straight walk through the wood at the top and constructing two simple rustic buildings, the Temple of Pan and the Hermitage. Although the temple had a Roman arch, its classicism would not be repeated by the mature Shenstone. This would have been about the time he was also (if the story is true) creating the formal avenue at Mickleton. Treadway Nash points out that 'The manner of laying out ground in the natural style was quite in its infancy when Mr. Shenstone began his improvements, and excepting the walk through the High Wood (which was his earliest attempt) very little of what was executed at first now remains unaltered.'[59] In 1743 the property was essentially pasture, with some fish-ponds and streams, and a degree of woodland, mostly oak and beech though a circle of firs on a swell may also predate Shenstone's arrival. An early project was Virgil's Grove, which Joseph Heely said transformed the site: 'From a once rude, unsightly, swampy glen, this small dell is become the pride of The Leasowes.'[60]

Shenstone's vision of how he wished The Leasowes to evolve took time to crystallise. He appears to have worked piecemeal initially, proceeding from that first straight walk through the wood to constructing a number of seats and inscriptions, together with an alcove and a serpentine strip of water. However, by 1746 his declared intention 'to embellish my whole farm'[61] indicates that a comprehensive scheme had by then come into his mind, and it has already been noted that in 1748 this scheme was granted the title of *ferme ornée* when Shenstone wrote to Graves. His first motivation was 'with an Eye to the Satisfaction I shall receive from its Beauty', but this later changed: 'I am now grown dependent upon the Friends it brings me, for the principal Enjoyment it affords.'[62]

By 1746, indeed, the basic structure of The Leasowes had been put in place. The poet Thomson came to visit, admired the views and was particularly taken with Virgil's Grove (colour fig. 44). An interview between Shenstone and Thomson discussing possible improvements to the Grove was published in the *Edinburgh Magazine* for 1800. The process from then on was one of refining, emphasising and embellishing. Some changes occurred – for example, the removal of the 'study' or summerhouse on an island in Beech Water when a path was moved – and there were many small additions, but the vision changed little from his ideas of 1746 (colour fig. 42 and 45). More sophisticated, perhaps, but not different. Implementation took longer, however, and the south-western part (Ruined Priory and pool) did not receive attention before the late 1750s.

In 1747 Virgil's Grove was improved, and a new path installed from the house. The terrace walk on the highest point was started – an unexpected piece of formality, but terrace walks were usually formal (cf the contemporary walk at Farnborough Hall, Warwickshire). Flowers were planted beside a stream and in Virgil's Grove, but Shenstone worried that flowers there made the spot look too much like a garden. They would also, surely, have militated against the atmosphere of dark seclusion and focused meditation that characterised the Grove. Two small islands appeared in a stream in the Grove, and a pebbled Gothic confection with pinnacles reared up beyond the Hermitage. Paths were extended, plantings put in place to enhance the setting of, for example, the urn to William Somervile, and the chalybeate spring in the Grove was given the Shenstone treatment by stonework and inscription. By the end of 1749 the path formed the complete circuit.[63]

The 1750s saw a process of consolidation, but there were no major works till late on in the decade. Christopher Gallagher discerns a change in Shenstone's thinking, namely that the works provided visual links across the landscape whereas previously links had generally been made by paths,[64] though that could be a development rather than a change in vision.

During 1757 further works appeared – a statue of Faunus (a gift from Dodsley), a Gothic screen, and above all the Ruined Priory, the most significant and noteworthy of Shenstone's garden buildings. This is shown in a watercolour by David Parkes from a 1791 drawing (colour fig. 37). The Priory even provided a source of income, since it incorporated a cottage which was let to a tenant. This marks the start of a serious remodelling of this lowest part of the grounds. From 1760 the laborious business of creating

57. Virgil's Grove, from *The Works in Verse and Prose of William Shenstone, Vol II* (1764)

the Priory Pool was in train – it took up to two years to fill it. Shenstone's death, on 11 February 1763, may even have meant that he never saw it in its glory, for Dodsley indicates that technical problems had prevented completion.

From 1763 a steady succession of owners depleted, neglected or altered the estate. John Parnell exclaimed, 'In the name of Order, Decency, &c., &c., what has Captain *Turnpenny* of Birmingham & Powell of Liverpool or any other traficking West Indian slave masters to do with urns Inscriptions mottoes, shady Recesses dedicated to Poets Muses, &c, &c.?'[65] Vandalism played its part, too, in spoiling Shenstone's poetic landscape – hooligans pitted their strength against urns and memorials. The basic structure survived, however, in sufficient fullness to make the descriptions of Heely and others valid if not reflective of Shenstone's garden at its height. It was not until the end of the century (1797) that the Birmingham and Worcestershire canal was dug, cutting across the bottom of Priory Pool and ruining the south-western aspect of the estate (colour fig. 38).

Two early descriptions survive, one by Joseph Spence in 1758, and the other by Thomas Hull c.1759, which eulogises Virgil's Grove and the long cascade near the Stamford root-house: these are given in the Riely article cited above. For a description of The Leasowes in Shenstone's time, Dodsley's account of the circuit will be followed in sequence, with comment as appropriate, especially from Shenstone himself in his letters. Quotations from Dodsley are all taken from the 1764 edition of Shenstone's works, Volume II, pp. 333-71. The account was written to give 'a friend' an impression of The Leasowes in order to preserve the memory of the beauties that time or posterity might destroy. He opens with the generalisation that Shenstone did not abuse Nature but opened up the natural beauties to their full extent. The hand of art was nowhere visible, though much thought and labour had gone into the operations.

Entrance to the grounds was at no.1 on the map, off what is now the Mucklow hill road, along the long serpentine green lane (2) which had a right turn to a ruined wall and the Priory Gate (3), a small gate within an arch (colour fig. 35). Here it should be mentioned that Dodsley's numbering in the text does not always correspond to the numbering in the plan, nor indeed are all the numbers in the text given on the plan (13, 20 and 38 are missing). The numbering is particularly muddled at this point – the Priory Gate is called 2 or 5 in the text, when it is neither, while 3 on Dodsley's map does double duty for the Priory Gate and the path down from the house. The numbering on the plan in fig. 58 (page 158) is based on Dodsley, but has been adjusted to make it compatible with the text both here and in Dodsley, except where the latter is self-contradictory.

The Priory Gate is the first 'object' encountered and also marks the start of the circuit. It sets the scene – a world of contemplation and retreat. The desired effect is romanticised by Shenstone in his watercolour (colour fig. 35), which depicts a figure, possibly a hermit, approaching the gate with rosary and crucifix. It also suggests an escape into an earlier, medieval time.

At this point, instead of launching on the circuit, most visitors chose to go up the right hand path to the house (2 on the plan) to leave their horses and luggage there, returning back across the grazing lawn down the left-hand path to a small gate which permits rejoining the circuit. By doing so, however, they would have pre-empted part of the climax to the circuit, Virgil's Grove. Turning left at the gate, the visitor keeps a stretch of water on the right (5), overshadowed by trees which render the scene 'cool, gloomy, solemn and sequestered.' This both contrasts with the open lawn and evokes a mood which is to be recaptured at the end of the walk.

Just down the valley, proceeding down the Priory Walk, the visitor

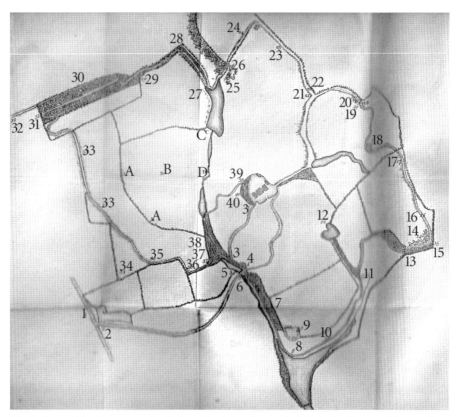

58. A plan of The Leasowes by Robert Dodsley, from *The Works in Verse and Prose of William Shenstone*, Vol II, (1764)

passes a small root-house, with an accompanying inscription:

> Here in cool grot, and mossy cell,
> We rural fays and faeries dwell;
> Tho' rarely seen by mortal eye,
> When the pale moon, ascending high,
> Darts thro' yon limes her quivering beams,
> We frisk it near these crystal streams.
>
> Her beams reflected from the wave,
> Afford the light our revels crave;
> The turf, with daisies broider'd o'er,
> Exceeds, we wot, the Parian floor;
> Nor yet for artful strains we call,
> But listen to the water's fall.

Three Great Eighteenth-Century Gardens

Would you then taste our tranquil scene,
Be sure your bosoms be serene;
Devoid of hate, devoid of strife,
Devoid of all that poisons life:
And much it 'vails you in their place,
To graft the love of human race.

And tread with awe these favour'd bowers,
Nor wound the shrubs, nor bruise the flowers;
So may your path with sweets abound!
So may your couch with rest be crown'd!
But harm betide the wayward swain,
Who dares our hallow'd haunts profane!

This is Shenstone at his (literally) most fey, summoning the vision of rural fairies. The Genius of the Place is at this point the Shakespeare of *A Midsummer Night's Dream*, for Shenstone attributed the above verse to Oberon in a letter.[66] But it must be remembered that for Shenstone the word 'fairy' had a double meaning, referring both to elvish spirits, as here, or to the fanciful world of the imagination (the *OED* confirms both uses). He also reveals a streak of then-fashionable antiquarianism.

Passing again through the Priory Gate (colour fig. 35), the visitor notes an inscription on the seat (6) beneath the ruined wall adjoining the Gate, this time giving the first of the Virgilian inscriptions (illustrated in David Parkes's watercolour, fig. 59, page 160):

Lucis habitamus opacis
Riparumque toros, et prata recentia rivis
Incolimus. (*Aeneid*, Book 6, 673-5)

[We dwell in shady groves; we make our beds on river banks and our abodes in meadows freshened with brooks]

The preceding words of the quotation – 'None of us has a fixed abode' – are presumably omitted because they carry an inappropriate suggestion of impermanence and unsettled wanderers.

A cascade is seen, while a break in the trees permits a view of Halesowen church and an attractive landscape. Thus, at the beginnings of the circuit, all the themes of the garden are announced: the sombre air of meditation,

On a feat beneath a ruinated wall, on entering the Priory Gate.

_____ Lucis habitamus opacis,
Riparumque toros et prata recentia rivis
Incolimus.

59. Inscription on a seat at the Priory Gate. Watercolour by David Parkes. Shropshire RO 6001/154

the cascades, the open lawns and the dense groves, Virgilian pastoral, and the English medieval past of priories and rural spirits, together with views of the surrounding landscape.

The valley and cascade, in fact, constitute a south-eastern extension of Virgil's Grove, so that the circuit turns full circle, though the Grove in its entirety eclipses this first glimpse. The path winds down the valley beside the stream, passing another bench which Dodsley observes is one of many simple seats constructed of two stumps and a transverse board. Each seat is carefully positioned, so the one at 7 provides a new vista to Halesowen church. The stream on the right, chattering over pebbles, pours into the triangular Priory Pool (8) which is connected to another piece of water below the estate, of about 20 acres, outside Shenstone's land and which was constructed from a chain of fishponds belonging to Hales Abbey.

Above the Priory Pool (colour fig. 38), on raised ground set back from the water, is the Ruined Priory (9), illustrated in an engraving (fig. 56, page 146). This is Shenstone's answer to the Ruined Castle at Hagley and shows much in common with it. Erected in 1757, nine years after Miller's castle, the Priory was allegedly built partly from stone from Hales Abbey, just as

col 30:
The Rotunda at Hagley

col 31: The Ruined
Castle at Hagley

col 32: View from Milton's Seat to Hagley Hall

col 33: The Leasowes: the farm with hayricks and barn by William Shenstone.
Wellesley College Library, Special Collections

col 34: Looking downstream towards the bridge in Virgil's Grove, The Leasowes

col 35: The Hermit at the Priory Gate, The Leasowes, by William Shenstone. Wellesley College Library, Special Collections

The Leasowes as it appeared in 1761, from a Drawing by Mr. D. Bond.

THE LEASOWES PRIORY. 1791.

col 36: The Leasowes: the Priory and the house. David Parkes, watercolour. Shropshire RO 6001/154

col 37: The Leasowes: the Priory by moonlight, 1791. David Parkes, watercolour. Shropshire RO 6001/154

col 38: The Priory Pool, The Leasowes

col 39: Gothic Seat at The Leasowes. David Parkes, watercolour. Shropshire RO 6001/154

col 40: The Leasowes: Virgil's Grove looking towards Wychbury Hill by William Shenstone. Wellesley College Library, Special Collections

col 41: The Leasowes: a seat from the far side of the serpentine stream, William Shenstone. Wellesley College Library, Special Collections

col 42: The Leasowes: Shenstone's summer-house or writing hut on a small island in the Beech Water with the spire of Halesowen Church in the distance. William Shenstone. Wellesley College Library, Special Collections

col 43: The Leasowes: Virgil's Grove by William Shenstone. Wellesley College Library, Special Collections

col 44: The Leasowes: Virgil's Grove by William Shenstone. Wellesley College Library, Special Collections

col 45: The Leasowes: Shenstone's summer-house or writing hut. Wellesley College Library, Special Collections

col 46: A view of the Beech Water at The Leasowes

col 47: The restored High Cascade at The Leasowes

that is said to have been plundered for the castle. It was similarly habitable, incorporating a cottage which was let to an old couple for £4 a year, which Shenstone seemed to think was a good rental,[67] though it was hardly calculated to swell his meagre income. It was a realistic portrayal of a ruined chapel, inspired perhaps by the ruined chapel at Woburn Farm as well as by the Hagley castle. Just as at Hagley there were appropriate furnishings, so in the Priory there was a Gothic parlour with seemingly antique wallpaper.[68] Parnell was, however, critical and said the building looked unfinished rather than a ruin.[69] By moonlight it looked strikingly romantic, as David Parkes's watercolour of 1791 shows (colour fig. 37).

The Priory is central to Shenstone's iconography, even though, according to Dodsley, he preferred it not to be viewed at this early part of the walk. First, the architecture is Gothic, which he uses elsewhere and which carries medieval associations. Second, it forms part (the commanding part) of an area with a particularly medieval/religious flavour – the Priory itself, the Priory Pool, the Priory Gate and the Priory Walk. These are heavy with the sense of meditation and retreat. Third, it is a ruin, which evokes sadness at transience and decay. In his *Unconnected Thoughts* Shenstone comments more than once on the effect of a ruin in a garden:

> A ruin, for instance, may ... afford that pleasing melancholy which proceeds from a reflexion on decayed magnificence[70] ... Ruinated structures appear to derive their power of pleasing, from the irregularity of surface, which is VARIETY; and the latitude they afford the imagination, to conceive an enlargement of their dimensions, or to recollect any events or circumstances appertaining to their pristine grandeur, so far as concerns grandeur and solemnity.[71]

The first steps of the circuit, therefore, establish nostalgia, a quiet melancholy and a sense that meditation and reflection are the way to approach what the garden has to offer.

The visitor proceeds along the path skirting the top of the pool up the valley on the eastern side (8, 10, 11). Dodsley comments that the pool is not only natural in appearance in a most pleasing way but that it appears to particular advantage when seen from Shenstone's house. The path curves up through the valley with the stream on the right and oak and beech shading the walk. No. 10 is a simple bench, giving a view of 'a fine amphitheatre of wood and thicket.' No. 11 is another seat beneath a spreading oak with the second Virgilian inscription:

Huc ades, O Meliboee! caper tibi salvus et hoedi;
Et si quid cessare potes, requiesce sub umbra. (*Eclogue 7*, 9-10)

[Come hither, Meliboeus! Your goat and kids are safe; and if you can
find time for idling, take your rest beneath the shade]

The tableau that presents itself is a lawn surrounded by hills and oaks, with
the statue of Faunus on a swell and an urn inscribed to William Somervile:

INGENIO ET AMICITIAE
GULIELMI SOMERVILLE

[To the genius and friendship of William Somervile]

with, on the reverse,

GS POSUIT
Debita spargens lacrima favillam
Vatis amici. (Horace, *Odes II*, 6)

[GS – i.e. Shenstone – placed this
Sprinkling with dutiful tears the ashes of a poet friend]

In the original, Horace himself is the 'poet friend', so Shenstone had to
change 'sparges' (May you sprinkle) to 'spargens' (sprinkling).

This urn (fig. 60, page 163) is the first of several, often to departed
friends, and Shenstone found them a powerful means of expressing
commemoration.

Rising from the seat 11 the visitor passes through a gate leading to a
willow thicket and then to a root-house dedicated to the Earl of Stamford,
set among chestnuts, larches and willows. It comprised a curving screen
with a seat and with soil on top, and had a rustic entrance (bottom right of
fig. 61, page 167). Apparently Stamford was present at the opening of the
cascade (12), a highlight of the circuit, which is fed by the heart-shaped pool
and which was the principal sight from the root-house, which was also
known as the 'Woodhouse'. Dodsley was much taken with the cascade: 'a
fairy vision, consisting of an irregular and romantic fall of water, very
unusual, one hundred and fifty yards in continuity, and a very striking
scene it affords. Other cascades may possibly have the advantage of a

60. Somervile's Urn.
Watercolour by David Parkes.
Shropshire RO 6001/154

greater descent, and a larger torrent, but a more wild and romantic appearance of water, and at the same time strictly natural, is what I never saw in
any place whatever.' The water rushed over rock, large stones and cinders.
He admits it is no Niagara but claims that in its scale it is perfect.

From here the path leads in the direction of 14 and 15, past a seat which
affords 'a scene of what Mr. Shenstone used to call his forest ground,
consisting of wild green slopes peeping through a dingle, or irregular
groups of trees, a confused mixture of savage and cultivated ground, held
up to the eye, and forming a landskip fit for the pencil of Salvator Rosa.'
This wilder sort of scene adds another dimension to the peaceful pastoral
quality that we are sometimes led to believe characterised The Leasowes.

Just below 14 is a bower of oaks inscribed to Dodsley himself (13, though
not marked on his plan) in these terms:

> To Mr. DODSLEY,
> Come then, my friend, thy sylvan taste display,
> Come hear thy Faunus tune his rustic lay;
> Ah, rather come, and in these dells disown
> The care of other strains, and tune thine own.

On the bank above is a statue of the piping Faunus in lead, modelled after
the antique and a common production of the lead yards (probably the work
of John Cheere). This statue, standing among shrubs, was a present from
Dodsley, hence the inscription. Some of the wilder view just mentioned

appears from this spot, while at the small bench nearby (15), the Priory comes into sight, seen beneath trees with solemn and dignified effect.

Between 15 and 16 are a small open grove and a dome of magnificent beeches, in the centre of which it had been intended to place an altar or a statue of the rural god Pan. This deity was, however, commemorated at the top of the garden. Another bench (16) quotes from Horace to allude to the secluded grove:

> Me gelidum nemus
> Nympharumque leves cum satyris chori
> Secernant populo. (*Odes I*, 1, closing lines)

> [Let the cool grove and the light-footed dancings of nymphs and
> satyrs mark me out from the crowd]

This is a probable change by Shenstone of the original 'secernunt' to indicate 'May I be marked out' rather than 'I am marked out'.

A distant hill crowned with a white farmhouse is seen, together with a clump of tall firs surrounding a pyramidal seat, to which the walk leads. On the way the Priory is seen at a different angle and distance from before, which is one of Shenstone's design tendencies, features approaching and receding. Somewhere in this part an urn was put up after Dodsley had drafted his description to commemorate Shenstone's brother Joseph, with this inscription:

> Fratri ejus unico.
> Fratrum amantissimo.
> Juvenum suavissimo.
> Hominum integerrimo.
> Postquam te fata tulerunt
> Ipsa Pales agros, atque ipse reliquit Apollo.
> GULIELMUS SHENSTONE.
> P.
> Aliorum moestitiae consulens.
> Et suae.

> [To his only brother/ Most loving of brothers/ Most sweet-natured
> of young men/ Most upright of persons. – After fate had carried you
> off, Pales herself, even Apollo himself deserted the fields (Virgil,

Eclogues V, 34-5). William Shenstone P(laced) (this urn) Having regard
to the grief of others/ As well as to his own]

Pales was the tutelary goddess of flocks and shepherds.

Shenstone had in fact recommended the above quotation from Virgil to
Lady Luxborough back in 1749 as suitable for inscribing on a memorial
pedestal, saying 'For I think it a *prime* good one, & what I wou'd use myself
upon Occasion.'[72] Dodsley's omission of any mention of the urn is puzzling,
because one would have expected it to have been erected soon after Joseph's
death, but Thomas Martyn, writing in 1766, is specific on the point that it
followed Dodsley's account, therefore presumably dating from the very
end of Shenstone's life.[73]

The path climbs up the hill to 17 (in the text), a small bench giving views
over opening countryside, the views extending further as one ascends.
Another seat (unnumbered but actually located at 17 on Dodsley's plan) is
'in the gothic form', on the back of which is a long inscription in English,
which Shenstone placed there because he thought there would otherwise
be lack of interest in that part of the garden, and the visitor's attention
needed to be sustained:

> Shepherd, would'st thou here obtain
> Pleasure unalloy'd with pain?
> Joy that suits the rural sphere?
> Gentle shepherd, lend an ear.
>
> Learn to relish calm delight,
> Verdant vales and fountains bright;
> Trees that nod on sloping hills,
> Caves that echo tinckling rills.
>
> If thou can'st no charm disclose
> In the simplest bud that blows;
> Go, forsake thy plain and fold,
> Join the crowd, and toil for gold.
>
> Tranquil pleasures never cloy;
> Banish each tumultuous joy:
> All but love – for love inspires
> Fonder wishes, warmer fires.

Love and all it's joys be thine –
Yet ere thou the reins resign,
Hear what reason seems to say,
Hear attentive, and obey.

'Crimson leaves the rose adorn,
'But beneath 'em lurks a thorn;
'Fair and flow'ry is the brake,
'Yet it hides the vengeful snake.

'Think not she, whose empty pride
'Dares the fleecy garb deride,
'Think not she who, light and vain,
'Scorns the sheep, can love the swain.

'Artless deed and simple dress,
'Mark the chosen shepherdess;
'Thoughts by decency controul'd,
'Well conceiv'd, and freely told.

'Sense that shuns each conscious air,
'Wit that falls ere well aware;
'Generous pity prone to sigh
'If her kid or lamkin die.

'Let not lucre, let not pride
'Draw thee from such charms aside;
'Have not those their proper sphere?
'Gentler passions triumph here.

'See, to sweeten thy repose,
'The blossom buds, the fountain flows;
'Lo! to crown thy healthful board,
'All that milk and fruits afford.

'Seek no more – the rest is vain;
'Pleasure ending soon in pain:
'Anguish lightly gilded o'er:
'Close thy wish, and seek no more.'

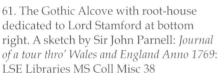

61. The Gothic Alcove with root-house dedicated to Lord Stamford at bottom right. A sketch by Sir John Parnell: *Journal of a tour thro' Wales and England Anno 1769*: LSE Libraries MS Coll Misc 38

62. A Gothic Seat. A sketch by Sir John Parnell: *Journal of a tour thro' Wales and England Anno 1769*: LSE Libraries MS Coll Misc 38

This Gothic Seat, in wood, is probably identifiable with the sketch by John Parnell in plan and elevation (fig. 62, above), though he places it in his ms at no. 30 on Dodsley's plan.

The path winds up still further to reach the clump of firs seen earlier, which arch over an octagonal seat (18), the back of which supports a goblet on a ledge inscribed 'To all friends round the Wrekin!', an old Shropshire toast referring to a large number of people holding hands to form a chain round the hill, which appears in the view about thirty miles away.

The octagonal seat, seen earlier as 'pyramidal' from a distance, provides eight different pictures or views which range from 'very romantic home scenes to very beautiful ones at a distance.' The scenes are very varied, giving an idea of virtually all the effects that landscape is capable of, from the gentle to the sublime, from the inhabited to the solitary. Further up the winding path a small thicket (19) is reached, and soon afterwards the pinnacled Gothic Alcove (20, not shown on the plan) which looks down on a slope bounded by oaks and beeches. The Alcove looked still in good shape in 1770 when sketched by Parnell (fig. 61, above), but he said it was about to collapse,[74] and David Parkes's sketch (fig. 63, page 168) shows it with some of the ornamentation missing. On the back of the Alcove is the inscription in old black print:

63. The Gothic Alcove. Watercolour by David Parkes. Shropshire RO 6001/154

O You that bathe in courtlye blysse,
 Or toyle in fortune's giddy spheare;
Do not too rashlye deeme amysse
 Of him, that bydes contented here.

Nor yet disdeigne the russet stoale,
 Which o'er each carlesse lymbe he flyngs:
Nor yet deryde the beechen bowle,
In whyche he quaffs the lympid springs.

Forgive him, if at eve or dawne,
Devoide of worldlye care he stray:
Or all beside some flowerye lawne,
He waste his inoffensive daye.

So may he pardonne fraud and strife,
If such in courtlye haunt he see:
For faults there beene in busye life,
From which these peaceful glennes are free.

The Alcove, often called 'my Gothick building' in Shenstone's letters, was originally conceived as a 'Hermit's Seat' to complement the Hermitage below, with a flooring of black and white pebbles. From this vantage point, a 'fine hanging wood' contrasts with a wild heath, while Shenstone's water effects are shown at their best. The inscription just quoted, in Shenstone's best pseudo-Spenser style, reveals Shenstone's great regard for Spenser and the medieval world that the earlier poet evokes.

A wicket gate (21) leads to another lawn, beyond which is 'a new theatre of wild shaggy precipices, hanging coppice ground and smooth round hills between' – we are approaching the highest point in the grounds. Another seat (22) is set beneath a beech, with the inscription:

> Hoc erat in votis: modus agri non ita magnus,
> Hortus ubi, et tecto vicinus jugis aquae fons,
> Et paulum sylvae super his foret. Auctius atque
> Dii melius fecere – (Horace, *Satires II*, 6, 1-4)

> [This was what I prayed for: a measure of land not all that large, where would be a garden and, near to the house, a spring of ever-flowing water and, to finish off, a modicum of woodland. The gods granted me more and better than I prayed for]

As the higher ground is reached, so more objects come into view – the house, the grounds at Enville and the Clee hills of Shropshire. Along the path is a small bench (23), to be followed by a seat (24) which looks down towards the Beech Water in a vista framed by oak and beech. Off the path, in a clump of beech, is a seat (25) round an oak chosen by and inscribed to Joseph Spence:

> IOSEPHO SPENCE,
> EXIMIO NOSTRO CRITONI;
> CUI DICARI VELLET
> MUSARUM OMNIUM ET GRATARUM CHORUS,
> DICAT AMICITIA.
> MDCCLVIII.

> [Friendship dedicates (this seat) to Joseph Spence, our most excellent Crito, to whom the chorus of all the Muses and the Graces would have wished it to be dedicated, 1758]

Crito was a wealthy disciple of Plato.

Further down the path is Lovers' Walk (26), which leads to the Beech Water, around which are a number of benches. An island is in the pool. At the top end is the Assignation Seat (27), with this inscription:

> Nerine Galatea! thymo mihi dulcior Hyblae,
> Candidior cygnis, hedera formosior alba!
> Cum primum pasti repetent praesepia tauri,
> Si qua tui Corydonis habet te cura, venito. (Virgil, *Eclogues VII*, 37-40)

> [Galatea, daughter of Nereus, sweeter to me than thyme of Hybla, more dazzling-white than swans, more beautiful than pure-white ivy, when first the fed bulls seek again their stalls, then, if you have any care for your Corydon, come]

Hybla was famed for its honey.

The Beech Water itself, as shown in Shenstone's drawing (colour fig. 42), revealed Halesowen church and steeple, with the Clent hills behind. The water was lined by alders on one side and oaks and beeches on the other, some of the beeches remaining to this day. Shenstone also indicates what appear to be poplars on one side, but the Lombardy poplar was not introduced into Britain until 1758. There may have been some raised at Whitton by the Duke of Argyll a little earlier, but Shenstone would have been unlikely to have had access to them, and in any case they would not have grown to the extent drawn. The summerhouse was intended as a study not as a decorative object in the scene, and had been built before Shenstone conceived his overall plan.[75] It was pulled down in July 1754.

Turning away from the water, up the hill in a north-west direction, the Lovers' Walk within a planting of hazels, climbs beside a bubbling stream to the right-angled corner marked by the urn to Maria Dolman (28) – fig. 64, opposite – whose tragic death at 21 moved Shenstone deeply, as the inscription indicates:

> PERAMABILI SUAE CONSOBRINAE M.D.
>
> AH MARIA
>
> PUELLARUM ELEGANTISSIMA,
>
> AH FLORE VENUSTATIS ABREPTA, VALE!
>
> HEU QUANTO MINUS EST
>
> CUM RELIQUIS VERSARI

64. The Urn dedicated to Maria Dolman. Watercolour by David Parkes.
Shropshire RO 6001/154

QUAM TUI MEMINISSE!

[To his most lovable kinswoman M.D. Ah, Maria, the most elegant of
maidens, Ah, snatched away in the flower of beauty, farewell. Alas!
How much less it means to be occupied with the living than with the
memory of you]

On another side was incised 'Et in Arcadia ego' [either 'I too was once in
Arcadia' or 'Even in Arcadia I (death) am present'], taken from the tomb-
centred painting by Nicolas Poussin. The urn, illustrated in fig. 64 page 169,
had been destroyed by 1770.

The path climbs steeply to another seat (29), among broken and rough
ground, and beyond to a small bench (unnumbered) with a line from Pope's
Eloisa to Abelard, 'Divine oblivion of low-thoughted care!' This is the only
reference to Pope, whom we might have expected to feature more prominently, as at Hagley. A further seat in the wood has a Virgilian inscription
to indicate the rural scene visible from it:

Hic latis otia fundis
Speluncae, vivique lacus, hic frigida Tempe
Mugitusque boum, mollesque sub arbores omni. (*Georgics II*, 468-70)

THE TEMPLE OF PAN.

[Here is leisure in widespread farmlands, here caves and living lakes
and cool vales, and the lowing of oxen and soft sleep under the trees]

Shenstone has replaced Virgil's 'at' by 'hic' twice to eliminate Virgil's context of contrasting country life with the world of town and business. 'Tempe' is used, as Arcadia or Eden are, as a symbol for any beautiful valley.

The path ascends still higher, to a small seat and another perched on a drop. Now a long straight walk passes along an alley in the wood, though Dodsley notes that the uneven surface of the walk, with its rises and falls, counters its apparent formality. The poet James Woodhouse mentions straight rows of cherry trees, silver birch and mountain ash.[76] Halfway along the walk a Gothic Seat (30) appears, giving a lofty view through the wood of the country falling away below. The crenellated seat, depicted in colour fig. 39, looks robust but the caption tells us it collapsed c.1771. There is, however, a puzzle regarding the seat. The Gothic construction sketched by Parnell (fig. 62, page 167) is placed by him at no. 30, but is very different from that illustrated by Parkes. However, Parnell refers in his text to two or three 'really pretty' seats with wooden pillars, 'mostly gothic',[77] and it is more likely that the sketch refers to one of those, at no. 17, as suggested earlier.

Many elements of distant landscape are seen, including a large wood at Hagley. At the end of the straight walk is a rustic building of rough, unhewn stone known as the Temple of Pan (31), illustrated by David Parkes (fig. 65,

66. Inscription.
Watercolour by
David Parkes.
Shropshire RO
6001/154

opposite). It bears emblems of Syrinx (Pan pipes) and the Tibia (ancient flute), with an inscription over the entrance:

> Pan primus calamos cera conjungere plures
> Edocuit; Pan curat oves, oviumque magistros. (Virgil, *Eclogues II*, 32-3)
>
> [Pan was the first to teach how to join several reeds together with wax;
> Pan has care of the flocks and of the guardians of the flocks]

Shenstone altered 'primum' to 'primus', but the sense is unchanged.

A final ascent brings the visitor to a high natural terrace, giving the ultimate viewpoint of everything previously seen, and more. In the middle of the terrace is a seat (32) which proclaims 'DIVINI GLORIA RURIS!' (Virgil, *Georgics I*, 168) [The glory of the divine countryside]. It is seen in fig. 66, above. The panorama splits into two – a huge bowl in front and a rich valley on the right. On the rim of the bowl in the distance are the Clee hills, the Wrekin, the Welsh mountains and Caer Caradoc, while the valley is fringed with woods, with a long winding vale 'rolling agreeably into the hollows'.

From the Temple of Pan the path goes down a slope, with seats at the two points given the number 33 on the plan. From the path the Gothic Screen (34), erected in 1757, is visible, backed by firs. By 'screen' Shenstone does not mean that it was flat – he advised Lady Luxborough to build a

Gothic screen, a seat, against a brick wall.[78] Such a seat, he suggested, should be a bench made of bars, for four people, with the back boarded. On the path itself is the next seat (35), also backed by fir, and dedicated to Lord Lyttelton, which suggests that Shenstone, though envious, bore no deep animosity towards him. The descent has been by now considerable, affording a striking view up the valley. The cascades and stream south of Beech Water are seen. Further down is a small seat (36), followed by another (37), which bears the motto:

> Rura mihi, et rigui placeant in vallibus amnes,
> Flumina amem, silvasque inglorius! (Virgil, *Georgics II*, 485-6)

> [Let the countryside be pleasing to me, and the running streams in the valleys; may I love rivers and woods, though they bring me no fame]

The climax of the circuit is 'the beautiful gloomy scene' of Virgil's Grove. Close to the entrance a small brick obelisk announces:

> p. virgilio maroni / lapis iste cum luco sacer esto.

> [To Publius Virgilius Maro let this stone and grove be consecrated]

This is illustrated in fig. 67, opposite. The character of the Grove is 'opake and gloomy', overhung with trees, including yew, and with an understorey of hazel and other trees, with streams and cascades between mossy banks dotted with primrose, violet, hyacinth, wood anemone and marigold. The first seat is dedicated to Thomson (38, not shown on the plan), with the inscription:

> CELEBERRIMO POETAE
> IACOBO THOMSON
> ROPE FONTES ILLI NON FASTIDITOS
> G.S. SEDEM HANC ORNAVIT.

> [To the most celebrated poet James Thomson, near to the springs not despised by him, G.S. (Shenstone) inscribed this seat]
> Quae tibi, quae tali reddam pro carmine dona?
> Nam neque me tantum venientis sibilus austri,
> Nec percussa juvant fluctu tam litora, nec quae

67. The obelisk in Virgil's Grove. Watercolour by David Parkes. Shropshire RO 6001/154

Saxosas inter decurrunt flumina valles. (Virgil, *Eclogues V*, 81-4)

[What gift can I give you in exchange for such a song? For neither the whistling of the rising south wind nor wave-beaten shore delights me as much, nor rivers that hurry down through rocky valleys]

This memorial came after Thomson's death in 1748, as Shenstone explained to Lady Luxborough: 'Your Ladyship will say, why do I raise an Urn to Thomson? The Pleasure *that* can afford must be of ye melancholy kind – Tis very true – But I can retire to Thomson's urn when I think *proper.*'[79] The seat, making Thomson an English Virgil, is perched on a steep bank from which to contemplate much of the Grove (colour figs. 40, 43 and 44). The water is seen pouring over cascades and down an arched niche of cinders and rock-work through fern, liverwort and aquatic weed to wind under a one-arch bridge. The principal cascade is seen overarched by trees. A seat lower down bears the verses:

> O let me haunt this peaceful shade;
> Nor let ambition e'er invade
> The tenants of this leafy bower
> That shun her paths, and slight her power.
>
> Hither the peaceful Halcyon flies
> From social meads, and open skies;

Pleas'd by this rill her course to steer,
And hide her sapphire plumage here.

The trout bedropt with crimson stains,
Forsakes the river's proud domains;
Forsakes sun's unwelcome gleam,
To lurk within this humble stream.

And sure I hear the Naiad say,
'Flow, flow, my stream, this devious way,
'Tho' lovely soft thy murmurs are,
'Thy waters lovely cool and fair.

'Flow, gentle stream, nor let the vain
'Thy small unsully'd stores disdain:
'Nor let the pensive sage repine,
'Whose latent course resembles thine.'

In the Grove the sight of water is sometimes lost, but never the sound (an effect Dodsley says the Chinese are fond of). The large cascade is surrounded by a kind of grottowork of native stone, overhung with trees, with a chalybeate spring at the head (colour fig. 47). The water contains iron, staining the surrounding rocks red. Such water was thought to have health-giving properties, the most famous example being at Tunbridge Wells. The spring has an iron bowl chained to it, and carved on a stone are the words:

FONS FERRUGINEUS
DIVAE QUAE SECESSU ASTO FRUI CONCEDIT

[Chalybeate spring/ To the goddess who granted the enjoyment of this retreat]

This simple inscription was chosen from seven variants set out in a letter to Richard Graves.[80] A stone seat forms part of the grottowork, inscribed:

INTUS AQUAE DULCIS, VIVOQUE SEDILIA SAXO;
NYMPHARUM DOMUS (VIRGIL, AENEID I, 167-8)

[Within are fresh waters, and seats of natural rock; a home for nymphs]

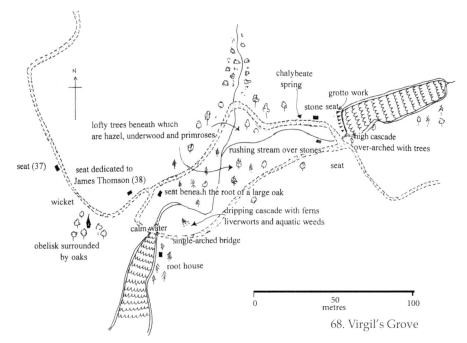

chalybeate
spring

grotto work

stone seat

high cascade
over-arched with trees

N

lofty trees beneath which
are hazel, underwood and primroses

rushing stream over stones

seat

seat (37)

seat dedicated to
James Thomson (38)

seat beneath the root of a large oak

wicket

dripping cascade with ferns
liverworts and aquatic weeds

calm water

single-arched bridge

obelisk surrounded
by oaks

root house

0   50   100
                         metres

68. Virgil's Grove

which was Shenstone's definition of a grotto, according to Dodsley. What the latter does not mention, however, is a bench below the spring which bears the inscription:

Claudite iam rivos, pueri; sat prata biberunt (Virgil, *Eclogues 3*, 111)

[Cut off the sluices now, lads; the fields have drunk enough]

The predominate tone in the Grove was gloom, but Shenstone introduced flowers to add colour and brightness: 'I have two or three Peonies in my grove, yᵗ I have planted amongst Fern and brambles in a gloomy Place by yᵉ water's side. You will not easily conceive how good an Effect they produce.'[81]

The depiction of Virgil's Grove by Thomas Smith and engraved subsequently by James Mason (fig. 69, page 178) presents a number of problems. It had a troubled history, and Shenstone did not enjoy the protracted process. In the summer of 1748 Smith, already known as a maker of garden views including Hagley and Belton, visited The Leasowes and 'behav'd wᵗʰ a Complaisance yᵗ made us wish to serve him. He shew'd us one *Painting* of a scene at Hagley. He took a Draught of wᵗ your Ladyship may remember *I* call "*Virgil's* Grove", *here*. This he purposes to insert in a smaller Collection; a Kind of Drawing-Book, wᶜʰ, If judge aright, will please me much beyond his larger Prints.'[82] However, at the same time Shenstone admitted

69. Tourists enjoying Virgil's Grove, from a painting by Thomas Smith of Derby, engraved by James Mason c1752

some reservations to Graves, saying he wished Smith had stayed longer and taken, say, four views instead of one, to form a small drawing-book collection of its own.[83]

Two years later he declared he liked Smith and appreciated many of his landscapes, and expressed the wish that all his views could be made prints by François Vivares, one of the most expressive and gifted engravers of the day. But he had misgivings about Smith's portrayal of the Grove – for example, an urn appeared too small (there is no urn in the finished engraving). 'The Picture of a Part of my grove will not [be] *good*, nor *like*; yet I cou'd have been easy had it been engrav'd by Vivares.'[84] By autumn 1751 he had turned totally against the artist: 'Mr. S- has so mangled and disfigured my *Grove*, that I dare not send it to your Ladyship, till he has altered the Plate, so as to render it less intolerable. Fluellin, as I remember, in Shakespeare [*Henry V*], speaking of the new Resemblance betwixt *Macedon* and *Monmouth*, observes, "There is a River in Macedon, there is a River also in Monmouth – peradventure, there be Fish in both. – Would you desire better Similitude?" S being a modest Man, has seemed to content himself with some such Degree of Resemblance: but I wish him well, and will cause him, one Day, to do the Place Justice, for his own Sake as well as mine – for his own, as his Piece will be seen by many who know the Place, and for mine, as the Place is known to afford the best Scene I have.'[85] Shenstone had evidently seen a proof plate, but does not record whether it was altered, or whether the result satisfied him. Probably not, for it does not present a realistic picture.

The path continues out of the top of the Grove northwards towards the house, past a seat under an oak and thence to the shrubbery which curves round the south-western side of the house. The shrubbery contains seats dedicated to two of Shenstone's closest friends, Graves and Jago. That to Graves is marked 39 on the plan, but is not numbered in the text, nor is that to Jago, marked 40 on the plan. The former seat is inscribed:

AMICITIAE ET MERITIS
RICHARDI GRAVES
IPSAE TE, TITYRE, PINUS,
IPSI TE FONTES, IPSA HAEC ARBUSTA VOCABANT. (Virgil, *Eclogues* I, 38-9)

[(Dedicated) to the friendship and merits of Richard Graves
The pines themselves, the very springs, these very orchards called out your name, Tityrus]

and the latter seat:

AMICITIAE ET MERITIS RICHARDI JAGO.
[(Dedicated) to the friendship and merits of Richard Jago]

Shenstone had intended to honour Thomas Percy with a similar seat in the shrubbery,[86] but nothing seems to have come of it.

The shrubbery itself burgeons with colour. James Woodhouse informs us of the contents of this well-stocked area. Trees and shrubs include phillyrea, laurel, laburnum, white and purple lilac, myrtle, orange-trees, tulip-trees, yellow-thorned barberry, syringa, acacia, laurustinus, dogwood, yew, bay, plane, arbor vitae, Scots and silver fir, larch, sycamore and silver-edged holly. Flowers include peony, geranium, roses, catch-fly, narcissus and daffodil, with raspberries also grown.[87] Beside the shrubbery is a dove menagerie. There is a statue of the Venus de Medici beside a goldfish pond and under a laburnum. She is given a poem:

'SEMI-REDUCTA VENUS.'
To Venus, Venus here retir'd,
    My sober vows I pay:
Not her on Paphian plains admir'd
    The bold, the pert, the gay.

70. Early-nineteenth-century print of Virgil's Grove by HF James, showing cascade and the statue of Venus moved from the shrubbery. British Library Board, K Top xxxvi.21.3.d

Not her, whose amorous leer prevail'd
　　To bribe the Phrygian boy;
Not her, who clad in armour fail'd,
　　To save disast'rous Troy.

Fresh rising from the foamy tide,
　　She every bosom warms;
While half withdrawn she seems to hide,
　　And half reveals, her charms.

Learn hence, ye boastful sons of taste,
　　Who plan the rural shade;
Learn hence to shun the vicious waste
　　Of pomp, at large display'd.

Let sweet concealment's magic art
    Your mazy bounds invest;
And while the sight unveils a part,
    Let fancy paint the rest.

Let coy reserve with cost unite
    To grace your wood or field;
No ray obtrusive pall the sight,
    In aught you paint, or build.

And far be driven the sumptuous glare
    Of gold, from British groves;
And far the meretricious air
    Of China's vain alcoves.

'Tis bashful beauty ever twines
    The most coercive chain;
'Tis she, that sov'reign rule declines,
    Who best deserves to reign.

Although Dodsley claimed some Chinese presence in Virgil's Grove, Shenstone is anxious to denounce it in his poem. This may be seen as an attempt to ally himself with others in the 1750s such as Gray and Walpole who vigorously rebutted the idea (espoused especially by the French) that China influenced the English landscape garden. While purporting (and starting out) to be a poem about Venus, it quickly transpires that it uses Venus merely as a means to talking about The Leasowes. The more lurid aspects of Venus are suppressed in a quieter approach to landscape gardening. In verse three, however, there is a titillation strikingly similar to the Bower of Bliss in Spenser's *The Faerie Queene*.

Dodsley omits certain features, either because they had disappeared during Shenstone's time (such as the summerhouse in Beech Water) or were away from the circuit. The Hermitage, which Shenstone dug out of the corner of a field around 1740, consisting of a cave with a cross on the top, was sited below where the Gothic Alcove (20) was subsequently created. At some point Lord Lyttelton criticised the Hermitage,[88] which evidently had gone by the time Dodsley wrote his account. The cross may have been transferred from the Hermitage to the Alcove (fig. 63, page 168). There were possibly two root-houses in Virgil's Grove, though only one is mentioned by Dodsley (unnumbered). The latter is depicted in the small engraving to be found in Dodsley's account which accompanies the poem to Venus by Shenstone (fig. 57, page 156).

Comments by contemporary visitors

A multitude of visitors sought out The Leasowes, some of them leading figures of the time such as Benjamin Franklin, Dr Johnson and John Wesley. They were drawn by the fame of the place and its special cultural character. Some have left descriptions, others not.

Comments were made in prose and verse. The poems were often left by Shenstone's friends or visitors, and a selection was printed at the end of Dodsley's description of the property. Most are conventional eighteenth-century poetic tributes, though some additional insights are provided by these verses. Lady Luxborough gave Nature the principal credit for what had been done;[89] Richard Graves, on the other hand, speaks of The Leasowes 'where art assumes the sweets of nature's face.'[90] While taking the opportunity to condemn the pleasures of the town as vain and idle, he asserts that a country wife will provide 'the genuine happiness of life', a somewhat pointed remark in view of Shenstone's confirmed bachelorhood.

An unknown woman ('Cotswouldia') sent a poem by post in 1761 which stresses the faery element ('Ye sportive elves') while happily conflating the classical and the medieval ('Whom Dryads honour, and whom Fairies love'),[91] just as Shenstone had done. Of more significance is Dodsley's account of his first visit to The Leasowes in 1754, which tries to explain why he was so enraptured. The poem is couched in strictly classical terms – Shenstone becomes Damon, and Muses, Dryads and Naiads abound – without a fairy or elf in sight. Having first attributed the beauties of the place to 'some sylvan god', he concludes it is all enchantment and that the spells are the 'incantations' inscribed everywhere. Shenstone himself is accordingly 'the great magician', the author and source of all the wonders to be beheld, rather than the sylvan deities previously invoked.[92]

'Arcadio', in penning some verses in 1756, sees as the key to Shenstone's design the wavy line, as advocated and popularised by Hogarth in his *Analysis of Beauty* three years earlier:

> Such is the WAVING LINE, they cry,
> For ever dear to Fancy's eye!
> Yon stream that wanders down the dale,
> The spiral wood, the winding vale,

Three Great Eighteenth-Century Gardens

The path which wrought with hidden skill,
Slow twining scales yon distant hill
With fir invested – all combine
To recommend the WAVING LINE.[93]

The implication is that Shenstone had fastened on to the serpentine line before Hogarth's exposition. The conclusion of the poem is that the source of the power of The Leasowes is simplicity, which would have pleased Shenstone greatly.

After his death the tributes continued to flow. In a twist to the celebrated epitaph on Vanbrugh's death – 'Lie heavy on him, Earth, for he / Laid many a heavy load on thee'[94] – a poem was left on a seat by an unknown admirer:

O EARTH! To his remains indulgent be,
Who so much care and cost bestow'd on thee! ...
Propitious earth! lie lightly on his head,
And ever on his tomb thy vernal glories spread![95]

If the reference to Vanbrugh was intentional, the author would seem to be saying that the natural elements, as shaped by Shenstone, are preferable to the artifice of architecture.

In 1771 Joseph Giles published a miscellany of poems, some of which had been revised or corrected by Shenstone. In particular he wrote a lengthy piece constituting 'A Poetical Description of the late Mr. SHENSTONE'S RURAL RETIREMENT', which had been composed in Shenstone's lifetime, amended by Shenstone and dedicated to Lady Luxborough (which dates it to no later than 1756). From a factual point of view it does not add to our knowledge of The Leasowes, but it corroborates the idea of a pastoral fantasy, where the Muses reign and where (as with Thomson at Hagley) the fancy is released:

Here may the thoughts expatiate free,
Embrace that friend, *Philosophy*,
The jarring croud forget:[96]

In David Parkes's portfolio of sketches and poems on The Leasowes there are a good many verses in Shenstone's memory by various hands, mostly some time after his death, but these are too trite and commonplace to bear reproduction.

James Woodhouse has already been mentioned as a (much younger) friend of Shenstone who may have helped him lay out the grounds. Wood-house's 'novel in verse', *The Life and Lucubrations of Crispinus Scriblerus*, contains a substantial section on The Leasowes written after Shenstone's death, full of nostalgia and bitterness that he has since been barred from visiting the place. There are also poems written to Shenstone in his sickness (also published by Dodsley in the 1764 edition of Shenstone's works), two elegies and an epistle to Shenstone 'In the Shades' (1784). The first elegy (June 1759) describes the visual and emotional impact of The Leasowes, with some religious motivation – 'To read her [Nature's] works, and seek her mighty Sire.'[97] But the longest piece is *The Lessowes: A Poem*, which fills in much of our knowledge of Shenstone's plantings. These have been indicated earlier, when describing the areas in question, in particular the shrubbery. Woodhouse, like others among his contemporaries, seizes on the role of fancy, or imagination, in experiencing The Leasowes. For example, the visitor can imagine the statue of Faunus playing its pipes:

> For fancy's ear can trace th'unreal sound,
> And hear from hills aërial tones rebound.[98]

Unusually, the normally visual quality of the imagination is here given an aural element, though Woodhouse may have taken his cue from Shenstone's dedication to Dodsley quoted earlier.

In prose, a number of authors used The Leasowes as material for a more general discourse on gardening and its history. George Mason, in *An Essay on Design in Gardening* (1768), attempts to analyse style through an historical approach. Shenstone is seen (along with Lyttelton) as following Southcote at Woburn Farm in creating vistas through the branches of a single tree, and improving on Southcote.[99] Mason had read *Unconnected Thoughts* as published in 1764, for he quotes Shenstone on the grotesque appearance of conical trees amid oaks or other forest trees.[100] He also credits Shenstone with the subtle management of keeping some parts seemingly neglected so as to render the succeeding scenes more beautiful.[101] He praises Shenstone for creating a garden which demonstrates, above all others, 'the most intimate *alliance with nature.*'[102]

It is surprising that Horace Walpole does not refer to The Leasowes in his essay *On Modern Gardening* (1770), but the same year saw the publication of Whately's *Observations on Modern Gardening*, which has already been mentioned as classifying The Leasowes as a farm (a pastoral farm) rather than a *ferme ornée*. Whately refers the reader to Dodsley for a detailed

Three Great Eighteenth-Century Gardens

description, but still devotes several pages to his visit. What Whately singles out are: the variety of scenes ('all the inclosures are totally different') and prospects, the range of hedge-type borders (quickset hedge fence, lofty hedgerow, a range of trees, a broken line of trees, a grove, coppice or thicket), and the inscriptions, as earlier mentioned. Whately concludes that at The Leasowes 'every natural advantage of the place within itself has been discovered, applied, contrasted, and carried to the utmost perfection, in the present taste, and with inexhaustible fancy.'[103]

Probably around 1770 comes the anonymous (the author is almost certainly Heely) and undated *A Description of Hagley, Envil and The Leasowes*. Since it proclaims that it is filling a need because there is a lack of description of the three estates, the date is unlikely to be any later. The first fifteen pages are taken up with some general observations about gardens and garden style, leading up to the proposition that the three properties follow Nature, whereas Le Nôtre had been 'puerile' and Hampton Court and Kensington Gardens were disgusting. In his tour of the property, the author describes plantings, the walks and the appearance of the farm and the grazing animals from time to time, and rhapsodises over Virgil's Grove: 'An exertion of the most lively and poetic fancy, it exactly marks the mind of the designer.'[104] He calls attention to the fact that Shenstone chose only native plantings: 'Indeed, when we consider The Leasowes as a Farm only, it would be taking too great a liberty, to throw into it those extragenious plants or trees, which (tho' not here) are a real ornament to a garden ... The rose, the althea, or the hypericum, which so sweetly become a shrubbery, would disgrace the simple banks of The Leasowes; a plain cowslip, a primrose, or a kingcup, in those recesses, is infinitely beyond the tulip, the carnation, or the auricula.'[105]

Many other visitors left descriptions without a context or agenda of garden history. In July 1755, one of the first to leave a description in Shenstone's time, Resta Patching, Quaker and wine merchant, paid a visit. He points out the separation of walks and pasture: 'He has laid out very pleasant Walks round his Fields, which are confined to the Hedge-side, without encroaching on the Pasture.'[106] In a rather fanciful comment on the cascades, Patching combines reality and 'fairy' imagination in a way that would have delighted Shenstone: 'Two Cascades are here remarkable for their Beauty and Simplicity; exceeding many Things of more costly Workmanship, having the Advantage of unaffected Nature on their Side, and are indeed so elegantly rude, so rural and romantic, as must inspire the Beholder with a Notion, that the poetic Descriptions of *Arcadia* and *Fairy-*

land are not altogether Fictions.'[107]

Arthur Young in 1770 said he could add little to Dodsley's account, but already at least one seat mentioned by Dodsley had disappeared. Young was particularly struck by the long cascade, near the root house dedicated to Stamford:

> [It] is astonishingly romantic; a large space of ground at your feet, for above an hundred and fifty yards, is thickly covered with the stems of fine oaks &c. a fall of water at the farther end of this ground first breaks to your view, and then forms twenty more before it reaches you, all broke into distinct sheets, wildly irregular, by the intervening and crossing stems of the trees above; their branches and leaves form a fine thick canopy of shade, which setts off most gloriously the sheets of water which here and there meet the sun beams and sparkle in the eye. This intermixture of wood and water is amazingly fine.[108]

John Parnell, also in 1770, complained that the succession of capitalist owners since Shenstone rendered the inscriptions ridiculous, since they knew nothing about poetry or nymphs (except the nymphs of the town).[109]

William Gilpin paid a visit in 1772, though his account was not published till twenty years later. He was rather critical, and thought that Shenstone had displayed great taste and elegance, but that there were too many urns, buildings and inscriptions, which were improper to a farm. The fields were too regular, and some views should be seen through trees. Although the pools were stagnant, Gilpin approved of Shenstone's use of rockwork to break the cascades and the streams.[110]

By the time Joseph Heely went round in the 1770s (his published account of 1777 says the description was based on earlier visits), many of the inscriptions, being flimsy, had disappeared, as had some of the seats, but the then owner, Mr Horne, intended to reinstate them.[111] Among other changes was the moving of Venus (and her accompanying verses) from the shrubbery to a position above the rock arch fountain in Virgil's Grove. Heely's description for the most part corroborates what we have already seen, but adds some details of plantings and is not uncritical. He considers the Priory Pool should have been sited lower down (outside Shenstone's property), that the visitor should not experience part of Virgil's Grove at the beginning and that the formal circle of Scots firs 'bears no relation to the character of The Leasowes.'[112] He judges that Shenstone 'knew that to surprize, was to please',[113] with examples such as the cheerful Lovers' Walk contrasting with the dreary ascent to reach it. He characterises The Leasowes 'as a farm only', not a garden or a park,[114] and declares that 'The glory of this truly arcadian farm rests on its simplicity',[115] confirming what many other visitors felt.

Richard Graves, in his satirical novel *Columella* (1779), follows an Oxford scholar who retired immediately to his small country estate 'and is now become a prey to low spirits, spleen, and, I am afraid, an incurable melancholy.'[116] The central figure is clearly modelled on Shenstone, though there are also references to Brown and to Charles Hamilton's hermit at Painshill. Two friends descend on Columella, expecting him to be supervising some improvement in his grounds 'or else perhaps reclined at the foot of some tree, or sitting in an alcove in his garden, reading Thompson's Seasons, or Shenstone's Works',[117] but find 'their philosophical friend running across the lawn, with a faggot-stick in one hand, and a book in the other, his hair about his ears, and one stocking about his heels, in a most violent paroxysm of rage',[118] chasing some pigs that had rooted up primroses and periwinkles in his shrubbery. There is a description of a cascade tumbling down rocks and over tree roots which might well have been based on the long cascade at The Leasowes. The friends say that Nature should claim most credit, though a hurt Columella protests that he hoped 'he had done something for Nature too' – an exchange which seems to have been modelled on Pitt and Shenstone quoted earlier – even though it was only copied from a cascade belonging to Bampfylde.[119] This is an unfair jibe at Shenstone, whose cascade predates Bampfylde's at Hestercombe and who did not visit that garden.

Many of the later descriptions reproduce (sometimes verbatim) the earlier accounts. As time went on, so these descriptions record the degeneration of the estate – William Marshall (1796) has already been cited for his disparaging comments, which included Virgil's 'dirty little obelisk' and finding some of the cascades dry.

Influence of The Leasowes
The Leasowes was frequently visited both during Shenstone's time and after his death when the estate was in rapid decline. For reasons advanced earlier, it was admired but not emulated at home, but visitors from abroad, under the spell of the English Landscape Garden, might sometimes draw on their experience of The Leasowes. The outstanding instance of this followed the visit of the Marquis de Girardin in 1763, who was inspired to imbue his estate of Ermenonville with the spirit of Shenstone. While overtly

owing much to Rousseau, and getting ideas from, for example, the Temple of Vesta at Tivoli, Girardin nonetheless gave many signs of why Ermenonville was known as the French Leasowes. It was a garden of inscriptions on the circuit around the lake, where one of the 'incidents' was a memorial to Shenstone, who featured also on one of the faces of an obelisk nearby. There were urns and funerary monuments, and references to rural contentment (the hut of Philemon and Baucis). He had a Hameau and productive areas such as a water-mill and brewery. The main plantings were of oak, beech, poplar and alder, all of which featured strongly at The Leasowes. Another French garden that shows some kinship with Shenstone in its inscriptions and farm-like approach was Watelet's Moulin-Joli, but there is no evidence that he knew, or knew of, The Leasowes.

Influence was felt the other side of the Atlantic, where Thomas Jefferson, as we have seen, used his knowledge and experience of The Leasowes in forming Monticello.

Arkadia, in Poland, was an important romantic garden of feeling, or sentiment, of the late eighteenth century. While owing much to Ermenonville (it even had an Island of Poplars as at the French site, as well as a cottage of Philemon and Baucis), the overall conception of an Arcadia undercut by thoughts of transience and mortality is not so far removed from The Leasowes. In Germany, Seifersdorfertal, set among thickly wooded hills and valleys, was a romantic or sentimental garden with a tendency towards the elegiac. It ranged widely in its literary references – German authors, Petrarch and two English writers, Laurence Sterne and Edward Young of the 'Graveyard' school of poetry. While there is no specific reference to Shenstone or The Leasowes, the spirit of the place is one with which he would readily have identified.

In Italy it was the poetry of Shenstone, perhaps, rather than The Leasowes itself, which inspired Melchiorre Cesarotti to create the garden at his villa at Selvazzano near Padua late in the century. It is said that this garden paid homage to both Shenstone and Thomson.[120]

There was, however, one example of a copy at home, and that was the diminutive creation of Sir Samuel Hellier at the Woodhouse, near Wolver-hampton.[121] In an eight-acre wood developed mainly between 1763 and 1773 Hellier devised a circuit with a number of glades or clearings within which various buildings were placed – a music room, hermitage, 'Handel's Temple', seats, root house, obelisk, grotto and a Druid's Temple. He had shrubs and flowers grown in the wood, but the closest connection with The Leasowes was the use of poetry boards, painted wooden tablets hung on

Three Great Eighteenth-Century Gardens

trees which gave quotations from Milton, Gilbert West and possibly others. The influence of Hagley is evident as well.

The most unexpected resurfacing of Shenstone in gardens came after a gap of two centuries. In the late twentieth century the Scottish poet Ian Hamilton Finlay, in creating his poetic and philosophical garden of Little Sparta, twenty-five miles south-west of Edinburgh, found relevance and resonances in Shenstone that could be applied to a modern approach to garden design. The garden is hard to define – emblematic, philosophical, poetic and sculpture garden are all terms that have been used – and it is definitely *sui generis*. But it harks back to earlier civilisations and cultures, and Shenstone is personally evoked. Within an area denoted 'English Park-land', there is a memorial to 'W. SHENSTONE 1714-63' in the form of a bronze cast of a wheelbarrow, suggestive of the practical work demanded of a creator who could not afford an army of labourers. There are connections with Rousseau and Ermenonville (temple to Philemon and Baucis, Julie's Garden), but Finlay also, along the lines of Shenstone's *Unconnected Thoughts on Gardening*, produced what at first were observations entitled *Unconnected Sentences on Gardening*, but which then became *Detached Sentences on Gardening*, with ambiguity in the word 'detached'. There are parallels in thinking between Shenstone and Finlay, especially in the use of allusion and inscription and in making optimum use of a relatively small estate.[122] The wheel came full circle with Finlay creating a stone bench at The Leasowes in the 1990s which slightly modifies Dodsley in an inscribed description, to reflect the worsened condition of the water in the gardens.

From this it appears that The Leasowes has relevance today, and that, despite the demands made by the golf course and the community walking areas, there would be merit in restoring at least part of Shenstone's original concept, in order to remind us that a garden can be far more than grass, water and trees, and that it can reverberate at a deep level to express thoughts and feelings about the transient nature of happiness; about beauty; about loss; in short, about *la condition humaine*.

AFTERWORD

WHILE THE THREE ESTATES WERE ESPECIALLY LUSTROUS GEMS IN THE WEST Midlands landscape, they also made a considerable contribution generally to the history of the progress of gardening in the middle and later years of the eighteenth century. The topography leads towards the Picturesque at a time when hills within the estate and mountains in the distance were starting to be exploited and cultivated for effect. At Enville the dramatic opening of the windows of the boathouse to view the frothing cascades, the passage from light to dark as one walked along the paths, and the single plank bridge across the cascades anticipate the Picturesque at Downton and other places. The naturalistic approach to layout is also prominent, with the advantage that even where the landscapes superseded a formal garden the result was much more natural than at some estates where the formal axes, though submerged, remained, as at Stowe or Wotton, Buckinghamshire. By use of artefacts – buildings, urns, seats, man-made cascades – the concept of the pictorial circuit garden was finely developed, bearing comparison with Stourhead, Painshill, West Wycombe and many other mid-century gardens. Imaginative plantings, with balance of light and shade, dense groves and open ones, aided the visual effect in a spirit very much of the time – a time of change, which the three properties exhibit.

The two literary gardens – Hagley and The Leasowes – stand out and cannot be matched elsewhere. Some gardens certainly contained literary allusions, such as Mount Edgcumbe, Cornwall, with its Thomson's Seat and Milton's Temple, and a re-creation of the Miltonic walls of Paradise in the amphitheatre, but the use of inscriptions at Hagley and especially at The Leasowes pushes them further ahead. Furthermore they may well have influenced such a site as the flower garden at Nuneham Courtenay, Oxford-shire (1770s), where inscriptions backed up the Rousseau-inspired plantings. Hagley, moreover, extended the boundaries of what a park might be consid-ered to be. Usually a park was distinct from the pleasure grounds, an area for sheep, cattle or deer, but at Hagley (as indeed at Enville) the features of interest were mostly at some distance from the house, making a consider-able tract of parkland in effect into pleasure grounds. The 'garden' element at Hagley was in fact quite small – the shrubberies near the house – so the whole estate was described as park, whereas (for example) William Gilpin sketched Painshill with a division between two almost equal areas of park and garden.

The buildings in the garden, particularly at Hagley and The Leasowes, bore associations either with people (e.g. Milton's Seat) or through usage, for example a hermitage or the Seat of Contemplation. Ruins, as discussed earlier, had their own resonances. None of these were confined to the trio, but such was their presence that the buildings would more emphatically cause the visitor to stop and contemplate than in some other gardens where similar buildings might only be frivolous or products of fashion, mere follies. The three gardens fed off each other, with ideas passing back and forth, and influenced others.

It was indeed a fortunate visitor who could go round Enville, Hagley and The Leasowes in their pomp.

Notes

Chapter 1 A Trio of Landscape Gardens

1 Michael Cousins, 'Hagley Park, Worcestershire', *Garden History* 35: Supplement 1, 2007, pp.74-7.

2 *Letters of William Shenstone*, ed. Duncan Mallam (Minneapolis: University of Minnesota Press, 1939), p.463.

3 *Victoria County History: Worcestershire*, Vol.I, p.238. Hales was accounted for under Worcestershire in 1154-5 (*Red Bk of Exch.* [Rolls Ser.], 656).

4 Ibid. Part of Halesowen, which was wholly included in Worcestershire in 1086, fell within Shropshire from the end of the eleventh century to the beginning of the eighteenth, but was finally transferred to Worcestershire under the acts of 1832 and 1844. Stat. 2 & 3 Will. IV, cap.64; 7 & 8 Vict. cap.61.

5 *Geological Survey of Great Britain (solid and drift)*, Sheet 167 (Dudley, 1967). British Regional Geology, Central England (London: HMSO, 1969), 3rd ed.

6 *Quart. Sess. R.* (Worcs. Hist. Soc.) Vol.89, p.262.

7 Ibid., p.397.

8 William Marshall, *On Planting and Rural Ornament* (London: G&W Nicols *et al*, 1796), Vol.I, p.327.

9 Shenstone, *Letters*, 6 March 1750, p.192.

10 *A Companion to The Leasowes, Hagley and Enville* (London, 1789), p.92.

11 Treadway Nash, *Collections for the History of Worcestershire*, 1781, Vol.I, pp.485-6.

12 Della Hooke, *The West Midlands* (London: English Heritage, 2006), p.87.

13 Margaret Gelling, *Studies in the Early History of Britain: The West Midlands in the Early Middle Ages* (Leicester: Leicester University Press, 1992), p.175.

14 Oliver Rackham, *The History of the Countryside* (London: JM Dent, 1986), p.173.

15 Ibid., p.78.

16 Oliver Rackham, *The Illustrated History of the Countryside* (London: BCA, 1994), p.59.

17 Assize R. 739, m.85.

18 Marie B Rowlands, *A Regional History of England: The West Midlands from AD 1000* (London: Longmans, 1987), p.59.

19 Ibid., p.115.

20 Enville Archives, B/1/1/13/3.

21 *Cal. Committee for Money*, iii, pp.1252-3.

22 Anthea Taigel and Tom Williamson, *Parks and Gardens* (London: Batsford, 1993), pp.48-9.

23 *Journal of the House of Lords 1739-68*: handwritten editions in the Enville archives.

24 (R Lawton, contributor), *An Historical Geography of England and Wales* (London: Academic Press, 1990), 2nd ed., Fig.11.1, p.286.

25 Mark Girouard, *Life in the English Country House* (New Haven: Yale University Press, 1978), p.188.

26 George Sheeran, 'Patriotic Views: Aristocratic Ideology and the Eighteenth-Century Landscape', *Landscapes* 7:2, Autumn 2006, p.6.

27 See quote from Treadway Nash in Hooke, *The West Midlands*, p.111.

28 Daniel Defoe, *A Tour through the Whole Island of Great Britain*, ed. Pat Roberts (Harmondsworth: Penguin, 1971), p.43.

29 *Selections from The Tatler and The Spectator*, ed. Robert J Allen (?: Rinehart Editions, 1970), pp.392-6. (Joseph Addison in *The Spectator*, no.409, Thursday 19 June, 1712)

30 *Passages from the Diaries of Mrs Philip Lybbe Powys*, ed. Emily J Climenson (London: Longman and Co., 1899), pp.165-6.

31 Adrian Tinniswood, *The Polite Tourist* (London: The National Trust, 1998), pp.94-6.

32 Shenstone, *Letters*, 3 June 1749, p.148.

33 William Toldervy, *England and Wales Described in a Series of Letters* (London, 1762), Vol.I, p.336.

34 See David R Coffin, *Gardens and Gardening in Papal Rome* (Princeton, NJ: Princeton University Press, 1991), pp.244-51.

35 Richard Graves, *Recollections of Some Particulars in the Life of the Late William Shenstone, Esq.* (London: J Dodsley, 1788), p.83.

36 Marshall, *On Planting*, p.326.

37 Michael Cousins, 'William Shenstone: Jealous of Hagley?', *Arcadian Greens Rural, New Arcadians Journal* 53-54, 2002, pp.60-73.

38 John Harris, 'Diverting Labyrinths', *Country Life*, 11 January 1990, p.64.

39 See Douglas DC Chambers, *The Planters of the English Landscape Garden* (New Haven: Yale University Press, 1993), p.6.

40 James Thomson, 'The Seasons', *The Poetical Works of James Thomson* (London: 1850), p.27.

41 David Lambert, 'William Shenstone and the Fairy Landscape', *The Georgian Group Report and Journal*, 1986, pp.67-73.

42 Mavis Batey, 'The Pleasures of the Imagination: Joseph Addison's Influence on Early Landscape Gardens', *Garden History* 33:2, Autumn 2005, pp.189-209.

43 *A New Display of the Beauties of England* (London, 1787), Vol.II, p.379.

44 Quoted in Helena Attlee, *Italian Gardens: A Cultural History* (London: Frances Lincoln, 2006), p.109.

45 *The Green Frog Service*, ed. Michael Raeburn, Ludmila Voronikhina, Andrew Nurnberg (London: Cacklegoose Press, 1995), pp.334-6.

46 Joseph Heely, *Letters on the Beauties of Hagley, Envil, and The Leasowes* (London, 1777), Vol.II, p.231.

Chapter 2 The *Ferme Ornée*

1 Miles Hadfield, *The English Landscape Garden* (Princes Risborough: Shire Books, 1977), p.40.

2 Robert Williams, 'Rural Economy and the Antique in the English Landscape Garden',

Journal of Garden History, 7:1, 1987, p.77.

3 Patrick Bowe, *Gardens of the Roman World* (London: Frances Lincoln, 2004), p.46.

4 See Douglas DC Chambers, *The Planters of the English Landscape Garden* (New Haven: Yale University Press, 1993), Chapter 12.

5 See David Coffin, *Gardens and Gardening in Papal Rome* (Princeton: Princeton University Press, 1991), Chapter 11 ('Flora et Pomona'), esp. pp.195, 205-6.

6 Ibid., Chapter 8 ('Garden Parks'), pp.138-58.

7 See Daniela Mignani, *The Medicean Villas by Giusto Utens* (Florence: Arnaud, 1991).

8 Ibid., pp.57-8.

9 Ibid., pp.53-4.

10 Joseph Spence, *Observations, Anecdotes, and Characters of Books and Men*, ed. J M Osborn (Oxford: Clarendon Press, 1966), I.603, p.250.

11 Quoted in *The Oxford Companion to Gardens* (London: Oxford University Press, 1986), p.186.

12 David Jacques, 'The Ferme Ornée', *The Ferme Ornée: Working with Nature*, Conference Proceedings of the Association of Garden Trusts (Staffordshire Gardens and Parks Trust, 1998), p.11.

13 John Smith, *England's Improvements Reviv'd* (1670), esp. pp.191-3.

14 *The Poems of Andrew Marvell*, ed. H Macdonald (London: Routledge and Kegan Paul, 1963), p.43, ll.31-2.

15 Timothy Nourse, *Campania Foelix, or, A Discourse of the Benefits and Improvements of Husbandry* (London: 1700), pp.1-2.

16 Ibid., p.334.

17 Joseph Addison, *The Spectator*, no.414, 25 June 1712.

18 Joseph Addison, *The Spectator*, no.477, 6 September 1712.

19 William A Brogden, 'The *Ferme Ornée* and Changing Attitudes to Agricultural Improvement', *British and American Gardens of the Eighteenth Century*, ed. Robert P Maccubbin and Peter Martin (Williamsburg: The Colonial Williamsburg Foundation, 1984), p.39.

20 Stephen Switzer, *Ichnographia Rustica* (London: 1742), Vol.III, p.vi.

21 Ibid.

22 Ibid., Appendix, pp.8-9.

23 Ibid., p.xvi.

24 Ibid., Appendix, pp.8-9.

25 Brogden, 'The *Ferme Ornée*', p.40.

26 Switzer, *Ichnographia Rustica*, p.46.

27 Ibid., pp.xv-xvi.

28 Batty Langley, *New Principles of Gardening* (London: 1728), pp.198 and 201.

29 Ian K S Cooke, 'Whiteknights and the Marquis of Blandford', *Garden History*, 20:1, spring 1992, p.29.

30 Horace Walpole, *The History of the Modern Taste in Gardening* (1770), ed. John Dixon Hunt (New York: Ursus Press, 1995), p.42.

31 Switzer, *Ichnographia Rustica*, Appendix, pp.9 and 11. See also Mavis Batey, 'The Pleasures of the Imagination: Joseph Addison's Influence on Early Landscape Gardens', *Garden History*, 33:2, autumn 2005, p.201.

32 'Imitations of Horace' (The Second Epistle of the Second Book of Horace), *Alexander Pope's Collected Poems*, ed. Bonamy Dobrée (London: Dent, 1986), ll.230ff.

33 For discussion of this point, see John Dixon Hunt, *Garden and Grove: The Italian Renaissance Garden in the English Imagination, 1600-1750* (London: Dent, 1986), p.188.

34 Peter Martin, *Pursuing Innocent Pleasures: The Gardening World of Alexander Pope* (Connecticut: Archon Books, 1984), p.71.

35 Ibid., p.127.

36 Michael Symes, Alison Hodges and John Harvey, 'The Plantings at Whitton', *Garden History*, 14:2, 1986, p.140.

37 Ibid.

38 Sir John Clerk of Penicuick, *The Country Seat* (1731), quoted in *The Genius of the Place: The English Landscape Garden 1620-1820*, ed. John Dixon Hunt and Peter Willis (London: Elek Books, 1975), p.202.

39 A A Tait, *The Landscape Garden in Scotland*, 1735-1835 (Edinburgh: Edinburgh University Press, 1980), pp.94-5.

40 Ray Desmond, *Kew: The History of the Royal Botanic Gardens* (London: Harvill Press, 1995), Plate 2 (between pp.46-7).

41 Gervase Jackson-Stops, *An English Arcadia 1600-1990* (London: The National Trust, 1991), p.98.

42 Mark Laird, *The Flowering of the Landscape Garden: English Pleasure Grounds 1720-1800* (Philadelphia: University of Pennsylvania Press, 1999), p.184.

43 John Martin Robinson, *Shugborough* (London: The National Trust, 1989), p.27.

44 Chambers, *The Planters of the English Landscape Garden*, p.177.

45 Richard Graves, *Recollections of Some Particulars of the Life of the late William Shenstone, Esq.* (London: J Dodsley, 1788), p.49.

46 *The Oxford Companion to Gardens*, p.186.

47 Dora Wiebenson, *The Picturesque Garden in France* (Princeton: Princeton University Press, 1978), pp.15-19.

48 Ibid., p.37.

49 Claude-Henri Watelet, *Essay on Gardens* (1774): *A Chapter in the French Picturesque*, ed. and trans. Samuel Danon (Philadelphia: Pennsylvania University Press, 2003), pp.25-33.

50 Wiebenson, *The Picturesque Garden*, p.99.

51 Ibid., p.104.

52 Publicity leaflet, *Veltrusy Landscape Park 2004*, produced by Studio Mac-Architecture,

responsible for the restoration of Veltrusy.

53 See Rudy J Favretti, 'Thomas Jefferson's "Ferme Ornée" at Monticello', *Proceedings of the American Antiquarian Society*, Vol 103, 1993, pp.17-29, and Paul Underwood, *Monticello: The Ferme Ornée*, HND in Landscape Design and Construction, University of Glamorgan, 2005.

54 *The Oxford Companion to Gardens*, p.380.

55 William L Beiswanger, 'The Temple in the Garden: Thomas Jefferson's View of the Monticello Landscape', *British and American Gardens in the Eighteenth Century*, ed. Robert P Maccubbin and Peter Martin (Williamsburg: The Colonial Williamsburg Foundation, 1984), p.181.

56 *The Oxford Companion to Gardens*, pp.384-5 and 597.

57 George C Rogers, 'Gardens and Landscapes in Eighteenth-Century South Carolina', *British and American Gardens*, p.152.

58 Ibid., p.153.

59 Ibid., p.154.

60 Barbara Orsolits, 'Drayton Hall and the Michaux Connection', from research for a historic preservation MA thesis, Georgia State University, 2002.

61 Spence, *Observations*, I.1125, p.424.

62 Ibid., I.1128, p.424.

63 See Michael Symes, *Fairest Scenes: Five Great Surrey Gardens* (Weybridge: Elmbridge Museum, 1988), pp.51-7.

64 Spence, *Observations*, I.1085, p.413.

65 Ibid., I, facing p.424.

66 Richard Warner, *An Historical and Descriptive Account of Bath and its Environs* (Bath, 1802), pp.106-7.

67 Michael Symes, 'Robert FitzGerald's tour of Surrey gardens', *Journal of Garden History*, 6:4, 1986, p.324.

68 [Henrietta Pye], *A Short Account of the Principal Seats and Gardens in and about Richmond and Kew* (Brentford, n.d.), pp.16-17.

69 Mavis Batey, *Alexander Pope: The Poet and the Landscape* (London: Barn Elms Publishing, 1999), p.32.

70 William Chambers, *A Dissertation on Oriental Gardening* (London: 1779 edition, orig. 1772), pp.89-90.

71 Thomas Whately, *Observations on Modern Gardening* (London: fifth edition, 1793, orig. 1770), p.165.

72 Ibid., p.181.

73 Ibid., p.182.

74 Ibid., p.185.

75 Ibid., pp.185-6.

76 Ibid., p.166.

77 Ibid., p.169.

78 Quoted in *The Genius of the Place*, p.335.

79 Stephen Bending, 'Uneasy Sensations: Shenstone, Retirement and Fame', *Arcadian Greens Rural, New Arcadians Journal* 53-54, 2002, p.38n5.

80 *Letters of William Shenstone*, ed. Duncan Mallam (Minneapolis: University of Minnesota Press, 1939), 21 August 1748, p.117.

81 William Shenstone, *The Works in Verse and Prose of William Shenstone, Esq.* (London: R & J Dodsley, 1764), Vol.II, p.373.

82 Shenstone, *Letters*, 30 May 1758, p.350.

83 Shenstone, *Works*, Vol.II, p.125.

84 William Marshall, *On Planting and Rural Ornament* (London: G Nicol, 1796), Vol I, p.320.

85 Joseph Heely, *Letters on the Beauties of Hagley, Envil, and The Leasowes* (London: R Baldwin, 1777), Vol.2, pp.88-9.

86 John Martin Robinson, *Temples of Delight: Stowe Landscape Gardens* (London: The National Trust/George Philip, 1990), p.103.

87 Anon. (William Mavor), *New Description of Blenheim*....(Oxford: 1803), 6th edition (originally 1787), p.93.

88 Whately, *Observations*, p.164.

Chapter 3 Enville

1 William Marshall, *On Planting and Rural Ornament* (London: G. & W. Nicols et. al., 1803), I, pp.327-334.

2 The Journal of Dr Richard Wilkes cited by Rev Stebbing Shaw, *The History and Antiquities of Staffordshire* (London: J. Nichols & Son, 1801), II, pp.269-270.

3 Enville Hall Archives, The Inventories of the Libraries at both Enville Hall and Dunham Massey (now NT) taken in 1760 and 1768 show their wide range of interests, Q1/2/1.

4 Ibid. 4th Earl's Personal Ledger, G/1/13/1.

5 Nottingham University Library, Portland Papers, Letter from Lady Henrietta Grey, née Cavendish Bentinck written at Envil 17 Dec 1763: PWF 4521.

6 Ibid., Letter from Lady Henrietta Grey, née Cavendish Bentinck to her brother 3rd Duke of Portland, Pl C 14/13.

7 Enville Hall Archives: Day Book Accounts 1761-1779,G/1/2/1/1.

8 *Letters of William Shenstone*, ed. Duncan Mallam (Minneapolis:University of Minnesota Press, 1939), Letter to Thomas Percy, 16 January 1763, p.463.

9 The John Rylands Library, Manchester, Stamford Papers, An Act for the sale of part of Lord Stamford's settled estate including the Manor of Stamford, and property in Nottinghamshire, Warwickshire and Derbyshire, EGR/3/7/3/4.

10 The John Rylands Library, Manchester, Stamford Papers, 2nd Earl of Warrington's Will,

EGR/1/8/12/3.

11 Domesday Book 1086: Staffordshire, Manor of Enville: woodland one league long by half a league wide.

12 Nottingham University Library, Portland Papers: Lady Henrietta Grey to her brother 3rd Duke of Portland, 1767 Jan 31, PwF/4555.

13 Nigel Tringham and MW Greenslade, *Victoria County History, The History of the County of Stafford*, (London: Oxford University Press for the Institute of Historical Research, 1984), XX, p.98.

14 Public Record Office, E326/11298.

15 Sampson Erdeswick, *A Survey of Staffordshire* (London for W. Mears, 1723) p.136.

16 Lichfield Record Office, Will and inventory of Sir Thomas Grey, 1565-66 Feb 12,ref. B/C/11

17 Enville Hall Archives, 2 maps
1. On vellum c.1650. It has no date and may well be a copy of an earlier map, but the information fits well with a Deed of 9 Charles I (1634) January 3, H/2/1.
2. An estate survey of 1688 by William Deeley: pen and wash on vellum roll, 1″ 20 perches, H/2/2.

18 Civil War information from John Sutton.

19 Enville Hall Archives, map of the Survey by Deeley (1688), H/2/2.

20 Robert Plot, *The Natural History of Staffordshire* (Oxford, 1686), p.121.

21 Richard Joseph Sulivan, *A Tour through part of England, Scotland Wales in 1778 in a series of Letters* (London:1785) II, pp.10-13.

22 The Royal Bank of Scotland Group Archives, Drummonds Bank customer account ledgers, accounts with 4th Earl of Stamford 1744-1762, DR/427/24-45.

23 Enville Hall Collection, three paintings by Anthony Devis showing the Cascades, a view across the Upper Pool to the Rotunda and the Shepherd's Bridge on Jordan's Pool.

24 John Laurence, *A New System of Agriculture, being a Complete Body of Husbandry and Gardening* (London: Thomas Woodward, 1726) and *A Dictionary of Husbandry and Gardening* (London: J. Nicholson, W. Taylor and W. Churchill, 1717).

25 Sandy Haynes, unpublished analysis of labour in the pleasure grounds and on the estate farm in the eighteenth century using the Day Book Accounts in the Enville Hall Archives 1761-1779, G/1/2/1/1.

26 Ibid., G/1/2/1/1.

27 Howard Colvin, *A Biographical Dictionary of British Architects 1600-1840* (New Haven and London: Yale University Press: 3rd edition, 1995), pp.93-95.

28 Enville Hall Archives, map of Lyndon Estate by Benjamin Booth in 1746, copied 1809, B/1/1/16.

29 Ibid., Estate Rent Rolls 1739-1781, E/3/1.

30 Ibid., Estate Rent Rolls 1782-1811, E/3/2.

31 *The Travels through England of Dr Richard Pococke, Bishop of Meath and Ossory*, ed. J J Cartwright (London: Camden Society,1889), II, p.231.

32 Enville Hall Archives, Day Book Accounts 1761-1779, G/1/2/1/1.

33 Ibid., Estate Survey c.1750, H/2/6.

34 James Rothwell, *Guide to Dunham Massey* (National Trust, 2000), pp.48-49.

35 Count Friedrich Kielmansegge, *Diary of a Journey to England, 1761-62*, trans. by Philippa Kielmansegg, (London: Longmans, 1902), p.37.

36 Enville Hall Archives, Bills and Vouchers, G/1/3/1823 and G/1/3/1824.

37 Howard Colvin, *A Biographical Dictionary of British Architects* (Yale, 3rd ed., 1995), pp.93-95.

38 Enville Hall Archives, 1760 Library Catalogue, Q/1/2/1.

39 Ibid., undated plan of the Home Farm, H/3/1.

40 Ibid., Day Book Accounts, 1761-1779, G/1/2/1/1 and correspondence between John Beckett, agent to Lord Grey 1819 March 20 describing repairs and painting, G/2/2/3/8/13

41 *A Companion to Hagley, The Leasowes & Enville* (London, 1789), p.101

42 *The Diaries of Sanderson Miller of Radway*, ed. William Hawkes (Bristol:The Dugdale Society in association with The Shakespeare Birthplace Trust, 2005), p.88.

43 Joseph Heely, *Letters on the Beauties of Hagley, Envil and The Leasowes* (London, 1777), II, p.68

44 Enville Hall Archives, 1760 Library Catalogue, Q/1/2/1.

45 Both Claude Lorrain and Nicolas Poussin were born in France. Lorrain was particularly noted for his treatment of light in the landscape. Much of their inspiration was taken from classical antiquity with scenes set in an idealised landscape. In the 1630s they spent time together sketching in the area around Rome known as the Campagna which had been celebrated in the writings of Horace and Virgil.

46 Batty Langley, *New Principles of Gardening*, (London, 1728), p.195.

47 Warwickshire County Record Office, Sanderson Miller's Engagement Book, CR 1382/1.

48 Shenstone, *Letters*, p.209.

49 Ibid., p.190.

50 Robert Plot, pp.337, diagram TAB XXXII.

51 Pierre Jean Grosley, *A Tour to London, or new observations on England and its inhabitants... translated from the French* (London, 1772), p.119.

52 Enville Hall Archives, Estate Survey c.1750, H/2/6.

53 Timothy Mowl, 'The Case of the Enville Museum', *Journal of Garden History* Vol. 3, No. 2, 1983 pp.134-143.

54 Miller, *Diaries*, p.59.

55 Ibid., p.60.

56 Shenstone, *Letters*, p.190.

57 Miller, *Diaries*, pp.96 and 99.

58 Shenstone, *Letters*, p.195.

59 Miller, *Diaries*, pp.133 and 193.

60 Shenstone, *Letters*, p.209

61 Pococke, *Travels*, II, p.231.

62 John Hill, *Eden or a Compleat Body of Gardening* (London, 1757), pp.633-636.

63 Jennifer Meir, *Sanderson Miller and His Landscapes* (Chichester: Phillimore, 2006).

64 Julia Ionides, *Thomas Farnolls Pritchard of Shrewsbury, Architect and 'Inventor of Cast iron Bridges'* (Ludlow: The Dog Rose Press, 1999), and in conversation with her.

65 Enville Hall Archives, 4th Earl of Stamford's ledger for 1767 records entries for pine-apples and seeds on 27 June, 6 July and 26 December, G/1/2/13/1.

66 Worcestershire Record Office, Kidderminster Collection, Edward Knight's Notebook, WOL.B/KNI 91-575032.

67 Enville Hall Archives, Day Book entry 1766 Aug 2 : sprig & glue at Gothic Room: 4d, G/1/2/1/1.

68 Ibid., Day Book entry, G/1/2/1/1.

69 Meir, *Miller*, pp.17-18.

70 Heely, *Letters*, II, pp.82-83.

71 Enville Hall Archives, Correspondence: 1838 September 29 : John Davenport (steward) writing to the 6th Earl of Stamford and Warrington – 'I have informed Mr Beddard that your Lordship wishes him to have all the movable seats in the garden cleaned and put in the old Billiard Room', G/2/2/11.

72 Enville Hall Archives, Vouchers and Bills, G/ 1/3 /1846.

73 *The Journal of Horticulture, Cottage Gardener and Country Gentleman*, three articles on the new gardens at Enville Hall serialised on 1864 November 1, 8 and 15.

74 Pococke, *Travels*, II, p.231.

75 Lilian Dickins and Mary Stanton, *An Eighteenth Century Correspondence* (London: John Murray, 1910), p.306.

76 *The Journal of Dr Richard Wilkes* cited by Rev Stebbing Shaw p.270.

77 Burghley House Archives, Attested Copy of Lord Stamford's Settlement on his marriage with Lady Mary Booth: 1736 May 8, Ex 81/13.

78 Enville Hall Archives, Family papers, F/3/5/5.

79 Ibid., proposed plans for landscaping, H/2/8 and Sandy Haynes, 'William Shenstone and the Enville Landscape', *Arcadian Greens Rural, New Arcadian Journal* 53/54, 2002 pp.76-80.

80 In conversation with Steffie Shields.

81 Rothwell, *Dunham Massey* (London: National Trust, 2000), pp.49-50.

82 Shenstone, *Letters*, p.190.

83 Enville Hall Collection, 'The Cascades appear to have been painted from the Chinese Temple and look up the whole run of pools and cascades to the large window of the

[Shenstone] Chapel on the hill above. 'The Rotunda as viewed from the Upper Cascade Pool at Enville Hall' by Anthony Devis (1729-1816). Anthony Devis painted 5 landscapes in oil for the 4th Earl of Stamford. On 28th June 1766 the 4th Earl's Personal Ledger records that Mr Devis was paid £215 16s 0d for the pictures, so they probably date from a few years before that.

84 Worcestershire Record Office, Kidderminster Collection, Edward Knight's Notebook, WOL.B/KNI 91-575032.

85 *The Works in Verse and Prose of William Shenstone, Esq.* (London: R and J Dodsley, 1764), II, pp.127, 130, 131.

86 Enville Hall Archives, Day Book , G/1/2/1/1
   1769 Jan 9 : Mr Bromfield for valuing Chinese Temple: 5s
   Jan 21 : Mr Wright valuing Chinese Temple: 5s
   1770 Jan 22 : Mr Wright's Bill for things to the house & taking down the Chinese Temple: £15 7s

87 Excavation by Sandy Haynes and Jane Bradney.

88 Enville Hall Archives, Day Book and photographs taken by what is now English Heritage in 1950s, G/1/2/1/1.

89 Heely, *Letters*, II, p.35.

90 Ibid., p.36.

91 Ibid., p.39-41.

92 Ibid., p.41.

93 Enville Hall Archives, Estate Vouchers and Bills, G/1/3/1773
   1773 Dec 25 John Guest's bill for work at Cold Bath £37 12s 8d
   Dec 29 Blacksmith at Bath - £3 14s 1d; Glazier at Do - £12 1s 0d

94 Ibid., Lyndon Deeds, B/1/1/17.

95 Ibid., Estate Survey c.1750, H/2/6.

96 Thomas Robins' sketchbook: Victoria & Albert Museum, Prints and Drawings Study Room, level D, The Sketchbook of Thomas Robins – drawing no. 131, Museum reference N.E. 1308: 125-2001.

97 Heely, *Letters*, II, pp.42 and 46.

98 Ibid., p.50.

99 Ibid., p.50.

100 Enville Hall Archives, Estate survey of 1688 by William Deeley: EnvArch H/2/2.

101 Worcestershire Record Office, Kidderminster Collection, Edward Knight's Notebook, WOL. B/KNI 91-575032.

102 Michael Raeburn, Ludmila Voronikhina and Andrew Nurnberg (eds.), *The Green Frog Service* (London: Cacklegoose Press,1995), view no. 757, p.336.

103 Enville Hall Archives, Vouchers and Bills,1768-1843, G/1/3/1809.

104 Heely, *Letters*, II, pp.59-60.

105 Enville Hall Archives, Day Book Accounts 1761-1779, G/1/2/1.

106 Marshall, *On Planting*, p.331.

107 Ibid., Day Book, G/1/2/1/1

    1761 June 13 : 4 Alveley men at Jordan's Pool: 6s

    June 19 : forty score live flounders to put in the pools: 7s

    Oct 26 : a doz rush baskets to move fish: 1s 6d

108 Enville Hall Archives, Estate Survey c.1750, H/2/6.

109 Worcester Record Office, Kidderminster Collection, Edward Knight's Notebook,
WOL.B/KNI 91-575032.

110 Enville Hall Collection, Anthony Devis, oil on canvas, *A man sitting reading by the Shepherd's Bridge on Jordan's Pool*: c.1765.

111 Enville Hall Archives, Vouchers and Bills, 1772 May 16, 1823 Sept, 1829 Sept 30,
G/1/3/1772, G/1/3/1823, G/1/3/1829.

112 Ibid., Day Book 1761-1779, G/1/2/1/1.

113 Ibid., Day Book 1761-1779, G/1/2/1/1.

    1767 Apr 18 : Waldrons Wag(gone)r for bringing 5 hen pheasants & four Guinea
fowls: 5s

    1770 Mar 24: carr. of a wild Turkey cock from Dunham: 5s

    Mar 31: keeper rearing 3 silver pheasants: 3s

    1771 Mar 18: Richard Huntley for his care in bringing a Chinese cock pheasant from
Longleat: 10s 6d

114 Osvald Sirén, *China and Gardens of Europe of the Eighteenth Century* (Washington:
Dumbarton Oaks, 1990 [originally published by The Ronald Press Company, 1950]),
p.42 and Plate 27 B.

115 Pococke, *Travels*, II, p.231.

116 Enville Hall Archives, Day Book 1767 April 11, G/1/2/1/1.

117 Heely, *Letters*, II, pp.71-75.

118 Mark Laird, *The Flowering of the Landscape Garden* (Philadelphia: University of
Pennsylvania Press, 1999), pp.109-114.

119 Pococke, *Travels*, II, p. 231.

120 Heely, *Letters*, pp.83-85.

121 Ibid., pp.83-84.

122 Enville Hall Archives. In the early 1780s Lord Grey measured and recorded some of
the various walks and drives with the distances between places of interest,
G/1/8/4/1: see appendix.

Chapter 4 Hagley

1 *Memoirs and Correspondence of George Lord Lyttelton*, ed. Robert Phillimore (London:
James Ridgway, 1845), p.33.

2 Rose Mary Davis, *The Good Lord Lyttelton: A Study in Eighteenth Century Politics and Culture* (Bethlehem, Pennsylvania: Times Publishing Co., 1939), p.111.

3 *The Poetical Works of Lord Lyttelton* (London: Joseph Wenman), p.70.

4 Rose Mary Davis, *Lyttelton*, p.146.

5 Hagley Hall Library, 3F 1.5. Quoted in Michael Cousins, 'Hagley Park, Worcestershire', *Garden History* 35: Suppl. 1, 2007, pp.17-18.

6 Rose Mary Davis, *Lyttelton*, p.144.

7 See Michael Symes, 'William Pitt the Elder: The *Gran Mago* of Landscape Gardening', *Garden History* 24:1, 1996, pp.126-36.

8 Rose Mary Davis, *Lyttelton*, p.168.

9 Lilian Dickins and Mary Stanton, *An Eighteenth Century Correspondence* (London: John Murray, 1910), p.430.

10 Rose Mary Davis, *Lyttelton*, p.171.

11 Michael Cousins, 'Hagley Park, Worcestershire', *Garden History* 35: Supplement 1, 2007, p.21.

12 *The Correspondence of Alexander Pope*, ed. George Sherburn (Oxford: Clarendon Press, 1956), Vol.IV, p.190.

13 Cousins, 'Hagley Park', p.74.

14 Thomas Whately, *Observations on Modern Gardening* (London: T Payne, 5th edition, 1793), p.198.

15 Ibid., p.209.

16 Ibid., p.201.

17 James Thomson, *The Seasons* (London: 1744), ll.904-54.

18 Quoted in Treadway Nash, *Collections for the History of Worcestershire* (London, 1781), Vol.I, p.486.

19 George Lyttelton, *Monody*, quoted in Davis, *Lyttelton*, p.136.

20 Joseph Heely, *Letters on the Beauties of Hagley, Envil and The Leasowes* (London, 1777), Vol.I, p.162.

21 John Parnell, *Journal of a tour thro' England and Wales, Anno 1769*, British Library of Political and Economic Science, MS, Coll. Misc. 38, Vol.III, p.68.

22 Whately, *Observations*, p.199.

23 George Mason, *An Essay on Design in Gardening* (London: Benjamin White, 1768), p.50.

24 *Horace Walpole's Correspondence*, ed. WS Lewis et al (New Haven: Yale University Press, 1937-83), XXXV, p.147.

25 Arthur Young, *A Six Months Tour Through the North of England* (London, 1770), Vol.III, p.350.

26 Cousins, 'Hagley Park', p.40.

27 *Letters of William Shenstone*, ed. Duncan Mallam (Minneapolis: University of Minnesota Press, 1939), 21 October 1751, p.233.

28 See Michael Cousins, 'Athenian Stuart's Doric porticoes', *Georgian Group Journal* 14,

2004, pp.48-54.

29 Cousins, 'Hagley Park', p.104.

30 Michael Symes, 'Flintwork, Freedom and Fantasy: The Landscape at West Wycombe Park, Buckinghamshire', *Garden History* 33:1, 2005, p.15.

31 Michael Bevington, '"The Watcher on the Column": The Prince's Column at Stowe, Buckinghamshire', *Follies* 6, 2006, p.54.

32 Betty Kemp, *Sir Francis Dashwood: An Eighteenth-Century Independent* (London: Macmillan, 1967), p.94n1.

33 *The Travels through England of Dr. Richard Pococke*, ed. JJ Cartwright (London: Camden Society, 1888), Vol.I, p.235.

34 Parnell, *Journal*, Vol.III, p.73.

35 Heely, *Letters*, Vol.I, p.221.

36 Thomas Maurice, *Hagley. A Descriptive Poem* (Oxford: author, 1776), p.19.

37 Pococke, *Travels*, Vol.I, pp.225-6.

38 Heely, *Letters*, Vol.I, p.133.

39 Maurice, *Hagley*, p.5.

40 Whately, *Observations*, p.210.

41 Pococke, *Travels*, Vol.I, p.226.

42 Robert Williams, 'The Leasowes, Hagley and Rural Inscriptions', *Arcadian Greens Rural, New Arcadians Journal* 53/54, 2002, p.53.

43 Anon., *A Description of Hagley, Envil and The Leasowes* (Birmingham, c.1770), p.85.

44 Cousins, 'Hagley Park', pp.96-100.

45 Mason, *Design*, p.47.

46 Jennifer Meir, *Sanderson Miller and his Landscapes* (Chichester: Phillimore, 2006), p.122.

47 Whately, *Observations*, p.203.

48 William Toldervy, *England and Wales Described in a Series of Letters* (London, 1762), Vol.I, p.342.

49 Walpole, *Correspondence*, XXXV, p.147.

50 Toldervy, *England and Wales Described*, Vol.I, p.342.

51 Cousins, 'Hagley Park', pp.81-2.

52 Ibid., pp.44-5.

53 Day Book at Enville Hall, 1 October 1768.

54 Heely, *Letters*, Vol.I, p.188.

55 Joseph Giles, *Miscellaneous Poems on Various Subjects and Occasions* (London, 1771), p.161.

56 Pococke, *Travels*, Vol.I, p.224.

57 *Letters to and from Henrietta, Countess of Suffolk*, ed. John W Croker (London, 1824), Vol.2, p.81.

58 Toldervy, *England and Wales Described*, Vol.I, p.339.

59 Whately, *Observations*, p.206.

60 See Cousins, 'Hagley Park', p.108.

61 Michael Bevington, *Stowe: The Garden and the Park* (Stowe: Capability Books, 1996), pp.95-6.

62 Meir, *Miller*, p.183.

63 Ibid., p.65.

64 Whately, *Observations*, p.208.

65 Ibid., pp.203-10.

66 Ibid., p.207.

67 Quoted in Cousins, 'Hagley Park', p.23.

68 Ibid., p.24.

69 Ibid., p.22.

70 Thomas, Baron Lyttelton, *Letters of the Late Lord Lyttelton*, ed. William Combe (London, 1780).

71 *Westminster Magazine*, XCI, Vol.8, May 1780, pp.249-50.

72 Michael Symes, 'Charles Hamilton at Bowood, Wiltshire', *Garden History* 34:2, 2006, pp.215-16.

73 Richard Warner, *A Tour Through the Northern Counties of England, and the Borders of Scotland* (Bath, 1802), Vol.I, p.69.

Chapter 5 The Leasowes

1 *The Works in Verse and Prose of William Shenstone, Esq.* (London: R & J Dodsley, 1764), Vol.I, p.ii.

2 Ibid.

3 Treadway Nash, *Collections for the History of Worcestershire* (1781), Vol.I, p.530.

4 *Letters of William Shenstone*, ed. Duncan Mallam (Minneapolis: University of Minnesota Press, 1939), p.62n.

5 Treadway Nash, *Collections for the History of Worcestershire* (1781), Vol.I, p.531.

6 Ibid., p.xviii.

7 Ibid.

8 See Michael Cousins, 'William Shenstone: Jealous of Hagley?', *Arcadian Greens Rural*, New Arcadians Journal 53/54, 2002, pp.60-72.

9 Jane Brown, *My Darling Heriott: Henrietta Luxborough, Poetic Gardener and Irrepressible Exile* (London: Harper Press, 2006), pp.66-72 and 76-80.

10 Ibid., p.160.

11 *The Life and Poetical Works of James Woodhouse (1735-1820)*, ed. Rev R I Woodhouse (London: Leadenhall Press, 1896), Vol.I, p.2.

12 A F B Williams, *The Life of William Pitt, 1st Earl of Chatham* (London: Longmans & Co, 1913).

13 Quoted in ibid.

14 Shenstone, *Works*, Vol.I, p.v.

15 Ibid.

16 Phillida Ballard et al, *A Lost Landscape: Matthew Boulton's Gardens at Soho* (Chichester: Phillimore & Co Ltd, 2009), p.6.

17 Shenstone, *Letters*, 1747, p.90.

18 Ibid., 15 August 1748, p.116.

19 Ibid., 18 October 1761, p.430.

20 Ibid., 13 November 1756, p.334.

21 Shenstone, *Works*, Vol.II, p.125.

22 Ibid., p.147.

23 Ibid., p.129.

24 Ibid., p.130.

25 Ibid., p.131.

26 Ibid., p.134.

27 Ibid.

28 Ibid., p.136.

29 Ibid., p.140.

30 Ibid., p.135.

31 Cousins, 'Jealous of Hagley?'.

32 Shenstone, *Letters*, 17 September 1747, p.83.

33 Ibid., 16 June 1748, p.109.

34 Ibid., 21 August 1748, p.118.

35 Ibid., 12 September 1749, p.162.

36 Ibid., autumn 1751, p.233.

37 Ibid., 26 December 1747, p.88.

38 Ibid., 30 (?) May 1744, p.72.

39 Ibid., 28 January 1750, p.188.

40 Ibid., 11 November 1753, p.281.

41 John Parnell, *Journal of a tour thro' England and Wales, Anno 1769*, British Library of Political and Economic Science, MS, Coll. Misc. 38, Vol.III, pp.96-7.

42 Humphry Repton, *Red Book for Shardeloes* (1794), quoted in John Phibbs, 'The View-Point', *Garden History*, 36:2, 2008, p.221.

43 See Dianne Barre, 'Sir Samuel Hellier (1736-84) and his Garden Buildings: Part of the Midlands "Garden Circuit" in the 1760s-70s?', *Garden History*, 36:2, 2008, p.310.

44 Shenstone, *Letters*, 3 June 1749, pp.148-9.

45 Thomas Whately, *Observations on Modern Gardening* (London: 5th ed., 1793), pp.173-4.

46 Ibid., p.174.

47 For a discussion of the inscriptions, see Robert Williams, 'The Leasowes, Hagley and Rural Inscriptions', *New Arcadian Journal* 53/54, pp.42-58.

48 Shenstone, *Letters*, 20 August 1749, p.159.

49 Whately, *Observations*, p.175.

50 Robert Williams, 'Rural Economy and the Antique in the English Landscape Garden',
   Journal of Garden History 7:1, pp.73-96 (pp.74-5).

51 Shenstone, *Letters*, 21 September 1747, p.85.

52 Quoted in Williams, *Life of Pitt*, p.192.

53 Shenstone, *Works*, Vol.II, p.143.

54 Shenstone, *Letters*, 9 July 1749, p.153.

55 Ibid., 26 November 1749, p.178.

56 Ibid., 3 June 1749, p.149.

57 Ibid., 15 March 1750, p.195.

58 John Riely, 'Shenstone's Walks: The Genesis of The Leasowes', *Apollo*, Vol.110, 1979,
   pp.202-9, and Christopher Gallagher, 'The Leasowes: A History of the Landscape',
   Garden History 24:2, 1996, pp.201-20.

59 Nash, *Worcestershire Collections*, Vol.I, p.530.

60 Joseph Heely, *Letters on the Beauties of Hagley, Envil and The Leasowes* (London: 1777),
   Vol.II, p.198.

61 Gallagher, 'The Leasowes', p.211.

62 Shenstone, *Letters*, October 1755, pp.330-1.

63 Ibid., 18 October 1749, pp.166-7.

64 Gallagher, 'The Leasowes', p.212.

65 Parnell, *Journal*, Vol.III, p.85.

66 Shenstone, *Letters*, 3 June 1749, p.150.

67 Ibid., 30 May 1758, pp.350-1.

68 David Coffin, *The English Garden: Meditation and Memorial* (Princeton, New Jersey:
   Princeton UP, 1994), p.45.

69 Parnell, *Journal*, Vol.III, p.111.

70 Shenstone, *Works*, Vol.II, p.126.

71 Ibid., p.131.

72 Shenstone, *Letters*, 3-8 November 1749, p.170.

73 Thomas Martyn, *The English Connoisseur* (London: L Davis and C Reymors, 1766), Vol.I,
   p.157.

74 Parnell, *Journal*, Vol.III, p.103.

75 Shenstone, *Letters*, 30 August 1749, pp.160-1.

76 Woodhouse, *Poems*, Vol.II, p.112.

77 Parnell, *Journal*, Vol.III, p.106.

78 Shenstone, *Letters*, 17 July 1754, p.299.

80 Ibid., 15 July 1753, pp.268-9.

81 Ibid., 4 June 1750, p.206.

82 Ibid., 16 June 1748, p.109.

83 Ibid., June 1748, p.111.

84 Ibid., 22 March 1750, p.197.

85 Ibid., (autumn 1751), p.234.

86 Ibid., 16 May 1762, p.444.

87 Woodhouse, *Poems*, Vol.II, pp.117-18.

88 Shenstone, *Letters*, 3 June 1749, p.149.

89 Shenstone, *Works*, Vol.II, p.373.

90 Ibid., p.375.

91 Ibid., p.372.

92 Ibid., pp.380-2.

93 Ibid., pp.384-5.

94 Abel Evans, *Epitaph on Sir John Vanbrugh, Architect of Blenheim Palace*, 1726.

95 Shenstone, *Works*, Vol.II, p.390.

96 (Joseph Giles), *Miscellaneous Poems on Various Subjects and Occasions* (London: 1771), p.4.

97 Woodhouse, *Poems*, Vol.I, p.97.

98 Ibid., p.106.

99 George Mason, *An Essay on Design in Gardening* (London: 1768), p.35.

100 Ibid., p.37.

101 Ibid., p.47.

102 Ibid., pp.50-1.

103 Whately, *Observations*, p.174.

104 Anon., *A Description of Hagley, Envil and The Leasowes* (Birmingham: n.d.), p.51.

105 Ibid., p.63.

106 (Resta Patching), *Four Topographical Letters* (Newcastle: 1757), p.57.

107 Ibid., pp.57-8.

108 Arthur Young, *A Six Months Tour Through the North of England* (London: 1770), Vol.III, pp.343-4.

109 Parnell, *Journal*, Vol.III, p.86.

110 William Gilpin, *Observations, Relative Chiefly to Picturesque Beauty, Made in the Year 1772, on Several Parts of England* (London: R Blamire, 3rd ed., 1792), pp.58-64.

111 Heely, *Beauties*, Vol.II, pp.99-100.

112 Ibid., p.147.

113 Ibid., p.167.

114 Ibid., p.228.

115 Ibid., p.226.

116 Richard Graves, *Columella; or, The Distressed Anchoret* (London: J Dodsley, 1779), Vol.I, p.8.

117 Ibid., pp.44-5.

118 Ibid., p.45.

119 Ibid., pp.127-8.

120 Helena Attlee, *Italian Gardens: A Cultural History* (London: Frances Lincoln, 2006), p.172.

121 Barre, 'Sir Samuel Hellier', pp.310-27.

122 Harry Gilonis, 'Emblematical and Expressive: The Gardenist Modes of William Shenstone and Ian Hamilton Finlay', *New Arcadians Journal* 53/54, pp.86-108.

A Chronology of the Gardens

The dates of buildings and features are for the beginning of construction

1709   Sir George Lyttelton born to Sir Thomas Lyttelton and Christian Temple Viscount Cobham's (Stowe) sister

1714   William Shenstone born

1716   Sanderson Miller born at Radway, Warwickshire
Lord Harry Grey, later the 4th Earl of Stamford born

1727   George II becomes King

1728/30   Sir George Lyttelton goes on the Grand Tour travelling through France and Italy where he spent most of his time in the major Italian cities

1731/34   possible first meeting between George Lyttelton and Alexander Pope

1732   William Shenstone admitted to Pembroke College, Oxford

1734   Philip Southcote begins to create his *ferme ornée* at Woburn Farm, Surrey

1736-9   Shenstone moves into The Leasowes with his tenants

1739   Harry Grey succeeds to the title of 4th Earl of Stamford and moves to Enville
Hagley: Pope made three sketches for garden buildings
Hagley: The Prince's Column; The Hermitage

c.1740   The Leasowes: the Temple of Pan and the Hermitage

1740/3   Enville: new stable block and brewhouse built beside the Hall

1743   Hagley: James Thomson wrote to Miss Young describing the park as having a stream with cascades and a pool, but no buildings

c.1743   Hagley: The Seat of Contemplation
The Leasowes: the summer-house on the Beech Water

1744   Hagley: James Thomson publishes *Spring* part of his poem *The Seasons* with references to Hagley
Hagley: Pope's Urn

c.1745   Enville: the creation of the Temple Pool
Hagley: Pope's Seat
The Leasowes: Shenstone began to extend his plan to make a
continuous circuit walk and to start work on Virgil's Grove

1746   Enville: Chinese Temple and Bridge; Rotunda
The Leasowes: a seat to Thomson in Virgil's Grove

1746/7   Hagley: Sir George Lyttelton's wife Lucy Fortescue died

c.1747   Enville: the *patte d'oie* on Round Hill with the Turning Seat; Grotto;
the Portico or Doric Temple or Summerhouse; the Gothic Seat
Hagley: the Stables and Coach House courtyard were built
The Leasowes: the improvement of Virgil's Grove

1747/8   Enville: Home Farm, architect William Baker
Hagley: The Ruin or the Sham Castle by Sanderson Miller
Hagley: The Cottage and plantations 'upon the Hill'

1748   Hagley: The Rotunda by John Pitt of Encombe

1749   Enville: first recorded visit of Sanderson Miller
Hagley: Thomson's Seat
The Leasowes: the circuit walk was complete; the Gothic alcove;
Urn dedicated to William Somervile. Shenstone writes he is
'embroidering my Grove with Flowers'

1750   The Leasowes: Lord Stamford visit and admires Virgil's Grove
Shenstone plants flowering shrubs and small trees
Enville: Gothic Greenhouse, Billiard Room or Museum and William
Shenstone's first visit; move to a more naturalistic design of the
landscape with the removal of hedges and sweeping curves
replacing straight lines
Hagley: The Stables by Sanderson Miller; Jacob's Well

1751   Death of Frederick Prince of Wales
Hagley: Dr Pococke describes the grotto, cascades and the Venus
which he saw on his visit, also the ridings cut into Wychbury Hill
The Leasowes: Shenstone leases the terrace beyond the wood

1752   Hagley: The Greenhouse and The Dairy by Sanderson Miller

1753   Hagley: Horace Walpole writes to Richard Bentley saying that the
Castle 'had the true rust of the Baron's Wars'
The Leasowes: the chalybeate spring with its iron bowl and
dedication to the goddess of health

1752/58 Enville: Ralph's Bastion; The Cascades; The Gothic Gateway; The Cottage or Hermitage; The Chapel; improvements to the Shepherd's Lodge and Lyndon in the Gothic taste

1754 Hagley Hall was rebuilt in Palladian style to designs by Sanderson Miller. It was built beside the old timber frame Hall
Hagley: Milton's Seat
The Leasowes: the summerhouse by the Beech Water is pulled down; two new cascades are constructed; Urn dedicated to Maria Dolman

1756 Hagley: Sanderson Miller draws designs for a Gothic Seat
Hagley: Hexagonal Temple built on Wychbury Hill

1757 The Leasowes: a statue of Faunus, a Gothic screen and the Ruined Priory

1758 Hagley: Temple of Theseus by James 'Athenian' Stuart
The Leasowes: dedication of a seat near the Beech Water to Joseph Spence

1759 Hagley: the new Hall is completed

1759/60 Lord George Harry Grey goes on the Grand Tour passing through Holland, Belgium and Switzerland on his way to Italy

1760 George III becomes King
The Leasowes: the start of creating the Priory Pool

1762 Hagley: The Palladian Bridge with 4 Ionic Pillars by Thomas Pitt, Lord Camelford

1763 February William Shenstone dies of a 'putrid fever'
Enville: the Chapel in Priest Wood is dedicated to his memory
the first mention of an ice house in the day book accounts

1764 Hagley: the obelisk

1765 Hagley: Shenstone's Urn

1767 Enville: the first mention of pines (pineapples)

1768 Enville: 4th Earl of Stamford dies and his son George Harry becomes 5th Earl

1769   Enville: The Chinese Temple and Bridge were taken down and The Boat House was built
        Hagley: Parnell's tour in which he sketched the various garden buildings such as the Hermitage and the Seat of Contemplation

1769/70 Enville: The Cascades were 'improved' by raising the dams and building sluices in order to give greater force to the water

1772   Enville: an Urn on a pedestal was erected, site unknown

1773   Enville: The Cold Bath
        Hagley: George Lyttelton dies and is succeeded by his son Thomas as the 2nd Lord Lyttelton

1775/80 Enville: the extension and modernising of the Hall to designs by John Hope

1777   Joseph Heely wrote *Letters on the Beauties of Hagley, Envil and The Leasowes*

A List of Walks and Drives at Enville written by Lord Grey, later 6th Earl of Stamford and Warrington, in the 1780s

	Miles	Qurs	Furlongs
Home Circuit			
From the Hall Door to the first Wicket beyond the Boat House	0	1	0
To the small Wicket near the third Cascade	0	1	0
By the Bastion to the Wicket coming out of the Round Hill	0	1	0
Thrô the Old Orchard to the Hall Door	0	1	0
Mile	1	0	0

	Miles	Qurs	Furlongs
Midland Circuit or Walk			
From the Hall Door by Jordan's Pool along the Path on the upper Side of the Cottage to the Spring close to the Foot - Path	0	2	0
To the Urn in the Wood	0	0	1
By the Seat at the Top of the Valley & along the Green Walk to the Foot - Path crossing the Ash Walk	0	0	2
To the first Wicket out of the Round Hill	0	0	1
Thrô the Old Orchard to the Hall Door	0	0	2
Mile	1	1	0

	Miles	Qurs	Furlongs
The General Walk			
From the Hall Door to the first Wicket beyond the Boat House	0	1	0
By the Cascades to the Wicket going into Priest - Wood	0	2	0
Thrô Priest - Wood by Shenstone's Chapel cross the Sheep Walk to ye second Yew - Tree with the Seat	0	2	0
To the Shepherd's Lodge	0	1	0
Thrô the Welch - Gate down the Foot - Path to the seat at the Top of the Valley	0	2	0
By the Urn to the Cottage Door	0	1	0
Over the Shepherd's Bridge to the Seat at the Top of the Parks	0	1	0
Down the Shrubbery to the Gothic Room, Green - House & to the Door of the Garden - Front	0	3	0
Mile	3	1	0

The Drive or Ride at Envil

	Miles	Qurs	Furlongs
From ye Front Door to ye Gate into ye Serpentine Walk	0	1	0
To ye Wicket by ye Mill Brook in Dᵒ.	0	1	0
White's Barn	0	1	0
Gate to Quarry Hawkes's	0	1	0
along Serpentine Walk to first Clump in Burnt Crofts	0	3	0
along ye Drive thro Priest - wood to first Yew Tree with Seat on ye outside	0	0	3
To large Clump of Hollies looking on Birch Wood	0	0	1
To Shepherd's Lodge	0	1	0
To 3 Hollies by Birch Wood by ye Lodge	0	1	0
To Welch - Gate	0	3	0
Down ye Green Walk thrô Gate at Top of ye Parks to ye Wicket by Gothic Room	0	3	0
Mile	4	1	0

The Cast of Characters

Ralph Allen (1693-1764) made a fortune as a sub-postmaster in Bath and saved the Post Office £1,500,000 over the next forty years by improving the postal services throughout England. He invested his money in the local stone quarries from which most of Georgian Bath is built. Allen was a great benefactor who helped to build the Royal Mineral Hospital. In 1742 he was elected Mayor and built Prior Park overlooking Bath for his own use. From 1757 until his death in 1764 he was MP for Bath.

John Baskerville (1706-1775) was born at Wolverley, Worcestershire, about four miles from Enville. When he was about 20 years he moved to Easy Hill, Birmingham where he became known as a stone-cutter and also taught calligraphy. He later set up a japanning business which was known for its high quality work. Baskerville was interested in developing the technology to give clearer printing and worked to produce better quality paper and ink as well as being the inventor of the typeface which bears his name and which was widely used in later eighteenth-century printing. He published a wide range of books for Cambridge University, an edition of Virgil, a folio Bible and also Dodsley's *Select Fables* (1761). He was a member of the Royal Society of Arts and a friend to many members of the Lunar Society, in particular Matthew Boulton.

William Henry Cavendish Bentinck, Duke of Portland (1738-1809) The 3rd Duke was the brother of Henrietta Cavendish Bentinck who married Lord George Harry Grey, later 5th Earl of Stamford. He was a staunch Whig who held high government posts between 1765 and 1782. He headed a coalition government in 1783. Portland was Vice-President, then President of the Foundling Hospital for abandoned children. He returned to high government office as Home Secretary under Pitt and was Prime Minister 1807-9.

Matthew Boulton (1728-1809) was born in Birmingham and followed in his father's business manufacturing small ornamental metal objects known as 'toys' such as buckles, buttons and handles. He bought land in Handsworth and founded the Soho Manufactory and Mint where he introduced modern production techniques which made a huge range of items in metal from toothpicks to coins to silver plate. He had wide ranging interests in both the sciences and the arts and was a member of the Lunar Society. His garden at Soho was greatly inspired by the landscape gardens of Painshill. Boulton was one of the most influential people of his time.

The Hon. George Byng, 3rd Viscount Torrington (1701-1750) A friend of the Greys. In 1719-1720 he went to Italy, where he joined his father and brother in Naples. He made his career in the Royal Horse Guards, achieving the rank of Major General.

Robert Dodsley (1703-1764) was born in Mansfield, Nottinghamshire. He was originally a footman and wrote a poem in 1729 entitled *Servitude* and later a satirical play called *The Toy Shop*. He later became a publisher and bookseller as well as a writer. He published works by some of the leading writers of the day such as Goldsmith, Pope and Samuel Johnson. Shenstone helped him to edit the six volumes of *Miscellanies*. He sent a copy of his poetry to Lord Grey at Enville on the recommendation of Lady Luxborough.

Maria Dolman There were two Marias; one was a cousin and the other a niece. Cousin Maria (1733-1754) was the daughter of Rev Thomas Dolman, vicar of Broome where Shenstone had spent part of his early life. Her father had married his mother's sister. Shenstone was very fond of her and after her early death from smallpox at the age of twenty-one he erected a gilt painted urn in Lover's Walk to her memory.

Lord Ferdinando Dudley Lea, 5th Baron Dudley (d.1757) was the son of William Lea of The Grange, Lapal, Halesowen a few miles from The Leasowes. His sister had married into the Shenstone family and he was a friend and neighbour of William Shenstone who was an executor of his will. Lord Ferdinando was a distant relative of Lord Ward's.

Lady Caroline Egerton (1724-1793) was the daughter of the 1st Duke of Bridgewater, who lived at Tatton Hall, Cheshire. Her sister, Louisa, married Lord Gower at Trentham. They were Cheshire neighbours and friends of the Booths of Dunham Massey; Lady Mary Booth was later to become became the 4th Countess of Stamford at Enville.

Henry Fielding (1707-1754) was born near Glastonbury, Somerset and was educated at Eton where he became friends with William Pitt the Elder. He studied classics and law, but lack of money meant that he abandoned his studies in favour of writing novels and satirical plays for the theatre including attacks on the government of Sir Robert Walpole. His best known work is *The History of Tom Jones* which was dedicated to Lord Lyttelton on whom the character of Squire Allworthy was possibly based, although Ralph Allen is another candidate. With his brother he established the Bow Street Runners.

Benjamin Franklin (1706-1790) was born in Boston, Mass., USA, but lived mainly in Philadelphia. He was one of the Founding Fathers of the United States of America. He was a man with many interests, a skilled printer, an ambassador, but most of all a scientist and inventor who tried to 'capture' electricity. He lived in England between 1757 and 1762 and visited The Leasowes in 1758. Franklin and John Baskerville worked together to improve the making of type and book production. He was a friend of Boulton and other members of the Lunar Society.

Frederick, Prince of Wales (1707-1751) was the eldest son of George II and father of George III and was greatly disliked by his parents. He had wide-ranging interests in art, literature and the sciences. In 1731 he leased the estate at Kew and was responsible for its expansion both botanically and architecturally. He was a figurehead for people dissatisfied with Walpole's government, such as the Lytteltons.

Morgan Graves (1707-1770) inherited the family estate at Mickleton in Gloucestershire in 1729. He was noted for his hospitality, but not his intellect. Shenstone , Whistler and Jago were all frequent visitors. Both Morgan and Shenstone shared a love of gardens and it is thought that the poet advised on improvements to the estate.

Richard Graves (1715-1804) was the younger brother of Morgan, and a fellow student with Shenstone at Pembroke College, Oxford sharing some of the same friends. He was forced into marrying Lucy Bartholomew in 1747 when she became pregnant and was ostracised by many. Later he became rector of Claverton near Bath, and was a friend of Ralph Allen who is buried in the churchyard there. Graves was a man of wide ranging interests – writing, poetry, novels, archaeology, numismatics, landscape gardening and modern and ancient literature. His acquaintances included Charles and John Wesley, the founders of the Methodist movement whom Graves satirised in *The Spiritual Quixote*, and Beau Nash, the King of Bath.

Amos Green (1734-1807) was first apprenticed to John Baskerville and later employed by Matthew Boulton painting trays and boxes. He specialised in flower, fruit and birds. He lived at Halesowen near to John Scott Hylton and was a friend of Shenstone's.

Lord Harry Grey, 4th Earl of Stamford (1716-1768) Lord Grey inherited the Enville estate in 1739 and spent the first sixteen years of his life there in beautifying his surroundings with the help of Shenstone and Sanderson Miller. Shenstone stayed at Enville and advised on the laying out of the grounds particularly around the Cascades. Lord Stamford tried to negotiate a pension for Shenstone.

The Hon. Charles Hamilton (1704-1786) was educated at Oxford and went twice on the Grand Tour. Hamilton became MP for Strabane in Ireland and in 1738 was made Clerk of the Household to Frederick, Prince of Wales. He is best known as the creator of Painshill and advised many others on the design of their gardens.

Frankie Holyoake was the son of Rev William Holyoake. He worked with Amos Green for Matthew Boulton at Snow Hill.

Rev William Holyoake (1694-1768) was the rector of Oldberrow and Lady Luxborough's chaplain who informed Shenstone of her death.

Thomas Hull (1728-1808) was the actor manager of the King's Theatre Birmingham and also the Bath Theatre for John Palmer. He appeared in London at Covent Garden. Richard Graves thought he spoke well but was an insipid actor. Hull also wrote a number of plays including *The Spanish Lady* and *Rosamund*. His *Select Letters* which were published 1778 include those from Shenstone, Whistler and Dodsley. He was author of adaptations from Shakespeare and French dramatists, oratorio librettos, two novels and translations.

Rev Richard Jago (1715-1781) The third son of the rector of Beaudesert in Warwickshire. He attended Solihull School and Oxford with Shenstone and with whom he shared a passion for gardening. He was curate, then rector of Snittersfield in Warwickshire. His poem *Edge-hill* was published in 1767 and he contributed to Dodsley's *Miscellany*. Towards the end of his life he revised many of his poems which were printed by his friend John Scott Hylton under the title *Poems Moral and Descriptive.*

Thomas Jefferson (1743-1826) In 1765 Jefferson obtained a copy of Shenstone's *Works* to add to his library, which would later contain Heely's *Letters on the Beauties of Hagley, Envil and The Leasowes*, Whately's *Observations* and Castell's *The Villas of the Ancients*. He saw garden design as an extension of the beauties of nature and incorporated some of Shenstone's ideas in his garden at Monticello, Virginia, USA.

Jefferson was the primary author of the draft of The American Declaration of Independence in 1776. Three years later he was elected Governor of Virginia. From 1785 to 1789 he was minister to France and whilst there made a visit to England in 1786 during which he visited The Leasowes. This was over twenty years after Shenstone's death and he was not impressed by the way in which it had been kept. In 1800 he was elected President of America.

Samuel Johnson (1709-1784) was born in Lichfield, Staffordshire, the son of a bookseller. He was a lexicographer, essayist, poet, wit and conversationalist. In 1755 he published the first comprehensive *Dictionary of the English Language* which remained the pre-eminent English dictionary for over 100 years. He later produced an annotated edition of Shakespeare and with his friend James Boswell made a memorable tour of The Hebrides which he described in *A Journal to the Western Isles of Scotland.*

William Kent (1685-1748) Sent to study in Rome where he met many influential people including the 3rd Earl of Burlington who became his patron. One of the leaders in the new naturalistic English landscape garden style which included Rousham, Stowe and the White House at Kew for Frederick, Prince of Wales.

Granville Leveson-Gower, Earl Gower (1721-1803) was the owner of the Trentham estate in North Staffordshire and many other smaller estates in Staffordshire and Shropshire. He became an MP for Bishops Castle and later Westminster. His second wife was Louisa Egerton of Tatton. In 1755 he became Lord Privy Seal. They were close friends of the Earl of Stamford's family.

Lady Luxborough (1699-1756) Henrietta was the daughter of Viscount St John and his French wife Angelica. Horace Walpole described her as 'lusty' and with 'a great black bush of hair.' She married Robert Knight, a Whig MP in 1727 and was later banished by him in 1736 to live at Barrels, Ullenhall, Warwickshire, after being accused of improper conduct with the Rev John Dalton. Her neighbours included William Somervile and Richard Jago who was curate at Snitterfield, and was a close friend of Shenstone, Graves and Lord Dudley. Barrels became the centre of a literary circle. She made a number of visits to Bath where she was acquainted with Samuel Richardson, the novelist who wrote *Clarissa,* Ralph Allen, Lady Huntingdon the prominent Methodist, Dr Oliver, the noted physician at Bath and William Hoare, the artist. She was a habituée of Frederick's and Leake's bookshop in Bath.

Lord George Lyttelton, 1st Baron Lyttelton (1709-1773) was the son of Sir Thomas and educated at Eton and Oxford. A relative of Lord Cobham's, he was a frequent visitor to Stowe. He was secretary to the Prince of Wales from 1732-44 and briefly Chancellor of the Exchequer. He was MP for Okehampton. Lyttelton published the poem *Monody* in 1747, *Dialogues of the Dead in* 1760 and *History of the Life of Henry II.* He was a friend of Alexander Pope, James Thomson, Henry Fielding and Shenstone, and was the driving force in the creation of the grounds at Hagley.

Sir Henry Mainwaring (1726-1797) inherited Peover Hall, Cheshire. Mainwaring accompanied Lord Grey, eldest son of 4th Earl of Stamford on their Grand Tour to Italy. (1759-1760)

Sanderson Miller (1716-1780) was born at Radway, Warwickshire. He inherited the estate when he was twenty-one and began to convert the Elizabethan house to the Gothic style. He was a gentleman architect who designed several notable buildings such as the Shire Hall at Warwick and the Great Hall at Lacock Abbey in Wiltshire. At Hagley he designed both the Hall in the Palladian style and the ruined Gothic sham castle. Miller also contributed to the design of some of the garden buildings at Enville, notably the Gothic Greenhouse. He worked mainly in the Midland counties and was a frequent visitor to Stowe.

Richard 'Beau' Nash (1674-1761) was born in Swansea and first visited Bath in 1705. He soon found employment as the aide-de-camp to the Master of Ceremonies, Captain Webster, who was later killed in a duel. Nash took over his post which arranged the life and social integration of the city. He was known as the 'King of Bath', but it was his elegant and expensive dress combined with overstated manners that earned him the nickname 'Beau'. Nash introduced rules for the smooth running of events in Bath which led to greater social integration.

Dr William Oliver (1695-1764) Dr Oliver was born in Cornwall and educated at Pembroke College, Cambridge. He moved to Bath in 1728 where he became a friend of Ralph Allen and Alexander Pope. He founded what is now the Royal National Hospital for Rheumatic Diseases with John Wood, Ralph Allen and Beau Nash, and in 1740 was appointed as the physician. Oliver is thought to have invented the Bath Bun which he then found was too fattening for his patients so he produced a healthier biscuit now known as a Bath Oliver.

Captain Outing was curate at Wootton Wawen, Warwickshire, and acted as Lady Luxborough's agent and secretary, often carrying letters between her and Shenstone.

Bishop Thomas Percy (1729-1811) was educated at Bridgnorth Grammar School, Shropshire, a friend of Samuel Johnson's and chaplain to George III and later the Bishop of Dromore, Ireland. He was an antiquarian and co-edited with Shenstone *Reliques of Ancient English Poetry*, published in 1765, which was a collection of ballads which he had found as a manuscript. It stimulated interest in traditional English and Scottish songs and stories. In 1771 he wrote *The Hermit of Warkworth.*

Thomas Pitt, 1st Lord Camelford (1737-1793) Born at Boconnoc, Cornwall, to Thomas who was the elder brother of William Pitt, Earl of Chatham and Christian, daughter of Sir Thomas Lyttelton of Hagley. Pitt was Member of Parliament for Old Sarum and later Okehampton. In 1762 he moved to Twickenham where his near neighbours were Horace Walpole and Alexander Pope. Pitt was a keen amateur architect who had befriended John Soane on his Italian tour. He designed several garden structures at Hagley and Boconnoc.

William Pitt the elder, 1st Earl of Chatham (1708-1778) was educated at Eton and Trinity College, Oxford. He was married to Hester Grenville, a niece of Richard Temple. His brother Thomas married Christian Lyttelton, daughter of Sir George, and they were the parents of Thomas Pitt. William Pitt was a keen gardener and offered advice to George Lyttelton on the laying out of the grounds at Hagley. He was so taken with The Leasowes that he offered Shenstone £200, through the offices of Sanderson Miller, to further develop his garden, an offer which was refused. He became one of the most celebrated of Prime Ministers.

Alexander Pope (1688-1744) was the son of a London linen merchant. He was considered to be an outstanding poet and published *An Essay on Criticism* in 1711 and a mock heroic poem entitled *The Rape of the Lock* the following year. This was followed by a translation of Homer's *Iliad*. He moved to Twickenham in 1719 where he created a garden and a grotto decorated with crystals, ores and marbles. His interest in geology grew and in 1739 he visited the Hotwell Spa at Bristol. He decided to redesign his grotto as a museum of mineralogy. In this he was helped by many people including Dr Oliver and Ralph Allen from Bath.

Samuel Richardson (1689-1761) was born in Mackworth, Derbyshire. He was apprenticed to John Wilde, a printer in London in 1719 and went on to found a printing and publishing company printing over 500 different books and journals during his lifetime. His second wife was Elizabeth Leake sister of the owner of Leake's bookshop in Bath. He printed the newspapers the *Daily Journal* and *Daily Gazette*. His first book published in 1740 was *Pamela: or Virtue Rewarded* which many people regard as the first English novel, but his most famous novel *Clarissa* was published in seven volumes between 1747 and 1748.

William Shenstone (1714-1763) was a noted poet and the influence of his garden designs at The Leasowes spread far beyond the West Midlands.

Admiral Thomas Smith (c.1707-1762) Admiral Smith was the illegitimate son of Sir Thomas Lyttelton and Sir George's half-brother. He lived close to Hagley at Rockingham Hall. Smith had the obelisk built and paid £300 for the building of the Temple of Theseus which was completed around the time of his death.

Utrecia Smith (c.1726-1746) The daughter of the Rev Smith of Mickleton. Utrecia was highly intelligent and widely read. She became a friend of Shenstone's and a close friend of Richard Graves whom she hoped would ask her to marry him. Allegedly she died of a broken heart. Shenstone wrote *Elegy IV*, *Ophelia's Urn*, in her memory.

Sir William Somervile (1675-1742) met Shenstone at Oxford. He was a noted poet and lived at Edstone, near Henley-in-Arden, where he became friendly with Lady Luxborough. His life was devoted to field sports which provided the subject of many of his poems. He wrote *The Chace* in 1735, *Hobbinol or The Rural Games* in 1740 and *Field Sports* in 1742.

Philip Southcote (1698-1758) bought Woburn Farm, Surrey in 1735 and was famed for the garden which he created to which the term *ferme ornée* was applied. It was a mixed farm, both arable and pasture, through which he made a circuit walk ornamented with fragrant shrubs and herbaceous plants. He was a friend of Pope, Kent and Burlington.

Rev Joseph Spence (1699-1768) was the son of a Hampshire clergyman and was educated at Eton and Oxford. He was a historian and literary scholar and was ordained in 1726. As well as his ecclesiastical duties, he was Professor of Poetry

(1728-1738) and later of Modern History at Oxford. He was also a critic and friend of Pope's. His most noted work was *Polymetis: or an enquiry concerning the agreements between the works of the Roman poets and the remains of the ancient artists*, published in 1747. In 1758 he visited Shenstone at The Leasowes.

Richard Temple, 1st Viscount Cobham (1675-1749) Temple first made his mark in the War of Spanish Succession (1701-1714) as on outstanding leader. Like the rest of his family he supported the Whigs, though went into opposition in 1733. He is chiefly remembered today as the main creator of the landscape gardens at Stowe with the help of some of the major designers of his day – Bridgeman, Vanbrugh, Kent, Gibbs and Brown. He was a cousin of the Lytteltons.

James Thomson (1700-1748) was born in Scotland, the son of a preacher and attended Edinburgh University. By 1720 he had several pieces of poetry accepted in the *Edinburgh Miscellany*. In 1725 he moved to London where he was employed as a tutor to Thomas Hamilton later 7th Earl of Haddington. Here he wrote the first part *Winter* of his poem *The Seasons* with *Summer* written in 1727 and *Spring* the following year. It was completed with *Autumn* in 1730. He managed to capture in these poems the drama of Nature. In 1738 he was introduced to Frederick, Prince of Wales who hearing of his impoverished circumstances granted him a pension of £100 a year. George Lyttelton became both a patron and friend. Thomson is thought to have written *Rule Britannia* which was part of an entertainment called *The Masque of Alfred* first performed in the gardens of Cliveden in 1740.

Frances Thynne (1699-1754) was the eldest child of Hon. Henry Thynne of Longleat, Wiltshire. On her marriage she became Countess of Hertford and later Duchess of Somerset. She had known the poets Elizabeth Singer and Anne Finch, Countess of Winchelsea, when she was growing up and published several poems anonymously. Frances was a great friend of Lady Luxborough and the Countess of Stamford. She was a patron of poets including James Thomson, Stephen Duck and William Shenstone who dedicated his ode *Rural Elegance* to her. Some of her letters to Lady Luxborough are in the British Library and the Bodleian, Oxford.

Horace Walpole, 4th Earl of Orford (1717-1797) was the youngest son of Sir Robert Walpole. He was educated at Eton and King's College, Cambridge where he became friends with Thomas Gray. In 1739 the two men went on the Grand Tour travelling through Florence and Tuscany. On his return he became MP for Callington in

Cornwall. He took possession in 1747 of a house at Twickenham known locally as Chopped Straw Hall. Over several years he doubled it in size and converted it into a 'Gothick' building with fan-vaulted ceilings. He was helped in this with his 'Committee of Taste' which consisted of John Chute, Richard Bentley and Walpole. In 1764 he published, under a pseudonym, the first 'Gothick' novel entitled *The Castle of Otranto*. He is remembered as a controversial polymath – a politician, playwright, art historian, novelist, letter writer and designer.

John Ward, 6th Lord Ward (1700-1774) The Wards owned two properties in Staffordshire: Dudley Castle which was built about 1070 and was bought by the family in the 1620s and Himley Hall. In 1740 John became 6th Lord Ward and was elected an MP. He decided to demolish the medieval Himley Hall and build a new Palladian mansion on the site. When Dudley Castle burnt down in 1750 the family moved to Himley permanently. The grounds were first laid out by Nathaniel Richmond in 1765 with later alterations by Capability Brown in the late 1770s.

Josiah Wedgwood (1730-1795) was born in Burslem, Stoke, the son of Thomas who was a potter. He created a cream-coloured ware known as Queen's Ware in 1765 and six years later built a factory called Etruria. Wedgwood realised the importance of canal transport for the distribution of goods. He was on the board of the Trent and Mersey Canal with James Brindley, the Duke of Bridgewater and the Earl of Stamford and was also a member of the Lunar Society. In 1773 Catherine the Great, Empress of Russia asked Wedgwood to produce a dinner and dessert service for her new palace designed in the English 'Gothick' style. The palace was built surrounded by a frog-populated marsh and was called La Grenouillère. It was to be decorated with views of England especially gardens. It became known as the Green Frog Service and has twenty-two pictures of Enville and three of Hagley on it.

John Wesley (1703-1791) and **Charles Wesley** (1707-1788) were two out of nineteen children born to Rev Samuel Wesley Rector of Epworth, Lincolnshire. John was educated at Charterhouse and Charles at Westminster, but both attended Christ Church, Oxford. John helped to found the 'Holy Club' which Charles later joined, dubbed 'The Methodists' because of the way in which they studied the Bible. John went back to Epworth, but felt that in order to reach out to more people he should preach in the open, often to thousands of people. They travelled thousands of miles and campaigned tirelessly on social issues. In 1782 John visited The Leasowes.

Mary West (Molly) (c.1704-1786) was a cousin of George Lyttelton's and married Captain Alexander Hood for whom Sanderson Miller designed a house at Cricket St. Thomas. She had an excellent eye for planting and was a frequent visitor to Hagley.

Anthony Whistler (1714-1754) was educated at Eton and Oxford where he met Shenstone, and although they had minor disagreements they were to become life-long friends. In 1736 Whistler wrote a mock heroic poem called *The Shuttlecock* and later contributed to Dodsley's *Miscellany*.

Other Lewis Windsor, Earl of Plymouth (1731-1771) lived at Hewell Grange, Worcestershire and was advised by Shenstone on the improvement of his lake which was recommended to be 'thrown into a broad Serpentine river'.

James Woodhouse (1735-1820) lived at Rowley near The Leasowes and was known as the 'cobbler poet'. He was befriended by Shenstone who encouraged his writing and allowed him to use his library, and introduced Woodhouse's work to his friends. In 1759 Woodhouse wrote an elegy to Shenstone. James Dodsley published Woodhouse's *Poems on Sundry Occasions* in 1764.

Bibliography

Archival and Manuscript Sources

British Library: Richard Pococke, Travels in 1755-6, Add MS 23000.

Burghley House Archives: Attested copy of Lord Stamford's settlement on the marriage with Lady Mary Booth, 8 May 1736, Ex 81/19.

Enville Hall Archives:

1760 Enville Library Catalogue, Q1/2/1.

4th Earl's Personal Ledger, G/1/13/1.

Day Book Accounts 1761-1779, G/1/2/1/1.

Estate Rent Rolls 1739-1781, E/3/1.

Estate Rent Rolls 1782-1811, E/3/2.

Vouchers and Bills, G/1/3/1772, G/1/3/1773, G/1/3/1809, G/1/3/1824, G/1/3/1829 and G/1/3/1846.

Correspondence: John Beckett to Lord Grey, 20 March 1819, G/2/2/3/8/13 and John Davenport to the 6th Earl of Stamford and Warrington, G/2/2/11.

Family Papers, F/3/5/5.

Lyndon Deeds, B/1/1/16.

Lord Grey's Walks and Rides, G/1/8/4/1.

Enville Hall Maps and Plans:

    c.1650, plan of the grounds surrounding Enville Hall, H/2/1.

    1688 estate survey of all the Grey estates in Staffordshire, Worcestershire and Shropshire by William Deeley, H/2/2.

    1746, copied in 1809, map of Lyndon Estate by Benjamin Booth, B/1/1/17.

    c.1750, Estate Survey, H/2/6.

    c.1752, proposed plan of improvements to the grounds, H/2/8.

    Undated plan of Home Farm, H/3/1.

    Survey of the Sheep walk.

Three oil paintings and one watercolour by Anthony Devis (1729-1816), showing the Cascades, a view across the upper pool to the Rotunda, the Shepherd's Bridge over Jordan's Pool and a view from near the Gothic Seat.

Two watercolours unsigned and undated of Gothic Gateway and Lyndon/Ralph's Bastion.

E Barber, pen and wash of Temple Pool and Boathouse.

Lady Katherine Grey's sketchbook.

Lichfield Record Office: Will and inventory of Sir Thomas Grey, B/C/11.

London School of Economics and Political Science: John Parnell, 'Journal of a tour thro' England and Wales, Anno 1769', MS Coll Misc 38.

Manchester University: The John Rylands Library, Stamford Papers, EGR/3/7//3/4 and EGR/18/12/3.

Nottingham University: Portland Papers, 31 January 1767, PWF/4555, and also PWF/4521 and Pl C 14/13.

The Royal Bank of Scotland Group Archives: Drummonds Bank Customer Accounts Ledgers, account with 4th Earl of Stamford, DR/427/24-45.

Shropshire Record Office: David Parkes, a book of poetry and watercolours, 6001/154.

Warwickshire County Record Office: Sanderson Miller's Engagement Book, CR1382/1.

Wellesley College, Massachusetts: Special Collections, watercolours by William Shenstone.

Worcestershire Record Office: Kidderminster Collection, Edward Knight's Notebook, WOL B/KNI 91-575032.

Contemporary Published Sources

including some later editions of contemporary accounts published up to 1900

Joseph Addison, *The Spectator*, nos 414 and 477, 1712.

A Companion to The Leasowes, Hagley & Enville, London, 1789.

A New Display of the Beauties of England, London, 1787.

William Chambers, *A Dissertation on Oriental Gardening*, London, 1772.

Sampson Erdeswick, *A Survey of Staffordshire*, London, 1723.

(Joseph Giles), *Miscellaneous Poems on Various Subjects and Occasions*, London, 1771.

William Gilpin, *Observations, relative chiefly to Picturesque Beauty, Made in the Year 1772, on Several Parts of England*, London, 1786.

Richard Graves, *Columella; or, The Distressed Anchoret*, London: J Dodsley, 1779.

Richard Graves, *Recollections of Some Particulars in the Life of the Late William Shenstone, Esq.*, London: J Dodsley, 1788.

Pierre-Jean Grosley, *A Tour to London, or new observations on England and its inhabitants...translated from the French*, London, 1772.

(Joseph Heely, attrib.), *A Description of Hagley, Envil and The Leasowes*, Birmingham, prob early 1770s.

Joseph Heely, *Letters on the Beauties of Hagley, Envil, and The Leasowes*, London, 1777.

John Hill, *Eden, or a Compleat Body of Gardening*, London, 1757.

Batty Langley, *New Principles of Gardening*, London, 1728.

John Laurence, *A New System of Agriculture, being a Complete Body of Husbandry and Gardening*, London: Thomas Woodward, 1726.

(George Lyttelton), *The Poetical Works of Lord Lyttelton*, London, 1785.

(George Lyttelton), *Memoirs and Correspondence of George Lord Lyttelton*, ed. Robert Phillimore, London: James Ridgeway, 1845.

(Thomas Lyttelton), *Letters of the Late Lord Lyttelton*, ed. Wm Coombs, London, 1780.

William Marshall, *On Planting and Rural Ornament*, London, 1796.London: G&W Nicols *et al*, 1803), third edition (orig. 1796)

Thomas Martyn, *The English Connoisseur*, London: L Davis and C Reymors, 1766.

George Mason, *An Essay on Design in Gardening*, London, 1768.

Treadway Nash, *Collections for the History of Worcestershire*, London, 1781.

Timothy Nourse, *Campania Foelix, or, A Discourse of the Benefits and Improvements of Husbandry*, London, 1700.

(Resta Patching), *Four Topographical Letters*, Newcastle, 1757.

Robert Plot, *The Natural History of Staffordshire*, Oxford, 1686.

(Richard Pococke), *The Travels through England of Dr Richard Pococke*, ed. JJ Cartwright, London: Camden Society, 1888-9.

(Mrs Philip Lybbe Powys), *Passages from the Diaries of Mrs Philip Lybbe Powys*, ed. Emily J Climenson, London: Longman and Co, 1899.

(Henrietta Pye), *A Short Account of the Principal Seats and Gardens in and about Richmond and Kew*, Brentford, n.d.

Stebbing Shaw, *The History and Antiquities of Staffordshire*, London, 1798-1801.

(William Shenstone), *The Works in Verse and Prose of William Shenstone, Esq.*, London: R&J Dodsley, 1764.

RJ Sulivan [Sullivan], *A Tour through Part of England, Scotland and Wales in 1778*, London, 1780.

Stephen Switzer, *Ichnographia Rustica*, London, 1742.

The Modern Universal Traveller, London, 1779.

James Thomson, *The Seasons*, revised ed., London, 1744.

Richard Warner, *A Tour Through the Northern Counties of England, and the Borders of Scotland*, Bath, 1802.

Richard Warner, *An Historical and Descriptive Account of Bath and Its Environs*, Bath, 1802.

Thomas Whately, *Observations on Modern Gardening*, London, 1770.

Arthur Young, *A Six Months Tour through the North of England*, London, 1770.

Modern published sources

An Historical Geography of England and Wales, London, Academic Press Ltd, 2nd ed., 1990.

Dianne Barre, 'Sir Samuel Hellier (1736-84) and his Garden Buildings: Part of the Midlands "Garden Circuit" in the 1760s-70s?', *Garden History*, 36:2, 2008.

Mavis Batey, *Alexander Pope: The Poet and the Landscape*, London: Barn Elms, 1999.

Mavis Batey, 'The Pleasures of the Imagination: Joseph Addison's Influence on Early Landscape Gardens', *Garden History*, 33:2, 2005.

Stephen Bending, 'Uneasy Sensations: Shenstone, Retirement and Fame', *Arcadian Greens Rural, New Arcadians Journal*, 53-4, 2002.

Michael Bevington, *Stowe, the Garden and the Park*, Stowe: Capability Books, 1994.

Patrick Bowe, *Gardens of the Roman World*, London: Frances Lincoln, 2004.

William A Brogden, 'The *Ferme Ornée* and Changing Attitudes to Agricultural Improvement', *British and American Gardens of the Eighteenth Century*, ed. Robert P Maccubbin and Peter Martin, Williamsburg: The Colonial Williamsburg Foundation, 1984.

Jane Brown, *My Darling Heriott: Henrietta Luxborough, Poetic Gardener and Irrepressible Exile*, London: Harper Press, 2006.

Douglas DC Chambers, *The Planters of the English Landscape Garden*, New Haven: Yale University Press, 1993.

David Coffin, *Gardens and Gardening in Papal Rome*, Princeton, NJ: Princeton University Press, 1991.

David Coffin, *The English Garden: Meditation and Memorial*, Princeton, NJ: Princeton University Press, 1994.

Howard Colvin, *A Bibliographical Dictionary of British Architects 1600-1840*, New Haven: Yale University Press, 3rd ed., 1995.

Ian Cooke, 'Whiteknights and the Marquis of Blandford', *Garden History*, 20:1, 1992.

Michael Cousins, 'William Shenstone: Jealous of Hagley?', *Arcadian Greens Rural, New Arcadians Journal*, 53-4, 2002.

Michael Cousins, 'Hagley Park, Worcestershire', *Garden History*, 35: Supplement 1, 2007.

Rose M Davis, *The Good Lord Lyttelton: A Study in Eighteenth Century Politics and Culture*, Bethlehem, PA: Times Publishing Co, 1939.

Daniel Defoe, *A Tour through the Whole Island of Great Britain*, ed. P Roberts, Harmondsworth: Penguin Books, 1971.

Ray Desmond, *Kew: The History of the Royal Botanic Gardens*, London: Harvill Press, 1995.

Lilian Dickins and Mary Stanton, *An Eighteenth Century Correspondence* [Sanderson Miller], London: John Murray, 1910.

Audrey Duggan, *The World of William Shenstone*, Studley Warwickshire: Brewin Books, 2004.

Rudy J Favretti, 'Thomas Jefferson's "Ferme Ornée" at Monticello', *Proceedings of the American Antiquarian Society*, 103, 1993.

Christopher Gallagher, 'The Leasowes: A History of the Landscape', *Garden History*, 24:2, 1996.

Margaret Gelling, *The West Midlands in the Early Middle Ages: Studies in the Early History of Britain*, Leicester: Leicester University Press, 1992.

Harry Gilonis, 'Emblematical and Expressive: the gardenist mode of William Shenstone and Ian Hamilton Finlay', *Arcadian Greens Rural, New Arcadians Journal*, 53-4, 2002.

Mark Girouard, *Life in the English Country House*, New Haven: Yale U. Press, 1978.

Sandy Haynes, 'William Shenstone and the Enville Landscape', *Arcadian Greens Rural, New Arcadians Journal,* 53-4, 2002.

Colin G Hey, *The Warwickshire Coterie: An Eighteenth Century Interlude*, Shipston-on-Stour: author, 1991.

Della Hooke, *The West Midlands*, London: English Heritage, 2006.

John Dixon Hunt, *Garden and Grove: The Italian Renaissance Garden in the English Imagination, 1660-1750*, London: Dent, 1986.

Julia Ionides, *Thomas Farnolls Pritchard of Shrewsbury, Architect and 'Inventor of Cast Iron Bridges'*, Ludlow: The Dog Rose Press, 1999.

Gervase Jackson-Stops, *An English Arcadia 1660-1990*, The National Trust, 1991.

David Jacques, 'The Ferme Ornée', *The Ferme Ornée: Working with Nature*, Conference Proceedings of the Association of Garden Trusts, Staffordshire Gardens and Parks Trust, 1998.

Count Friedrich Kielmansegge, *Diary of A Journey to England, 1761-62*, trans. Philippa Kielmansegg, London: Longmans, 1902.

Mark Laird, *The Flowering of the Landscape Garden: English Pleasure Grounds 1720-1800*, Philadelphia: University of Pennsylvania Press, 1999.

David Lambert, 'William Shenstone and the Fairy Landscape', *The Georgian Group Report and Journal*, 1986.

Peter Martin, *Pursuing Innocent Pleasures: The Gardening World of Alexander Pope*, Connecticut: Archon Books, 1984.

Jennifer Meir, *Sanderson Miller and his Landscapes*, Chichester: Phillimore & Co 2006.

Daniela Mignani, *The Medicean Villas by Giusto Utens*, Florence: Arnaud, 1991.

(Sanderson Miller), *The Diaries of Sanderson Miller of Radway*, ed. William Hawkes, Warwick: Dugdale Society, 2005.

Timothy Mowl, 'The Case of the Enville Museum', *Journal of Garden History*, 3:2, 1983.

(Alexander Pope), *The Correspondence of Alexander Pope*, ed. George Sherburn, Oxford: Clarendon Press, 1956.

Roy Porter, *Pleasure in the Eighteenth Century*, London: Macmillan, 1996.

Oliver Rackham, *The History of the Countryside*, London: Dent, 1986.

Oliver Rackham, *The Illustrated History of the Countryside*, London: BCA, 1994.

John Riely, 'Shenstone's walks: the genius of The Leasowes', *Apollo*, 110:211, 1979.

John Martin Robinson, *Temples of Delight: Stowe Landscape Gardens*, London: The National Trust/George Philip, 1990.

George C Rogers, 'Gardens and Landscapes in Eighteenth-Century South Carolina', *British and American Gardens in the Eighteenth Century*, ed. RP Maccubbin and P Martin, Williamsburg: The Colonial Williamsburg Foundation, 1984.

James Rothwell, *Guide to Dunham Massey*, London: The National Trust, 2000.

Marie B Rowlands, *A Regional History of England: The West Midlands from AD 1000*,

London: Longmans, 1987.

James Sambrook, 'Parnell's Garden Tours: Hagley and The Leasowes', *British and American Gardens in the Eighteenth Century*, ed. Robert P Maccubbin and Peter Martin, Williamsburg: The Colonial Williamsburg Foundation, 1984.

George Sheeran, 'Patriotic Views: Aristocratic Ideology and the Eighteenth-Century Landscape', *Landscapes*, 7:2, 2006.

(William Shenstone), *The Letters of William Shenstone*, ed. Marjorie Williams, Oxford: Basil Blackwell, 1939.

(William Shenstone), *Letters of William Shenstone*, ed. Duncan Mallam, Minneapolis: University of Minnesota Press, 1939.

Osvald Sirén, *China and Gardens of Europe of the Eighteenth Century*, Washington: Dumbarton Oaks, 1990 (orig. edition, 1950).

Joseph Spence, *Observations, Anecdotes, and Characters of Books and Men*, ed. JM Osborn, Oxford: Clarendon Press, 1966.

Michael Symes, *Fairest Scenes: Five Great Surrey Gardens*, Weybridge: Elmbridge Museum, 1988.

Anthea Taigel and Tom Williamson, *Parks and Gardens*, London: Batsford, 1993.

A A Tait, *The Landscape Garden in Scotland, 1735-85*, Edinburgh: Edinburgh University Press, 1980.

The Genius of the Place: The English Landscape Garden 1620-1820, ed. John Dixon Hunt and Peter Willis, London: Elek Books, 1975.

The Green Frog Service, ed. Michael Raeburn, Ludmila Voronikhina and Andrew Nurnberg, London: Cacklegoose Press, 1995.

The Oxford Companion to Gardens, London: Oxford University Press, 1986.

Adrian Tinniswood, *The Polite Tourist*, London: The National Trust, 1998.

Victoria County History: The History of the County of Staffordshire, London: Oxford University Press, 1984.

(Horace Walpole), *Horace Walpole's Correspondence*, ed. WS Lewis, New Haven: Yale University Press, 1937-83.

Horace Walpole, *The History of the Modern Taste in Gardening* [1770], ed. John Dixon Hunt, New York: Ursus Press, 1995.

Claude-Henri Watelet, *Essay on Gardens* [1774]: *A Chapter in the French Picturesque*, ed. and trans. Samuel Danon, Philadelphia: University of Pennsylvania Press, 2003.

Dora Wiebenson, *The Picturesque Garden in France*, Princeton, NJ: Princeton University Press, 1978.

A F B Williams, *The Life of William Pitt, 1st Earl of Chatham*, London: Longmans, 1913.

Robert Williams, 'Rural Economy and the Antique in the English Landscape Garden', *Journal of Garden History*, 7:1, 1987.

Robert Williams, 'The Leasowes, Hagley and rural inscriptions', *Arcadian Greens Rural, New Arcadians Journal*, 53-4, 2002.

INDEX